The Three
Sustainabilities

The Three Sustainabilities

Energy, Economy, Time

ALLAN STOEKL

UNIVERSITY OF MINNESOTA PRESS

MINNEAPOLIS • LONDON

A portion of a version of chapter 2 was published as "Urban Ecology,"
in *Fueling Culture 101: Words for Energy and Environment*, ed. Imre Szeman,
Jennifer Wenzel, and Patricia Yaeger, 361–64 (New York: Fordham
University Press, 2017). A portion of chapter 5 was published in a different
form as "Solar Le Corbusier," in *Philosophy and the City*, ed. Keith Jacobs
and Jeff Malpas, 83–102 (London: Rowman and Littlefield, 2019).

Published by the University of Minnesota Press
111 Third Avenue South, Suite 290
Minneapolis, MN 55401–2520
http://www.upress.umn.edu

ISBN 978-1-5179-0817-1 (hc)
ISBN 978-1-5179-0818-8 (pb)
Library of Congress record available at https://lccn.loc.gov/2021023175.

Printed in the United States of America on acid-free paper

The University of Minnesota is an equal-opportunity educator and
employer.

Contents

Introduction

Sustainability, n. **b.** *spec.* The property of being environmentally sustainable; the degree to which a process or enterprise is able to be maintained or continued while avoiding the long-term depletion of natural resources.

—*Oxford English Dictionary*

"Sustainability"—why write a book about it? Hasn't it been discredited?[1] Or isn't its meaning self-evident? Isn't it just shorthand for some impossible capitalist future? Or what everybody dreams of, and everybody knows will never happen? The ecological version of utopia, a perfect space of fulfillment—in other words, no-space? Or what we have to attain in order to survive? But who is "we"? And what is survival? Shorthand for doing nothing of any significance and feeling good about it? Just a word?

Or is working toward sustainability the last hope for the planet? But whose planet? And whose sustainability? Rocks? Iron ore? Animals? People? Rich first-world white people? Everybody? Is it a word we need without knowing why we really need it?

Stacy Alaimo pronounces the most severe evaluation of "sustainability." Alaimo sees the word as implying that "we can fix the world in such a way as to ensure 'it' will keep providing for 'us.'" She concludes: "Rather than approaching this world as a warehouse of inert things we wish to pile up for later use, we must hold ourselves accountable to a materiality that is never merely an external, blank or inert space but the active, emergent substance of ourselves and others."[2] So forget sustainability.

I'm certainly in agreement with at least a variant of this position, as I hope the final chapters of this book will demonstrate. But is "sustainability" itself, the word, or for that matter variants and euphemisms, so easily jettisoned? Alaimo herself doesn't seem to think so; after all, earlier in the book, she writes: "I live in the belly of one of the most ravenous, *least sustainable* beasts—not just the United States, but Texas" (95, emphasis added). True, she may be using the term (or its adjectival variant) here "ironically," but the point is, ironic or not, she still makes use of it. Texas is indeed dependent on fossil fuels (like the rest of the developed world), both their extraction and their refining; life is famously lived large there (like everywhere else, but supposedly a bit more so), with plenty of driving, shopping, driving to shopping, and so on. That is to say, Alaimo uses the word because, presumably, there is nothing else that can do its work. It or some variant of it is useful, and will continue to be useful. But what is, in the end, its work?

I would like to argue that "sustainability" still has a role to play in discourse, in our political unconscious. The word will sustain itself, if only as a recurrence of ever-larger or more contestable or ironic meanings, or as a place marker, the "x" of what cannot be definitively formulated or eliminated. Because, most fundamentally, not just the human is sustained, or sustains itself. Sustainability in the larger sense is about time, and objects (living and inanimate): all the aspects of how objects are in time, and pass—or do not pass—away. With or without us, depending on how we imagine both them and ourselves (as humans). The fact of their temporality—their genesis, their stubbornness, their oblivion, their residue—and our role, or lack of role, in that temporality (and hence the "passing" of ourselves) confronts us on a daily basis. Objects in time—and the moral and physical conundrums that that movement, or lack of movement, implies—is the subject of this book. And so too is energy transformation, conservation, and loss—but energy is precisely not an object (though known only through objects: fuel, heated things, movement of things, electrical discharge, etc.).

Sustainability (the word) will be sustainable, I think, following another, related definition of the word: "sustainable, adj. . . . 2. Capable of being upheld or defended as valid, correct, or true" *(OED)*. But what is truth in relation to sustainability?

The larger objection to "sustainability" might be that it has become nothing more than a cliché. But as Jean Paulhan reminds us in his fundamental book *The Flowers of Tarbes* (1940), all we have in language are clichés, words that are ground down through overuse. There is no escaping them. To escape clichés is to escape language itself, by trying to devise one's own pristine and ultimately private language. The problem is that this new language itself then becomes a cliché as soon as it goes out into the world.

(Paulhan's example is the stylistic experimentation of the surrealists.) True, language is policed, in the endless effort to weed out hurtful or insulting words. But worn-out words? They are all we have, and the true challenge is to master rhetoric—another thing we cannot escape—in order to effectively express ourselves, using the figures of speech, words, and grammar that have been handed down to us, for good or ill. When we are attentive to what we have, the elements of language at our disposal are not worn out, but capable of expressing what is worth expressing. That's the ideal, anyway . . .

"Sustainability" in the context of environmentalism and resource "conservation" (another word) is often defined through three "pillars": it entails an economic model, a political or social one, and finally an ecological or environmental model.[3] Each of these is inseparable from the others, and each evokes a future to which we inevitably turn: the economic invites us to consider the modes of development that would respect the ecological; the political proposes the structures by which these economic reforms can be implemented through governmental or quasi- or nongovernmental means; and, finally, the ecological grounds the other two, in that their very legitimacy depends on a "sustaining" of "natural resources" (living and inert) that will ensure, as the World Commission on Environment and Development (the Brundtland Commission) (in the volume *Our Common Future* [1987]) puts it, that "development meets the needs of the present without compromising the ability of future generations to meet their own needs."[4] All three pillars work together, in other words, to further certain values: social justice (equitable distribution, "meeting the needs of the present"), prosperity ("development," steady state [nongrowth]), and the indefinite future (of human "generations").

From the perspective of traditional ethics, one cannot argue with this, as long as the human remains the primary subject not only of social history but of environmental history. Nevertheless, I would like, very briefly, to examine each of these "pillars" with reference to a book, or books, that could be said to convey some of the underlying ideas, or ideals, behind it. I think doing this can lead us to understand why these models might need to be supplemented, so to speak, with a few more scenarios, ones that move out at orthogonal angles from established doctrine. What, after all, happens when we consider sustaining stuff from the point of view, if such a thing could be posited, of the stuff (living, inanimate), which is not necessarily concerned with a task of sustaining humans? And what can we say about

humans and their (self-)sustainability after we consider their position not
as an essential one in relation to everything else, but instead as tangential,
marginal, obscure?

First, we might consider the economic and political sustainability models. In Harvard economist Jeffrey D. Sachs's massive tome, *The Age of Sustainable Development*, we find the political itself broken down into three
categories: "economic development, social inclusion, and environmental
sustainability" (5). Later, sustainable development has no fewer than eight
components:

1. Eradicate extreme poverty and hunger.
2. Achieve universal primary education.
3. Promote gender equality and empower women.
4. Reduce child mortality.
5. Improve maternal health.
6. Combat HIV/AIDS, malaria, and other diseases.
7. Ensure environmental sustainability.
8. A global partnership for development.[5]

We can all agree on these goals, but it is unclear how the overarching term,
"sustainability," links up with the only goal that actually mentions sustainability, down the list at number 7. Without any critique of the capitalist
consumer model of production/consumption/disposal, Sachs enumerates
goals that will certainly add to humanity's well-being, but that are not necessarily reconcilable with number 7, if that entry means, as the *OED* has
it, "avoiding the long-term depletion of natural resources." Certainly most
of the other goals (2, 3, 4, 5) could be said to aid in population reduction,
as women who are educated, empowered, and healthy feel less need to
have large families. That's all good, of course, but Sachs does not indicate
how a global society in which extreme poverty has been reduced will manage to "avoid depletion of natural resources" as long as world population
continues to grow. His conservative model of population growth foresees
world population peaking "around 2050 at 8.3 billion and then gradually
declin[ing] to 6.8 billion, by 2100" (210).

The point here is not to criticize the essential goal of ending world poverty, but to note the difficulty of conceiving a model of development without a thoroughgoing critique of consumerism and its driver, capitalism.
Sachs does genuflect in the direction of anticonsumerism: "In the end, if our

societies are driven overwhelmingly by the goal of increased incomes and consumerism, we are unlikely to achieve the kind of happiness and life satisfaction that we desire" (66). But nowhere does Sachs indicate how what he calls development and consumerism can be uncoupled; this passing glance to consumerism's danger, and to the healing potential of the traditions of world religions (219–28), are the only real indications that there may be a conflict between development goals 2, 3, 4, and 5 and number 7 (however "sustainability" is to be defined). The need to somehow elaborate a completely different ethics of consumption and indeed wealth, at variance with that promulgated by capitalism for the last several hundred years, is simply not central to Sachs's project.

Some measure of the problem is indicated, I think, by the fact that "sustainable development" is defined, on p. 145, by . . . sustainability. The definition is circular. Sustainable development is nothing more than number 7, "environmental sustainability"—which Sachs himself does not really define outside of the parameters of development, and all the other add-ons (numbers 1 to 8, minus 7) that go to make it up. A larger sustainability, in other words, can only be defined through another, more limited, sustainability— which can only be fully defined through the larger one.

Cognitive dissonance,[6] in which contradictory opinions or options must be simultaneously held, characterizes a good number of formulations of sustainability. We must believe that sustainability can be achieved, on a worldwide basis, if we use the term to define something that most likely would not lead to a larger sustainability, in any sense of the term. We painfully—or contentedly—conceal from ourselves the fact that environmental sustainability is radically incompatible with a larger "developmental" sustainability that is not adequately formulated *against* consumerism (and hence capitalism as we know it). Development is never disentangled from growth. The very use of the first term (development) to help define the second (sustainability) shows the extent of this dissonance.

Ecological sustainability, the third member of the sustainability triad, according to Willis Jenkins, "focus[es] directly on the health of the living world. . . . From an anthropocentric point of view essential natural resources should be sustained, as should those ecological systems and regenerative processes on which human systems rely."[7] Jenkins also notes an "ecocentric" (presumably non-anthropocentric) sustainability in which "species should be sustained for their intrinsic value." But how could this intrinsic value be determined outside the purview of human demands and needs?

Ecological sustainability, then, is principally an anthropocentric notion, and as such it leads to a larger set of questions: What is it for humans to identify (aesthetically?) with "other species" to a sufficient extent that their "intrinsic" value can be recognized? What is this identification? How do we measure ourselves against and identify with "species," or an entire biosphere, that must be sustained? Since humans are presumably an integral part of this "ecological" sustainability, we must find ourselves in a world in which we both are the authors of ecological damage—the threat to sustainability—and the authors of ecological amelioration (to the point of sustainability). What does this in turn tell us about human consciousness, which is able to carry out both selfish ecological degradation and selfless salvation? How does such a disproportionate (monstrous?) consciousness (or will) arise in the world? How does it see itself, and the human? Given its monstrosity, can its self-perception ever be accurate? How does the selfish, unseeing "me" transform itself, once and for all, into the noble, perceptive "me"? How is this global ethical revolution to be carried out? What would a full identification of the human with all "other species" entail? How will such identification salvage the human, given its tendency to destroy?

In the case of William Rees and Mathis Wackernagel, sustainability can be *measured*. Here it is not a question of a multiplicity of factors, some quantifiable, some not ("a global partnership for development") that we saw in Sachs. Instead, Rees and Wackernagel have a sophisticated and very specific method of determining quantities of nutrients and resources necessary to continued human life, which includes energy resources, materials, and so on ("ecological footprint" analysis).[8] Through their formulae, they are able to indicate this consumption, measured in hectares. Here we can see quite clearly when we are overconsuming, and when we are not: now, through their method of calculation, we can determine whether, per capita, our society (our nation, in effect) is consuming more than the earth can continue (indefinitely) to provide. In other words, as Rees and Wackernagel point out, "Today, there are only about 1.5 hectares of [productive] land for each person, including wilderness areas that probably shouldn't be used for any other purpose." The point, of course, is that first-worlders are overconsuming: "The present per capita ecological footprints of North Americans (4–5 ha) represents three times their fair share of the Earth's bounty. By extrapolation, if everyone on Earth lived like the average North American, the total land requirement would exceed 26 billion hectares. However there are fewer than 9 billion hectares of such land on Earth" (238).

Ecological sustainability analysis is, literally, the most down to earth: we are down there, with the other animals, we are animals; the earth has a limited carrying capacity, and we violate it. Now the interesting thing here, I think, is that this method results in a kind of anthropocentric whiplash. We are both *different* as humans, since we are causing the problem, but also in that we can see the problem, and presumably correct it. In other words, we can lessen our ecological footprint. At the same time, however, we are *just like* any other species of animal, no different, since we are bound by the same ecological constraints, the same rules. We pass through the anthropocentric and come out the other side.

No one would argue that the human population should be reduced by the sudden appearance of predators or viruses.[9] But seeing humans as just another species also makes clear our difference: we need to *formulate* sustainability. Sustainability itself is a measure of the human, because animals are quite content without it. Animals are indifferent to sustainability. Sustainability is the mark of the nobility and the degradation of the human. (Nobility because humans see the need for it, are conscious of its necessity, and formulate models of it; degradation because humans have created the very crisis that they alone can remedy.) The very need to formulate sustainability, and somehow to impose it (on ourselves and upon all other species) indicates that we are just another species. If we were angels who don't have to eat and excrete we would not have to worry about it. And yet we would like to be on the side of the angels, working to save the planet. We need to worry about sustaining our environment: this is the curse of consciousness, which always finds itself on the outs with the environment—opposed to it, objectifying it, negating-destroying-using it, turning it into a "for us," but also seeing it as an "in itself" that must be recognized, somehow affirmed as it is, "saved" (but through that very gesture, maddeningly, turning it into a "for us"). Yet the human is only fully human, fully recognizing itself in its compromised status, at the cost of recognizing itself as no different from the animal.

There can never be perfect ecological sustainability, then, because it depends on a cognitive dissonance in which we are both animal and human, above the "natural" world in our ability to analyze and save it, but below it in our wanton destruction of it. Sustainability is only possible in the duality of poison and cure, the *pharmakon* in which we recognize what we have done but are able (we hope) to remediate it. And yet at the same time, we recognize the irremediable damage—the world is now fully human, it has lost the pristine innocence it had before we sullied it with our subjectivity, with our destruction and our amelioration. Sustainability as conceived in this context can never be one, never be simple; it promises a future of balanced accounts that is fundamentally unstable since the accounts can only be balanced by a consciousness both noble and base, a human consciousness that rightly sees itself as inseparable from the animal in its needs but also in its unconcern (indeed much worse than animals because it knows the perversity of its wanton acts). We humans are the angels who serve and the devils who destroy, shouting *non serviam*.

In *Cradle to Cradle: Remaking the Way We Make Things*, William McDonough and Michael Braungart propose an ingenious solution to the ills of environmental degradation. Pollution on a planetary scale is caused by the fact that the things we use are not properly destined for recycling— or what they call "upcycling." Nowadays stuff, if recycled at all, is only "downcycled," because things are not designed to be recycled; steel from automobiles, when melted down, is contaminated with paint and plastic; it cannot replace "virgin" ore in making new metal products. Aluminum is similarly degraded in its second use, paper and plastic as well. Often, recycled materials can make only inferior products, all the while generating additional unusable material offscourings that must be thrown "away." And a third recycling is even more problematic. McDonough and Braungart instead propose a kind of perfect recycling in which nothing is lost or degraded; objects are designed to be recycled indefinitely, in a timeless, perfectly closed economy:

> Carpeting designed as a true technical nutrient would be made of safe materials designed to be truly recycled as raw material for fresh carpeting, and the delivery system for its service would cost the same or less than buying it.[10]

The biological metaphors used here are important: raw materials are now "technical nutrients" because the production process is seen less as a mechanical or even social operation than a kind of natural one: stuff is reused in the same way that natural systems reuse stuff. Nothing goes to waste, and there is no "away." There is no difference between human-authored recycling and the recycling "out there," "in nature."

There might not be an "away," but there is a human awareness, and that's the rub. It's both there and not there, crucial and invisible. It's the curse and the solution. Here the authors write of ants:

As part of their daily activity, they:

—safely and effectively handle their own material wastes and those of other species

—grow and harvest their own food while nurturing the ecosystem of which they are a part

—construct houses, farms, dumps, cemeteries, living quarters, and food-storage facilities from materials that can be truly recycled

—create disinfectants and medicines that are healthy, safe, and biodegradable

—maintain healthy soil for the entire planet. (79)

If only we could be as perfect as the ants. They have no history, no self-awareness (presumably—at least no human self-awareness: they have nurseries and farms, but no universities), no word for sustainability. And yet they do it.

But if they don't have the word, are they really sustainable? True, McDonough and Braungart don't use the word either (in this sense they're like the ants), but their euphemism for it, "cradle to cradle" (which McDonough attempted to copyright) conveys very well the great desire to give everything back, to continue indefinitely, generation after generation, in a kind of steady state circular movement, and to be aware of the process. No buying and selling, just leasing the "use" of things—but presumably capitalism will continue. No consumerism though—by implication at least, it's gone, since one cannot indulge in it while only leasing . . .

But how closed is this closed economy? How can ants, or environments, be sustainable if they don't care about it? Or will we have to think about another kind of sustainability that would encompass a world where not only no creatures worry about sustaining, but where all systems produce an excess that cannot be sustained, that inevitably is lost? After all, all animal species produce *too much*—too many offspring, too much stuff, too much waste. Trees try to cover the landscape, beavers try to populate streams with more beavers, deer certainly try to get in everywhere. Ants too, no doubt. It's rule by excess. Most die before they can reproduce; there's no steady state, at least not for individuals, and not in the long run. If there is a larger sustainability, it's one of systems, eco and otherwise, but systems that themselves only continue for a while, always producing more, always losing most of the more they produce, eventually dying out or off . . . It's only humans who try to come up with a model of an eco-economy that never produces too much, that's a perfectly closed system, sustainability in the sense of a finitude that limits precisely humans' tendency to produce too much. A self-reflexive sustainability, in other words, that triumphs over the vagaries of time. Here's anthropocentric whiplash again: eco-sustainability tries to mimic the "natural"—the ants—all the while proposing something that has never before existed in the world, and could not be less "natural": self-engendered limits to growth, conscious mastery over the natural through the ultimate appeal to and identification with the natural.

Finally, putting all three "pillars" together we can, with Jenkins, imagine "sustaining the cultural conditions needed to realize ecological personhood, civic identity, or even personal faith through ecological membership."[11] Jenkins cites Val Plumwood and Norma Wirzba in support of this position, but I would also mention Bill McKibben's book *Deep Economy: The Wealth of Communities and the Durable Future* as a prime example of a theory of a larger cultural sustainability.

McKibben's book is perhaps the most sustained effort out there to rethink the bases of politics and economy and ecology in such a way that a "durable" future will be possible. "Durable" here stands in for "sustainable," no doubt, a telling euphemism because it enables McKibben to stress not only simple temporal survival (the *OED*'s first definition of durability: "**1.** Capable of lasting or continuing in existence; persistent, lasting; not transitory, permanent."), but also the ability of something quite physical to withstand change (hence the *OED*'s second sense of the word: "**2.a.** Able to withstand change, decay, or wear," and perhaps most important the subsidiary sense: "**b.** *spec.* Designating a class of goods the usefulness of which continues over a period of time, as distinguished from goods produced for immediate consumption").

The second category of goods provides an alternative to most goods we know in the consumerist, globalized world. Thus "durable" as a word conveys very well both the temporal aspect of a desired ecologically aware society—capable of going on indefinitely—and the deeper values behind the physical world to be established and maintained.

McKibben's very engaging book posits the simple fact that we are happier in small-scale communities where everyone knows everyone else, and in which all work together. Such communities have been shown empirically to be more healthful: our bodies are programmed to operate best in a local environment in which we are concerned most with working with others. "We have a surplus of individualism and a deficit of companionship," McKibben writes. "Humans seem to be genetically wired for community."[12]

And it's not simply a matter of having a strong circle of friends: McKibben stresses the economic aspect of this. Local production and consumption, small-scale farming, artisanal craftspersonship, all necessarily challenge the faceless pump and dump logic of global capitalism (although McKibben nowhere in his book explicitly critiques capitalism in itself).

So the local is good for the planet, and is good for our personal health. A small-scale world will involve much less consumption of goods, a much smaller ecological footprint, but a much greater level of psychological health. McKibben writes:

> Every measure of psychological health points to the same conclusion: people "who are married, who have good friends, and who are close to their families are happier than those who are not," says the Swarthmore psychologist Barry Schwartz. "People who participate in religious communities are happier than those who [do] not." Which is striking, Schwartz adds, because social ties "actually decrease freedom of choice." To be a good friend is hard work. (109)

McKibben goes on to cite the example of the Old Order Amish, who "live a life poor in appliances but rich in community, [and who have] a depression rate about one tenth of their neighbors," despite the fact that their community too suffers from "drug abuse, wife beating, and social tension" (112). It's interesting that McKibben cites the Amish as models for his version of community. Of course he does and he doesn't; his version of community, which he sees among his neighbors, in the small-scale farmers and craftspersons of Vermont, does not entail adherence to seventeenth-century religious beliefs and cultural practices. But at the same time, the example is telling: the Amish are an excellent example of a resolutely local community, whose life is made possible by a system of belief that coexists with great difficulty with modernity. The Amish are an extreme example, but note that Schwartz also mentions membership in a "religious community." Given our existence in a relentlessly secular civilization in which a majority of people claim to believe in God but rarely go to church—and not even that in Europe (where at least people are honest enough to say they're atheists)—we can, however, ask: How can we attain a local existence (as defined by McKibben) that seems to depend on modes of belief (religious, technological) that have largely been superseded in the modern world?

The most obvious example of this, then, is religion, but in a way, participating in a fully local—and communitarian—existence demands a similar willing suspension of disbelief. McKibben would have us maintain our current cultural sophistication, reading contemporary psychologists and social thinkers, plugged in to the internet and all its conflicting versions of truth, where we learn about, and then can struggle against, the forces that are changing the global climate. We will have to do a fairly agile dance, thinking globally while acting locally. But how to act locally? How to separate the details of *belief* in a local life, which may entail much more than the local, with the *recognition* of the necessity of the local? How can we, in other words, engage wholeheartedly with others on a local level, engaging in localized belief, when all the while we are thinking that we are doing so for the sake of our own personal psychological health, and for the health of the planet? How can we, for example, "believe" in a "religion" while all the while we know it is mainly a tonic that will help us sustain our sanity? How do we go back home once we have bathed fully in the global, secularized world of consumption and simulation? How do we affirm the low carbon lifestyle while we jet around the world trying to understand and change it?

We think of Pascal's old dictum: go through the motions and you will believe. "The sign of the cross, holy water, etc." You wager on belief in God to save your soul—you have an infinity to gain and nothing to lose. Today we would say, after McKibben: you have a world of durability to gain, a healthy mind in a healthy world, and nothing to lose (but your pollution). But how to believe, all the while ensconced in a pragmatics of success (even ecological success)? I will participate in my community—because it's good for me . . . To do so I will have to travel the world . . . I will believe because it's useful . . . Again, cognitive dissonance: belief without belief. Or one kind of belief coexisting awkwardly with another. What motions should we go through, what holy water should we dip into? We have to believe in a religion, belong in our locale, when our civilization tells us not to, and when we can only affirm the local by going global through our globalizing powers of reason. Belief and belonging suddenly take on the aspect of revolt, which inspires not comfort but a sense of separation and refusal.

The closed economy of sustainability, then, is not perfectly sealed, a cradle to cradle, seamless and durable whole in which nothing is lost, but in which presumably nothing can be added either (to add to it would break open its circularity). Sustainability, in its localized, political version entails a radical and no doubt traumatic break from the present, the opening of

another time, and not just the continuation of the present one, whatever
and whenever it might be (the present without a fallen future).

Can other versions of sustainability be developed? By whom? What
would they be like? If we still need a theory of sustainability—how things
overall, and objects (animate and inanimate) in particular, play out over
time, how a given desirable environmental state of affairs is to be maintained (or more to the point, sustains itself)—then, I would argue, we should
think outside the box of the three pillars, though the concerns they represent would still be addressed, perhaps indirectly, by other versions, and fictions, of sustaining.

Perhaps one way to look at alternative sustainabilities would be through
the lens of "scale critique." As Derek Woods points out, rather than seeing
the Anthropocene from only one scale—a hierarchical one, with "Man" at
the top, author and victim of ("his" own) environmental degradation, it is
more fruitful to consider different scales of time and space as a whole, much
as in the discontinuous changes in scale represented by the film *Powers of
Ten* and Google Earth.[13]

In a similar way, Woods argues, the "author" of the Anthropocene is not
a single anthropomorphic identity, but rather an "assemblage" of different-
scaled magnitudes. Such a series of assemblages, Woods argues, is "horizontal," a conglomeration of causes and effects, agencies or agents of all
different sorts, working together, or at cross purposes, and resulting in what
many are calling the Anthropocene (more on Woods's version or scale critique in chapter 2).

I would argue that we can approach sustainability in a similar way: rather
than a tightly knit conjunction of three aspects, always with the indefinite
preservation (or "flourishing," as they say nowadays) of the human at its
apex and goal, a scale-critique sustainability would stress the heterogeneous
elements, the jumble of different scales, that go to make a sustainable reason whose "subject," if we choose to use the word (as Woods does), is both
a summit and perhaps the catastrophic fall of an all-embracing and universal knowledge of the interactions of stuff (living and nonliving). Just as
a scale-critiqued Anthropocene would still have within its purview some
tweaking that would allow the planet to go on without frying to a crisp, so
too sustainability could be seen now as a science of continuation, an absolute knowledge of going on, but without the satisfaction of the human at
its summit. The human, if not "Man," would be in there somewhere, but
challenged as the unique scale (and hence measure) on a number of levels:

not just human presence, human stardom, but also human subjectivity as agency, human reproduction as the fulfillment of natural law, human consciousness as reflexive and permanent selfhood, and so on.

The scale-critique of sustainability, then, ultimately results, rather than in a presiding subjectivity, in a proliferation of disproportionate sustainabilities, which couple with each other, conflict, break apart, and reunite in a nonhierarchical fashion. For our purposes, I have isolated three of them, which conjoin (or proliferate) in mock-Hegelian synthesis.

First-order, or unqualified, sustainability will be one to which the human species is largely irrelevant (chapter 1). This sustainability rigorously resists any characterization (qualification) that might be applied to it (inevitably for human ends), and is therefore useless (unqualified) for any task a human might want to burden it with. It engages the great unthinkable behind Jeffrey Sachs's book. That massive book never once considers the glaring question: Why should humans be sustained, or sustain themselves? Are they significantly different from nonhumans (organic and nonorganic)? Ecology for scholars like Sachs is inseparable from the humans within it: it serves as their base, the source of wealth at their disposal (hence "ecological economics"), and it must be massaged in such a way that humans will survive into, one has to assume, the indefinite future (but for how long is never specified). But what if we zoom back a bit, both in space and time—or forward, for that matter? Why are humans so central to creation? They certainly are in various theological models, but if those models too are zoomed beyond in our scale-critique, the human sacred quickly recedes.

Who says we have to sustain what we have right now, and not at some other (historical, cultural, geological) conjunction? Why is right now preferable to some other period? Who says the human has to be sustained by the human, or that the planetary ecologies need humans to sustain them? Given the right (or wrong, as the case may be) scale, we aren't even a factor. Put several scales together (as Pascal did) and we become very difficult to situate, monstrous in our homelessness, our little-bigness. Franz Kafka once stated: "There is plenty of hope, an infinite amount of hope, but not for us."[14] We could just as easily say: "There is plenty of sustainability, an infinite amount of sustainability, but not for us." Or indeed for us, but on an unknowable scale. Why should we be so central to sustainability? Nothing we do is going to have much of an impact on Antares. Black holes can take care of themselves. But what is sustainability without us, or with us, but only as the infinitesimally small or the grotesquely large?

In its most rigorous formulation, first-order sustainability is analogous to dark matter, situated in an unstable zone where its effect can be felt but where it evades knowledge (as one would expect, given its status outside the parameters of the necessity of human awareness). Is the universe devoid of consciousness? Does its function sustain itself without humans because we are nowhere, or at only the most insignificant vanishing point (since our species will soon be extinct)? But then how do we come to be here at all? Are we an anomaly, with no coherent place in the scheme of things? Or, on the contrary, is consciousness everywhere in the universe, and are we simply one insignificant example of it? How did our consciousness, which we usually take as the capstone of creation, come to exist at all? And what is its "existence," anyway? Is there any real difference between an omnipresence of consciousness, of which the human mind would be just a minor example, and the preeminence of human consciousness in an (otherwise) enigmatically empty universe, the universe of things?[15] But if we discount our observing consciousness, our perspective, how can we say that what exists "out there," which apparently sustains itself, really does so? Metastatements on first-order sustainability appear to be resistant to any empirical knowledge. And yet when we look at the sky, we know that the heavenly bodies are out there, somehow self-sustaining, for a while at least.

Central to the considerations of this first section of the book, and to the other two that follow as well, will be the question of the city, and of the energy that powers it. One of the greatest environmental issues of our day is energy use in cities: the need to reduce urban energy inputs, the inherent efficiency of the city versus the country, the inefficiency of current cities. Cities, of course, are giant assemblages—hyperobjects, if you will—operating on a number of different scales, so a consideration of the city will be necessary, even in the context of a sustainability that can be seen as operative outside the imperative of the human (chapter 2). Does urban ecology "need" the human? What is the city without humans (as agents or subjects of perishability or sustainability), or humans as now configured (in various ways)? What of humans only as animals, or as primarily observers of (other) animals' traces?[16] Are there nonhuman cities? Ants' nests? Hives? Species that can never be properly localized? Cities of simulacral but absent humans: statues, icons, or humans whose "presence" cannot be simply or straightforwardly ascertained (or separated from animals or things)? Sustainability, both in its traditional variants and in any scale-critique variant, will necessarily consider the problem of energy and its relation to bodies, animate and inanimate, in movement, in growth, in death, in cities. Cities are conglomerations, junctions of energy conservation and expenditure systems, and even in their decline, their incoherence, their speed, they could be considered as agents—and victims—of sustainability.

But first-order sustainability in a strange way generates the second. The human is finally revealed, insignificant as it might be, as the minder of machines and the things they make (chapter 3). But it is an unconscious minding: we mind the world as we mind the road when we drive (Heidegger's "ready-to-hand"). The world, the machine, minds itself. Our consciousness simply melds with the task at hand, that of driving, that of functioning. This is a version of first-order sustainability in which "we" are nothing more than elements in a world of objects that can seemingly sustain themselves without us. Our consciousness, situated always in a body, is that of the proper functioning of machines, without focus on the machines as separate, recalcitrant objects. This is the world of statues that glorify this relation, and that might very well also reflect critically upon it. And this is the world of the consumer who doesn't stop to think much about his or her consuming (or driving). Drivers remain blissfully ignorant of their carbon footprint. Wall-E works in a ruined world of trash, focused only on the task; "he" doesn't even need to be human. But when the machine of rhetoric flips, when the machine and the icon of the human (the statue) revolts, we can know ourselves as outside the world of machines, and in that case, the world of language and devices needs us to observe and maintain it—just as our car needs our attention when it stops working (Heidegger's "present-at-hand"). This is the result of an anamorphosis, the aftereffect of the rhetorical conjunction of figure and grammar that is at the basis of, if not identical to, consciousness. Initially there was sheer meaning, sheer self-sustaining aside from maintenance and measurement, even aside from us. Now we know the world, we attend to its rhetoric (of which we are an aftereffect) and service its machines; we are separate from it but vital to it. We have passed (and always re-pass) the unthinkable but unavoidable border—the anamorphosis's edge—between the two modes.

Second-order, or restricted, sustainability, following from the first, will be the concern of the three central chapters of this book. Let's assume for a moment that, for whatever reason, the presence of humans, no matter how tweaked (and humans have always been cyborgs, inseparable from their tools) is somehow important to "the" world (a tautology: the world of humans!), or at least to *a* world with which it is somehow associated. Humans have the responsibility to measure it, know it, sustain it, keep the machines running, if only to help themselves. They see its limitations, its finitude. They assume their own presence for the indefinite future, and, since humans rely on "natural capital," they must assure continuing supplies of resources. Ecology and its embodiment in/as economics will serve humans, but humans will necessarily serve ecology, in its most practical avatars (sustainably run farms, organic orchards, nature preserves [involuntary or not], etc.). In this second-order variant I want to examine a bit the grounds for and consequences of a sustainable thinking that values the human above all.

"Saving the world," no matter how necessary, is never entirely innocent. I argue in these chapters that classical, human-oriented sustainability depends on certain political gestures that can be traced back to traditions of energetic and technocratic theory. Energy supplies are finite, and depletable; everything in second-order sustainability flows from this. I'll look at energy economics from the early part of the twentieth century, and Technocracy Inc., a movement of the 1930s influenced by economic crisis and by the mass political movements of the era (chapter 4). I note that one of the key thinkers of Technocracy, M. King Hubbert, was also the prophet of "peak oil" celebrated by many sustainability proponents of the early 2000s. Thus many of the problems inherent in Technocracy are reproduced in later, widely known approaches to sustainability. My point is not to criticize the need to be aware of and adapt to the finitude of resources, but to note that a purely instrumental conception of the object—as repository of embodied energy—presupposes a certain relation with that object that is itself technological. That is, (second-order) sustainability is a purely pragmatic orientation that requires measurement, top-down decision making, and self-discipline (or enforced discipline) on the part of the population. All well and good, but this means that subjectivity itself then becomes an object, a unit that is to be re-formed, through coercion if necessary, so that consumption in the right way will ensure a healthy planet. A purely rational measure of the object and its finitude depends on a rational mass subjectivity that will either conquer its own irrational desire to consume (and expend), or have that desire more or less forcibly extirpated.

There is nevertheless a contemplative side to a rigorous second-order sustainability. We see this quite clearly in Le Corbusier, for whom a rational solar world is also one of withdrawal and meditation (chapter 5). Pascal's

withdrawal into a room is ultimately Le Cobrusier's ideal: the entire intri-
cate and fundamentally static city he plans has as its ultimate goal the silent
contemplation of a subject alone in the "machine for living." But this withdrawal is under a larger Kantian imperative, one that, as we will see, entails
a kind of sadistic superego, one very much in tune with an ethics of imperative conservation. Already in Le Corbusier this rigor starts to crack:
the heterogeneity of Le Corbusier's meaning-giving sun also spins off a
subversive double, the residue of the subjectivity (with its whiff of bourgeois self-pleasuring) whose "pathology" is its very individuality before
the ethical imperative. This pathology can be associated with Georges
Bataille's notion of a violence and insubordination of the object that Le
Corbusier's model would, on the surface at least, master. The heterogeneity of a "sovereign" subject is generated through the affirmation of a rigorously rational ethics that has no place for a pathological consciousness
or an insubordinate object. The cell of the supremely rational meditator,
blissfully unaware of the supporting mechanism, morphs into the regions
of the madman proclaiming an eternal return that is slightly out of phase
(the phase of deviant subjectivity). The ideal city reveals just beyond (or
inside) its borders a labyrinth at the center of which is the death of the
empire of reason.

The triumph of the second order, then, is also its downfall. The third
technocratic figure I will examine is Ernst Jünger, whose affectless technological world of production and energy flows is supremely irrational: it
is a world of total mobilization, the subordination of all useful activity to
the destruction of and by its own products in war (chapter 6). This cult
of modernity, "rational" use of resources, and destruction of excess in the
cruelest manner possible—typified by the relentless back and forth movement of the machine gun—is answered by Walter Benjamin, who, like
Jünger, bases his model of technology in the repetitive movements of the
machine. But Benjamin's machine is also an aesthetic one—the motion
picture camera—and his avowed Marxism, established in opposition to
Jünger's protofascism, is based in this very (photographic) model of repetition. But Benjamin's model also entails a repetition of history itself: liberation is to come from the pileup of the ruins of capitalism, hurled forward
through the blind and uncertain repetitions of moments of history, into
the next moment of social development. Jünger is blissfully ignorant of
the fuel that powers his explosive aesthetico-political combine. Benjamin
recognizes, on the contrary, that fuel in and as the very historical ruins that

undergird, but also clog and destabilize, the capitalist enterprise. The object now is revealed to be not only a stable repository of (recycled) energetic inputs, but an explosive avatar of an unknowable future, blasted forward as a wreck from the past. The old fetish explodes commodity fetishism. This future is not utopian—that is the province of a changeless and pristine second-order sustainability. Rather it is messianic (without a Messiah), the (cinematic?) "aperture" through which we see a world perhaps (as in Kafka) always beyond our grasp, a promise as much as a fulfillment.[17]

Those ruins are what third-order, or general, sustainability recycles, and from which it derives its energy. Its energy is not the power that necessarily lights houses or drives engines, nor is it somehow embodied in the ecological footprint of useful and ultimately consumable things; it is the energy of the object in its power as fetish and avatar of the death of closed systems of knowledge and analysis (chapter 7). This sacred energy has its own economy, its own power, its own model of repetition. It is the power of the fetish in revolt and degradation: the object now reveals itself in withdrawal, bearing a repulsive or compulsive charge. We see this already in the monstrous conjunction of sustainability and resilience; the latter impossibly "supplants" sustainability (whose defiance of time cannot be supplanted), supplementing sustainability's time-negating return with a temporality that engages a nonrecuperable return (the loss of entropy) *within* a system that is "always already," in relation to what comes after. This opening to a defectively recurrent time is the opening to the messianic (in Benjamin's formulation), but one that both faces the past *and* the future.

Third-order sustainability is that of the excess produced by any ecological, social, or intellectual system, as first noted by Bataille in *The Accursed Share*. The problem is how to "face" such a negativity, recognizing its imperviousness to simple reappropriation. This negativity, in excess, "out of a job," not only opens the historical and conceptual system that would contain it, it puts in question the discrete subjectivity that would know and contain manipulated and conserved objects. Hence meditation (chapter 8): this is the practice of subjectivity in contact with the expenditure that opens a messianic aperture in its closed scale of development and permanence. In meditation the object returns not as that which assures stolid utility, but as a flaming, time-saturated element opening the *ipse* to impersonality, ecstasy, and death. The affirmation of time and death in meditation is the acceptance of that which most challenges the finite limits of an appropriating self. Accepting temporality (hence *another* sustainability), melding with it, means accepting the loss of limits (personal, cultural, urban) erected precisely to fend off the vicissitudes of time.

Finally, the object as radical withdrawal in affirmation of time and unrecoverable energy meets the economy in which a larger social sustainability can be affirmed (chapter 9). Sustaining involves a subject open to radical consumption—not the stockpiling and "use" of the capitalist economy, but the consumption of sacred objects in pleasure and communion. An economy based on this consumption consumes that which has already been consumed, but in a sacred fashion; scrounging and gifting in the ruins replace accumulation and dumping.[18] The logic of the scrounge is the logic of an economy at and after the end of capitalism, which is also the end of the world, since capitalism, with its energetic regime, has entirely made the world that we know. We cannot "foresee" this other world: we are as blind as Benjamin's (and Klee's) angel, facing backward but rushing forward or facing forward and looking into the face of the unknowable and unpredictable. This future is infinitely distant, we cannot kill it, and yet in blindly seeing it, subjectivity itself mutates, shifting from one of exclusion and consolidation to that of the recognition of the mortal wound in "us," the inner experience of the loss of appropriable matter.

Hence Pascal in his cell, in Le Corbusier's city, but the economy of the city, and the subjectivity of the meditator before the finitude of time and life, are transformed, in an anamorphosis, from a technical construct into a gift economy of sacred and subversive things. Second-order sustainability can never be escaped or evaded; we will always be *subject* to it, measuring, calculating, and working to preserve endangered resources and species. The effort to imagine a perfect eternal return in which what was lost is restored always reasserts itself (but with resilience it is invaginated). The classical mechanics of the end of history will prevail as sustainability, in perpetuity: no more damage can be done and hence nothing more can happen. But in a rhetorical transfer that is also a transfer in the vision of the object and time, there is another subjectivity, one that does not grasp and promote itself, but rather communicates in the moment of radical loss, and another object, which unites a society of lovers only by splitting them in the opening of erotism and death. (Third-order) sustainability is not the goal but the aftereffect, the result of the gaze backwards: the subject (the *ipse*), and the object (charged with *mana*), are consumed, as the base expenditure entails the recognition of the unrecognizable surplus. This sustainability "means" the saving, but also the ecstatic scrounging and spending, of the lost world, the uncontrollable movement of time and change against the endlessness of the end. The messianic arising out of, and against, the utopian—perhaps.

There are two limits to growth, braided together: the limit of the not enough, the impossibility of ever having enough to grow forever, and the limit to growth in the saturated field; in the latter case growth will continue, ever more will be consumed, but sustainable consumption in this case entails not conservation and reduction but the necessary flaming consumption, on all levels, of the "accursed share." These two limits are not incompatible; when the limits to the first growth appear, one finds oneself already in the realm of the second, the realm of the expenditure of the very logic of growth, and thus the logic of capitalism. Sustainability in this second limit now propounds another consumption, one of subjectivity itself, and of the object as inert and disposable. This expenditure is not, cannot be, purely logical, since the consumption of any surplus not devoted to further growth is a non-sense, a violation of the laws of utility that govern the modern world and its economic laws of energy. Sovereignty passes from the unconditioned grounding of a coherent world to the general sustainability of the subject face-to-face with the economy of the squandering universe. Infused, perhaps, with consciousness, but devoid of a putative human subjectivity that would only, in delusion, *conserve,* this universe of first-order sustainability returns to intersect with a third-order posthuman economy reestablished "on the scale of the universe."

An added note: My title is evidently inspired by that of Félix Guattari's book, *The Three Ecologies.* As is well known, in that work Guattari conceives of ecology not only on the environmental plane, but on the mental and social planes as well. The present work should not be read as a critique of Guattari, but perhaps only as a preface. It considers ecology, and the larger aspects of sustainability in which it is to be conceived, not in and as a single *tranche* of time (a conception nevertheless desirable in any second-order sustainability), but as a multiplicity of braided and conflicting temporalities. Ecology implies a system of interrelations, second-order cybernetic loops, and the transformations of those loops. I would argue, however, that any given ecology (such as any earth ecology incorporating humans) cannot be seen as a static endpoint, or as a necessarily desirable endpoint (the definitive presence of aspects of the human in an ecology, for example). Since life emerged on the planet, there have been an enormous number of ecologies, some more long-lasting than others. Some ecologies were, no doubt, from a human perspective, quite unpleasant (the initial ecology of the cyanobacteria, the ecology of fauna and flora shortly after the impact of an asteroid, etc.). Some ecologies have been sustained for millions of years, others probably for no more than a few days or a few decades. The larger question then arises: Which ecology, how to arrive at it, how to sustain it? And, of course, how is one to characterize the sustaining of that, or any given, desired ecology? All this involves questions of sustainability disproportion,[19] of the subject and of the object in mutation, in ecstasy, before death. In other words, a general theory of sustainability. In this book I have simply tried to think about the question of sustainability *in relation to time*—that is, I've tried to sketch out different approaches to a sustaining of an ecology, with or without, before, during, and after, "us," in the anamorphoses of our rhetoric-consciousness, approaches that can account for different modes (some more desirable, from a human perspective, than others) of the expenditure of energy.

Unqualified Sustainability

1 Objects, Energy, the Chora

The vexed problem of the Anthropocene epoch, one could argue, is nothing more than that of sustainability writ large. If "man" changes "the earth," interfering to such an extent that the climate of the planet changes, a new geological and climatological era is not only in question; what's really in question is the ability of "man" to rein in the changes "he" has wrought, in order to preserve the way of life "he" has known for at least the last century or so. The Anthropocene is not a neutral term like the Pleistocene or the Holocene; it implies catastrophic change, and extinction events, the likes of which have been attributed, heretofore, to things like the impact of asteroids on the earth. What's scary about the Anthropocene is that it promises, or announces, the end of the Anthropocene; extreme climate change, one can easily imagine, will lead to the extinction not only of significant portions of all currently living species, but of the species *Homo sapiens* as we now know it. We have met the enemy, and "he" is us—in our capacity as changers of the planet.

So we imagine not so much escaping the Anthropocene as ameliorating it so that it no longer continues to do ("us," the environment with which we are familiar) harm. But humans, scientists will be quick to point out, are not the first to trigger an ecological crisis due to the production of harmful waste gasses. Cyanobacteria, as Dorion Sagan points out, "mutated two billion years ago, causing the greatest pollution crisis in planetary history." He goes on to state:

> The release of oxygen (O_2) from water (H_2O) must have been a horror show for any beings that could feel. The killingly reactive gas accumulated in the

oceans and atmosphere on a global scale. Many life-forms, beginning with the green bacteria that first released oxygen gas as waste from photosynthesis (before life evolved metabolic means and behavioral stratagems to tolerate and then exploit the reactive gas), must have perished.[1]

The larger point here, of course, would be that organisms subsequently evolved to tolerate and then absorb, and make use of (and depend upon), the "poisonous" oxygen. Die-off and evolution go together; planetary ecological crisis is a relative term, based above all on a certain temporal perspective. From the perspective of many one-celled organisms, the overpopulation of cyanobacteria was a "horror show" on a certain day (or a certain millennium) two billion years ago. But from a different scale, ours "today," the crisis was necessary; indeed it set the stage for what came later. The same can be said for the extinction of the dinosaurs, and so on.

We can say, then, as a first statement about sustainability, that it is time-conditioned, even beyond being species-conditioned. We might speak of short-term sustainabilities (the sustainability that would have ensured the survival of the bacteria that thrived before cyanobacteria; our own sustainability as humans); but we could also speak of longer-term sustainability, on the scale of billions of years (that of the sun, of galaxies). The temporality of a black hole is not human temporality. So sustainability might be species-conditioned, but then again on a much longer timescale it goes beyond the survival of any given species, or any species at all.

From this perspective, sustainability might not even involve ecology. But it certainly entails energy, energy flows, and things (matter, objects). For something, anything, to sustain itself, energy must continue to be expended—and to flow through, so to speak. As Sagan goes on to say:

> Vladimir Vernadsky understood living matter as an energetically infused moving mineral, an impure form of water, a "geological force." Part of an Earth-solar process, humankind and technology ride on the multi-billion-year transduction of solar energy. . . . Life, including all human life and technics, is essentially a solar energetic phenomenon.[2]

From this perspective, the sun's sustainability is inseparable from the sustainability of life on the planet, and the sustainabilities of any number of species, both living now and (more likely, in terms of overall numbers) extinct. We, and our fellow species, are, as Sagan points out, epiphenomena of the sun's energy flows; life on earth reduces the "energy gradient" between the heat of the sun (5,400 Kelvin) and the coldness of outer space (2.7 Kelvin)—lessening heat, recycling waste, organically reproducing.

If there is a macrosustainability—the sustainability of genera rather than species, the sustainability of stars rather than starfish—there is also a micro version. Within a species—any species—there is a tendency to appropriate as much energy as possible, and of course reproduce as much as possible. If conditions are favorable, and there is more than enough food, and a paucity of predators, a species will proliferate. While a "climax" ecosystem entails a provisional balance between various species, "disturbed" or "colonized" ecosystems often leave openings for colonizers, who are capable of appropriating large amounts of food-energy for themselves. The classic example is the rabbit, introduced in Australia in 1859; it was an exotic species that discovered a lot of food-energy and not many predators. The result: a population "bloom." But blooms are usually followed by "die-offs," since the rapidly expanding population soon overshoots available food resources. The field is saturated, and growth cannot continue. If the exotic species does not go extinct, it eventually finds a niche, and equilibrium gradually returns, for a while at least.[3]

This is a parable of sustainability, now on a smaller, species scale. The invasive species may indeed be able to sustain itself, but not in a bloom where the species takes over an ecosystem and shoves aside a lot of other organisms. Eventually the limit is reached. Where do we situate sustainability in the case of the Australian rabbit? In its short-term sustaining of a population that outstrips the carrying capacity of the continent? Or in the later, greatly reduced numbers where it eventually finds an ecological niche? It should be stressed, however, that even the later sustainability is not perfectly stable; predator and prey populations seesaw, as the oversupply of one group leads to the diminishing of the other.

This is a common situation among animal or plant populations in any number of ecologies, but the important thing as far as sustainability goes is that the crucial term here is "energy." By this I mean, following Dorian Sagan, that the larger function of ecologies and of organisms within ecologies is the capture, retention, and recycling of energy. Organisms and populations of organisms are energy-recycling devices, caught in cycles of flourishing and collapse. Entropy is at the basis of this process; evolution itself is an aftereffect of entropy, in that the very necessity of the capture of energy is due to its inevitable dissipation.

The obvious conclusion when considering the Anthropocene is that humans, with all their technological savvy, are no different from any other exotic species. There is nothing particularly human about the Anthropocene; it is merely a population bloom of *Homo sapiens,* but on a planetary scale rather than a local one. The difference lies in the fact that a particular adaptation, called intelligence, has allowed humans, by various means, such as the processing and burning of fossil fuels, to appropriate more energy to themselves (relative to other organisms) than any other animal has been able to do, at least in recent geological history. (Cyanobacteria may have had an even more spectacular bloom, but their appropriation presumably did not entail the use of intelligence, at least as defined by humans.) As in any population bloom, humans have appropriated the lion's share of energy in their ecosystems, and the result has been predictable.

Sustainability is usually interpreted as meaning the human population of the earth should be sustained, presumably at the current levels, into the indefinite future. (Time is linear but static; the same stuff always happens, so there is perfect repetition lodged within perpetuity.) The current explosion of technical and cultural production is simply due to the use of intelligence / language to maximize energy flows to the species. This means that humans are no different from animals in their most basic relation: to energy. Humans are just one more species, doing what all other species do, and for this reason they do not deserve their own special definition of sustainability. If we consider rabbit sustainability—since we are now considering that word in relation to specific animal populations—there is nothing in it that demands that it be used to characterize the survival of a species at the height of its bloom. On the contrary—since animal blooms always seem to imply a die-off when energy sources have been exhausted—sustainability conceived from a long-term perspective would seem to be more appropriate in the context of a reduced population securely situated in a climax ecology.

Humans from this perspective are merely an energy-effect, and their long-term survival—what we like to call the sustainability of their lives, their civilizations—is dependent on those flows. What is certain is that *there is* sustainability, in different and perhaps radically disparate timescales. What are sustained within limits are the larger energy flows, energy dispositions across matter and time—what Timothy Morton calls "hyperobjects." Morton considers something like global warming a hyperobject, and global warming is, finally, a matter of energy disposition: growing amounts of

CO_2 in the atmosphere trap, precisely, (heat) energy, which results in any number of ecological/climatological effects. Species in their bloom/dieoff cycles could also be considered as hyperobjects.

After too quickly dismissing the term "sustainability," Morton notes:

> Objects can't be reduced to smaller objects or dissolved upward into larger ones. . . . Objects compose an untotalizable nonwhole set that defies holism and reductionism. There is thus no top object that gives all objects value and meaning, and no bottom object to which they can be reduced.[4]

God is dead (the ultimate top object is missing), and there is no essence that sums everything up from below (the proletariat?). In other words, objects are channelers of energy, taking it in, expelling it, without a stable circumscribing totality (a "world"). Energy, for its part, is not something that can be isolated by itself, as an object, in a simple series of closed relations, outside of its effects as it is expended. Species are conservers and channelers of energy, which can never be stable (energy is always being appropriated and expended; it is always in too great a quantity, or too little, in its passing-through and disposal).

How then can we say that there is sustainability, but not for us?

Because, on the first, most basic level, from the perspective of energetic sustainability, there is no human. At its greatest extension, humanity, prizing itself, does what any other species does at the height of its bloom. It takes over all space and tries to continue appropriating space and energy until it has saturated the universe. It cannot imagine anything else, and it justifies this saturation with various philosophies. We can argue that sustainability is always there, is always a fortunate feature of species' interactions with their environments. But since humans are not in any profound sense different from any other species that blooms, there is no reason to think that a self-directed sustainability, where limits are arbitrarily imposed from within, is possible. Sustainability is not human. It is an effect of time (it obviously could not take place without it), and time is an effect of sustainability (what is sustained generates its own timescale). Human intelligence, like any other energy appropriation strategy, has never been about sustainability. It's about blooming. Sustainability as a product of human intelligence is just a subset of strategies used to effect and guarantee the bloom, by ensuring the maintenance of human populations in the largest numbers possible and assuring their consumption of adequate and carefully quantified and renewed amounts of energy / matter. That's fine, and there are certainly (quite legitimate) strategies for generating this version of sustainability (which I'll call second-order sustainability, and will discuss in part 2 of this book). But primary sustainability has nothing to do with this sort of notion on the part of this or any other species. No species has a right to a comfortable perpetuity. (Immortality is a religious notion and has nothing to do with scientific inquiry.) Energy flows cannot be controlled in that way. Our species could die off tomorrow and the planet, not to mention the universe, would remain quite sustainable. Sustainability is merely the continuation of certain energy flows (capture and expenditure) over certain periods of time. It is, in other words, the interrelation of energy, objects (whether living or dead)[5] and time.

In this primary sustainability, there is no waste (or dirt); matter outside of its proper place makes no sense in the context of worlds without humans. It is humans that do the placing. But what then can one say about the place or placing of first-order sustainability? Sustaining, "holding up" (its etymological sense) does not require someone (a subjectivity or individual / collective will) to do the holding or a unidirectionality to determine the proper place of the "up." But what can be posited in their absence?

We can step back a moment and pose a more fundamental issue: the *what* of sustainability. What needs to be sustained? Classic sustainability theory, epitomized by the Brundtland commission, sees sustainability as an exclusively human issue. We should not be too quick to criticize this characterization, though; after all, what can we know, what can we experience, that is *not* human? Sustainability, as it is generally understood, is only a logical consequence of a Kantian position, "correlationism." For Immanuel Kant, in critic Steven Shaviro's formulation, human skepticism was resolved by arguing that the "realities 'out there' must be organized in accordance with the conditions imposed by our minds."[6] Today we largely take this position for granted; we are not solipsists: yes, there is an "outside," but it is always mediated by our perceptions of space and time, by our categorizations of things, by our language and measurement. There is material, there is reality, but we are inseparable from it. And it goes without saying that what used to be called "nature" also exists in this correlationist warp: as soon as we walk into "nature," it is no longer nature, or natural. It is fully humanized because it is we who perceive it, measure it, know it, set ourselves in opposition to it, and thereby alter it. So the Brundtland Commission's emphasis on *our* future in all its avatars is not out of place, or absurd; it is bound up with the very way reality exists, since reality can never be perceived or grasped—can never exist—outside of our interventions, perceptions, and needs.

Criticizing sustainability as overly anthropomorphic, then, is not so easy: What could possibly be outside of our own development, our self-sustaining? How could we ever know it? What is real beyond our world? And what, for this reason, could be more important than preserving our world?

This leads to an interesting problem: if our world, or whatever we want to call it, is so fragile, so in need of conserving or sustaining, how can we say it is our only world? Speaking hypothetically for a moment, we could imagine a complete failure of sustainability: the Anthropocene winds down to its grisly finale, mass die-off of humans ensues, and the world bakes without us. But that future, that fear, presupposes our absence. But how is such a thing thinkable when we have just determined that all that exists is both *in itself* and, necessarily, *for itself*? How can we posit a sustainability that defines itself against a reality—the world without us—that cannot exist for us, and which for that reason literally cannot exist? A human world that doesn't sustain itself leads directly to a world that can never be of interest for us, because we could never know it, perceive it (however sustainable, on its own terms, it might be). The risk faced by sustainability is more remote than a tiny planet in another galaxy, completely beyond our telescopic powers of perception. At least we could imagine someday, somehow perceiving that planet (through the development of more powerful telescopes, etc.); a world without us is even more remote—infinitely remote. Or, conversely, if that other world, the one without us, which we fear and hate, *is* real, what becomes of "us"? And what becomes of (our own) sustainability, and the value we attach to it?

A whole school of philosophy has recently come to approach this problem. The recognition of the Anthropocene has, for the first time, ironically but interestingly enough, helped us posit our radical absence, at a moment when our influence on the earth would seem to be at its greatest. For this school, known loosely as that of "speculative realism" or "object-oriented ontology," the correlationism of Kant no longer applies. Reality—objects—somehow exist beyond our feeble orbit. This observation is both perfectly obvious and intellectually scandalous. For we all assume that the limits of the world are determined by my perception, my language, my concepts. And we all assume, at the same time, that there is stuff out there that we don't know, that we cannot know. But how to reconcile these two opposing positions?

What if there is no "world," no enclosed, encapsulating totality, no safe harbor in which we can know and act? What if that plane of reality where our perception and language have not or cannot penetrate, where our existence is irrelevant, is the "real"?

We don't know anything about it: we don't know its limits, and indeed we don't know if it has limits. Limits are not necessary to it. We can speculate about this reality—hence the term "speculative realism"—but it is not a question of our perception of it. Or even of our thought of it. Speculation here enters a paradoxical phase in which speculation itself must withdraw before that which defies it; but at the same time it affirms itself, and the reality necessarily beyond its grasp. As Shaviro notes, *"Pace* Kant, we must think outside of our own thought, and we must positively conceive the existence of things outside our own conceptions of them."[7]

But why this imperative, this "must"? It's almost as if there is a new duty now, toward a "universe of things" that is utterly indifferent to us, and we enter into a conceiving beyond conception. Perhaps one way of approaching the problem is through objects. "Reality," "the Real," are giant words, and the phenomenological tradition has bequeathed to us a conception of "the Real"—the state of things beyond or below our perception and action— that is gluey, repugnant. It is precisely not objectival, because that tradition conceives of objects as things we use, things we manipulate and know. Hence the gooey dripping stains in Maurice Blanchot's novels (his version of Levinas's *Il y a*), or the melting and horrifying tree roots in Antoine Roquentin's vision in Sartre's *Nausea*. This is a world of the abject, more a philosophical problem (the impossibility of the world without us), or the aftereffect of a bad mescaline trip. The melting goo shows only too clearly that defined objects have no place in this supposed de-anthropomorphized reality.

Speculative realists like Graham Harman are after something quite different, and for this reason they embrace the object rather than dismiss it. But this would only seem to displace the problem: if reality is somehow conceived beyond the possibility of conceiving, how could the object be grasped—both literally and figuratively—beyond perception?

Much of Harman's work derives from Martin Heidegger (as well as, but in a different way from, Blanchot, Levinas, and Sartre), and Harman's focus in Heidegger is precisely on Heidegger's object. Heidegger's critique of technology, elaborated mainly in the 1940s and 50s, entails the realization that the real problem lies in the way modernity conceives of the object: things now are fully knowable, fully serviceable, and all of reality is nothing more than a collection of stuff to be measured off into discrete units of raw material, fabricated, put to use, used up, or just "wasted," and then thrown "away." Hence a kind of total moral degradation has been achieved: the world of agribusiness, the "tourism industry," and much worse. All life, plant and animal as well as human, is reduced to the status of mere measurable raw material.[8] All this today makes perfect sense, in our era of the self-conscious Anthropocene, where the planetary "standing reserve" has been both created by humanity (in its image) and in its degradation threatens to turn around and destroy its author.

Harman's reading of Heidegger focuses on another object, one that would serve as an alternative to the objects that seem to stand before us in plain sight, fully known, manipulated, and consumed. These correlationist objects, if we can call them that, can exist only for us; they conceal nothing from us, they give up everything to our perception and our demands. They have nothing more to give; they are fully captive within our modes of perception, our life world. Heidegger's objects, on the other hand, turn away, conceal, reveal slowly. There is a dimension, many dimensions, an infinity of dimensions, that we can never know and use. Objects in Harman's version of Heidegger are not even dependent on the human. As he writes of Heidegger's 1949 essay "Insight into What Is":

> What is a jug? It is not only a container, but a container that stands independently of itself. . . . Heidegger draws a distinction between objects and things. "Object" is a negative term, used to describe entities only in their presence-at-hand. But "thing" is a positive term referring to entities in their proper reality. The jug is not just an object, since it remains a container whether we look at it or not. Although this was already true of equipment in Heidegger's early writings, the emphasis in that period was on the need for human Dasein to be present for any reality to exist at all: without Dasein, there would be no truth and no world. By 1949, Heidegger's thinking about things had shifted in a subtle way. He now emphasizes that the thinghood of the jug is not dependent on whether Dasein looks at it or not.[9]

The important thing here is not to insist on Heidegger's terminology of "object" versus "thing" (for in the end, from the perspective of philosophers like Harman, all objects turn out to be things in the Heideggerian sense), but rather to stress the independence of the thing (or the object) from the human gaze, and indeed human awareness. The human cannot encapsulate or totalize the thinghood of the thing, and the thing itself cannot totalize itself in relation to other things. Its thinghood is always partial, fragmentary, and all relations between things contain that element of the distant, concealed, and unknowable. Harman, again on Heidegger, notes:

> The world is both visible ("cleared") and hidden, and this is the meaning of the Greek word for truth: *aletheia*. But *aletheia* is not something under human control, since unconcealment always requires concealment as well.[10]

The important step here for Harman and other speculative realist critics is to strip the human from the "thinghood of the thing"—to posit a thing, even an artifact, in no way dependent on the human, its awareness, its gaze, or whatever. The next stage of this thinking allows for an anti (or un) correlationist universe in which the human is not necessary for the reality of the thing. Objects, in other words, don't need us to exist, they have their independence in the fact that their (self) concealment is in a sense definitive. Since they are never fully "present at hand," or just plain present, to each other or to us, human dominion over the object, and indeed over all of creation, is sidelined. And our self-revelation is inevitably equally partial. The very thinghood of the thing consists in the marginalization of the necessity of human consciousness for the thing's existence (indeed the definition of "existence" could consist in the withdrawal of human consciousness in the thingness of the thing).

The philosopher Quentin Meillassoux has pushed this further, positing a universe in which unconcealment (to the human, *Dasein*) is not just partial, but irrelevant. For Meillassoux, there is a world "capable of subsisting without being given to us or to any other perceiver: a world that is capable of existing whether we exist or not." This is a world "that is essentially unaffected by whether or not anyone thinks it."[11]

One can well imagine that we're not far from a philosophical theorization of a "world without us," in the formulation of Eugene Thacker.[12] The Anthropocene, which contains within itself its own negation (total human dominion amounts to the almost instantaneous [in geological time] extinction of the human), leads inevitably to a philosophy of the radical absence of the human.

One can go a bit further and consider thought itself as a thing (in the Heideggerian sense), thoroughly stripped of its anthropocentric mooring. Thought itself, from the perspective of Ray Brassier, takes on the passivity and radical autonomy of the world without us.[13] Thought and thought about thought (and so on to infinity . . .) is therefore, in Shaviro's formulation, "epiphenomenal, illusory, and entirely without efficacy."[14] We are at the antipodes of Descartes: I think now, and therefore I am not (I as a fully self-conscious entity, existing through my thought); my thought accomplishes nothing, and it certainly does not guarantee my existence, or my capacity to subsequently know the world. It is just more stuff, circulating on its own, with moments of contact with other stuff, but also always withdrawn, always radically partial ("concealed"), and even, we might say, radically insufficient. At the moment of our most intense conscious activity, we ourselves are a world without us.

This leads Shaviro to coin a term, "eliminativism," to indicate this world that has no need of us, our perceptions, or our plans, to exist. We are by now a long way from Heidegger, for whom the critique of technology was clearly meant to, in the end, lead to a world where a greater respect for the autonomy, and even dignity, of things would somehow save us (redefined as *Dasein*). Now our salvation is inseparable from our inexistence; the world can indeed sustain itself perfectly well without us. Indeed it always has. Shaviro writes of Brassier's "nihilism," but this approach can be linked to a radical affirmation of the earth: the elimination of the human, and its complex of perception, transformation, and use, opens the field to a world[15] that can once again do its thing on its own, as it had for billions of years before the rather sudden appearance of *Homo sapiens*. Our thought from this perspective is no different from the appearance of the first cyanobacteria, creating one world and destroying another; a world is in our absence. I think, therefore I am not. Or I do not think (or perceive), therefore it is.

This way of thinking—thought as just another thing among things (indeed, how could it be any different from things, once God and Man have died?) leads to another, concurrent possibility: all things think. Descartes is attacked from the other side. Now thought is omnipresent, since it's no different from things, but by the same token, once again, it's removed and partial, to all else and to itself, so in principle it will be nonperceivable. My pencil is just as capable of thought as I am, but of course there is no way to perceive it. But why shouldn't it be? The universe of things is also one of thoughts, but thoughts separated from themselves, concealed, partial, fragmentary, or perhaps melding but unaware of their very melding, or the extent and contours of their melding. The ultimate removal of the anthropocentric gaze is to posit thought not just in animals (where it's fairly easily noticeable), but in everything. Maybe thought is necessary for the existence of the world, but not human thought, and not even communicable thought. It's a universe of solipsistic things, charged with the movement of thought.[16]

There is one area where thought and the object might intersect: that of agency. But thing agency, like human agency (as we know from psychoanalysis) is charged with opacities, realms of unknowability, the sliding of signifiers. Another name for this agency might be "vibrancy." Things are not dead, passive, inert, or glutinous. They move, they act, they respond; materialism that posits objects passively waiting for our use is very much the result of the kind of "enframing" that Heidegger analyzed. Their movement may be precisely what causes the extremes of the radical absence of human consciousness and will ("eliminativism") and the universality of some kind of consciousness through agency (Shaviro includes in this agency sentience, intentionality, vitality, possession of powers)[17] to come together. Jane Bennett, whose work is often cited in the context of the "vibrancy" of matter, has this to say:

> [Had] the sun not glinted on the black glove, I might not have seen the rat; had the rat not been there, I might not have noticed the bottle cap, and so on. But they *were* all there just as they were, so I caught a glimpse of an energetic vitality inside each of these things, things that I generally conceived of as inert. In this assemblage, *objects* appeared as *things*, that is, as vivid entities not entirely reducible to the contexts in which (human) subjects set them, never entirely exhausted by their semiotics.[18]

Bennett here maintains (unlike some others) the Heideggerian distinction between object and thing; as we saw before, in this opposition, "object" entails the inert stuff that "Man" forms, unthinkingly uses and discards; "things" are never fully graspable, always engaged in a play of concealment and revelation. But note as well something that Heidegger, or few, if any, speculative realists stress: this concealment/revelation is a matter of an "energetic vitality." Bennett, I think, is on to something here. We in fact could argue that the vibrancy of things is a matter of the expenditure of energy. At this point it really becomes difficult to distinguish between objects and things—a distinction I will not maintain—because both consist of embodied energy (or "emergy," as Howard Odum puts it[19]).

What seems lacking in most of the discussions on the part of speculative realists like Harman and Brassier, then, is the connection between objects in their thinghood and their expended or expendable energy. An object is inseparable from its carbon footprint, the totality of all the energy inputs that go to make it up. The pitcher so beloved of Heidegger (and Harman) is an object constituted not simply by its use but by the void it contains, which is, we might say, shot through with energy—the energy of the formulation of its clay, of the work that went into forming it (on the part of the potter), of the heat that fired it, and so on. And, as with all objects, plenty of energy is expended just maintaining it, making sure it doesn't get lost or damaged, keeping it heated, cleaning it, repairing it. Maintaining a void around it, not just in it. Even getting rid of it, disposing of it, requires energy (it has to be compacted, driven to the landfill when it no longer gives us joy). Just maintaining stuff, and then getting rid of it, is energy intensive, as any collector knows (and we are all collectors). But all that energy is human oriented; Bennett could cite the energy of objects not under our purview, the parameters of whose operation is still to a large extent beyond our grasp: the "big bang," the physics of black holes, and so on. This energy obviously goes beyond all the fairly puny human efforts to harness it, just as "things" (in the Heideggerian sense) go beyond the efforts to contain them, and fully exhaust them. Just as there is an "object-oriented ontology," we could speak of an "energy-oriented ontology." If "we" are "made of energy," if life and everything else is a "solar energetic phenomenon," then the vicissitudes of the object are the movements of its energy; the end of the passive and inert object is to be found not only in the Heideggerian "thing," but in a Heideggerian energy. The two in their revelation/concealment might be one and the same.

Of course it's up to us to consider that energy, because Heidegger's thing was more "things." If objects are nothing but the ("embodied") energy that makes them up, where then is the energy? I can see a pitcher, even stick my nose into its void, but I cannot "see" energy itself. In revealing itself to me—in kinetic energy, potential energy, chemical energy, nuclear energy—it conceals itself. It never reveals itself as such, a thing sitting there on my table, but only in its conversion, when it passes from one form to another, and the loss entailed in that conversion (entropy). Its revelation is its loss. The chemical energy in gasoline is converted to heat energy, which in the piston is converted to kinetic energy, and so the car moves. But in its very conversions, when I think I can somehow grasp it, it also escapes: there is something always missing in its conversions. There is entropy.

Now it's true that, in principle, I can calculate the entropy in energetic conversions. Energy, like the object, can be formulated as a "presence at hand." But this presence is even more elusive than that of the object: at least I can take hold of a pitcher, turn it under my gaze, give myself the illusion that I have "grasped" it. But energy? As the physicist Richard Feynman wrote:

> [Energy] is not a description of a mechanism, or anything concrete; it is just a strange fact that we can calculate some number and when we finish watching nature go through her tricks and calculate the number again, it is the same. [. . .] We have no knowledge of what energy is. We do not have a picture that energy comes in little blobs of a definite amount.[20]

One can also note that "the energy concept was not at all a descriptive entity," but merely the "mathematical expression of invariance through time, the reification of a stable external world independent of our activity or inquiry."[21] Independent, yes; but as we've seen in the notion of correlationism, this very independence can be turned around, so that energy, like any other aspect of the "stable external world," can be said to exist only to the extent that we perceive it, measure it, describe it, situate it in our own space and time–based experience. Correlationism, rather than being opposed to a science that measures independent things, is in fact characteristic of science.

So what then could we say about a Heideggerian energy, which we could imagine at the basis of Bennett's "vibrancy" of things? Feynman, cited above, makes clear what's at stake: energy never was something that we could imagine as a stable, inert object, just sitting there waiting for us to prod it, break it down, and thoroughly know it. Energy from the first conceals itself, makes it clear that we know only our own activity of measurement and calculation; in other words, we know it by not knowing it, by delineating it in such a way that we think we can manipulate it, all the while not describing it, not capturing it, not really having any idea what it is, not knowing where it comes from (let alone how to call it into existence), or where it goes. It conceals itself in its revelation: its revelation is always fundamentally incomplete, and scarily fleeting (we worry about "running out of energy"). Energy, in other words, does not even give us the illusion of presence-at-hand. To believe we have attained that lofty goal of knowledge and utility is an act of self-deception of the first order.

This self-deception may be said to have its foundation in the first and second laws of thermodynamics, which are quite contradictory until unraveled through a kind of intellectual legerdemain. The first law states that energy in the universe is constant; it can neither be created nor lost. It can be transferred and changed, however (from chemical to kinetic to heat, for example). This law would seem to presuppose a clockwork (mechanical, Newtonian) universe, one whose laws can run backward or forward, irrespective, in other words, of the passage of time.

The second law, however, takes into account the fact that the "heat engine" that Sadi Carnot first cited to understand the mechanics of energy transfer could not run backward. In the second law, the total entropy of an isolated system can only increase over time. Energy transformations were discovered by William Thomson (Lord Kelvin) to be irreversible; there is always some energy dissipated (where?); the engine cannot be run backwards to provide a full accounting of the energy that first went into it. The term entropy, coined by Rudolf Clausius, is thus the precise measure (first in an engine) of the progressive dispersion of heat (or of any other form of energy). The positing of entropy as an unavoidable double of energy is, in other words, an indication of the irreversibility of time: time's arrow.[22] Time is not perfectly circular (or repetitious), nor can the circular be situated somehow in or as the perpetual.

How are these two seemingly contradictory laws related? Thomson attempted to reconcile the two laws by noting that energy does not simply disappear, but only "'runs down' to less useful forms." Cara New Daggett, for her part, notes the anthropocentric orientation of Thomson's argument.[23] Entropy enables the two laws to be reconciled; energy is still conserved, as per the first law, but in the second it's only lost *to human use*, according to precise formulae. Indeed the very characterization of energy as the "power to do work" indicates that, from the first, energy has been conceived as something humans can make use of to do other stuff. We can say that energy can only be conceived of, known, measured, as "ready to hand," ready to do a job. Energy is what energy does, for humans. Entropy solves the problem of the seeming contradiction of the two laws, but does so by making necessary the conception of a linear, irreversible, and human time. A time, we could add, that we conveniently already know: our time, the time of our daily lives. This is the time of our perception (the story of human experience, birth to death), correlationist time, which happily dovetails perfectly with the scientifically demonstrated (but weird) existence of an energy whose prime characteristic, at least according to human scientists, is to do "work." On one side of the temporal barrier, so to speak, is energy, circular; on the other side is work, a function of entropy. Nevertheless, keep the cycle of energy production / use going long enough, and eventually everything dissolves into "chaos" (maximum disorder). This of course was the great, haunting fear of the nineteenth century, which imagined, in the distant future, a cold and dead universe, where the last bit of "useable" energy had been put to use, and nothing was left but heat death—unadulterated entropy. As Clausius put it, the two terms, energy and entropy, sound alike because they are "allied":

1. The energy of the universe is constant.
2. The entropy of the universe tends to a maximum.[24]

From this double perspective, entropy was indeed scary, because it implied the complete absence of humans in two different ways; either their absence through the absence of unidirectional work, from the get-go, or, conversely, their absence at the end of their allocated temporality.

I would argue that the linearity of time also implies a linear separation of the first and second laws. First, time is circular, and then this circularity is opened out to linearity. First, there is energy, the circularity of energy and no-time (or a circular time in which nothing can happen, an eternal return in which no work can be done); then there is linearity, and the passage from energy to entropy via "work." The first law is superseded by the second, but also, we could say in good Hegelian fashion, maintained.[25] This *Aufhebung* of energy is nothing more than the demand that energy both be all and nothing, as perceived from a human perspective, and that this all to nothing pass in an ordered, linear fashion (the first law is negated, but retained and raised up on a higher level, in the second: this is the movement of time, of history, of useful work). In the passage from all to nothing, from full energy, at the "big bang," to heat death, presumably at the end, energy passes from sheer presence to itself—the first law—to sheer absence from itself, sheer entropy, at the end. But it remains energy—nothing is lost. What separates the two is nothing more than the demand that energy be useful, that time pass. In the doing of work, there is time—human time, at least, time we can perceive and know. But at the same time, even at and after the end, energy remains, it abides even in the timelessness of the end: maximum entropy still entails the constancy of energy. It's dispersed to be sure, nil to the max, but conserved all the same.

Now let's go back to the speculative realists' idea of the "world without us"—the world of stuff that exists without the correlationist demand that the world and its limits be necessarily coterminous with the human world—the world of human language, human perception. If we continue with this line of thought, displacing it from objects to energy, we will have to also consider energy without us, and time without us. Of course, per definition, we cannot say what these would "be," but we can say that energy as it has been formulated in the clearly demarcated first and second laws is entirely within the parameters of human perceptions and needs. Energy without presence, so to speak, would still be identified with the autonomy of things—as Bennett has noted—and with time, but it would not have to be beholden to human, "lived," time. It's common knowledge, at least since Einstein's Special Theory of Relativity, that time is not necessarily anthropomorphic; it can curve, it is related to space, there could even be some kind of time travel. The universe defies the anthropomorphic. If, as Daggett notes, the second law of thermodynamics has opened the possibility of the theories of relativity and quantum mechanics,[26] we could argue that it also opens the possibility of realities that have nothing to do even with the calculations of those theories. We go from speculative realism to speculative energy and time: speculative energetics.

This would also imply, perhaps, a non-Hegelian energy—that is, an energy in which there is no *Aufhebung* linking the first and second theories. The first would not be negated, preserved, and raised up to a higher level in the second. One can speculate, and narrate any number of non-anthropomorphic fictions of the relations between the two laws: the law of energy and the law of entropy, of no-time and linear time, may interpenetrate, with entropy scattered throughout, as in bubbles. Or perhaps energy is scattered throughout entropy. Linear time is scattered in no-time or circular time. Or just as monstrous, there is a region of energy that contains within it a region of entropy: the first law is not sublated in the second, but instead the two are quite distinct, with the second "invaginated," surrounded but ignored by, the first. Or perhaps the two are not distinct at all, but muddled together, or dappling each other, so that time is always off, always on, and energy is always expended but never is (again).

These possibilities cannot be known—to know them (say, scientifically) is, paradoxically, to deny their reality. The problem now, however, is how to think the relation between the first and second laws of thermodynamics. How are they derived, how are they conjoined? If the second is somehow generated out of the first, linear time will also arise: the time of entropy replacing, supplanting, or supplementing the circular eternity of the first. But to presuppose this progression is already to suppose the second law: it is the law of time, after all. The second law is generated out of the first, thanks to nothing other than the second law (linear time), which existed somehow all along, out of time, yet also generating time in time. Instead of this conundrum, we might posit a chora of time and energy. The chora (also spelled Khôra: space, place) in Plato's *Timaeus* is the matrix out of which forms are generated. Plato addresses a fundamental problem of his theory of forms: how does a timeless, perfect form generate a temporalized, imperfect object? What is the connection, the moment of transition between the two?

> Wherefore also we must acknowledge that there is one kind of being which is always the same, uncreated and indestructible, never receiving anything into itself from without, nor itself going out to any other, but invisible and imperceptible by any sense, and of which the contemplation is granted to intelligence only. And there is another nature of the same name with it, and like to it, perceived by sense, created, always in motion, becoming in place and again vanishing out of place, which is apprehended by opinion and sense. And there is a third nature, which is space, and is eternal, and admits not of destruction and provides a home for all created things, and is apprehended without the help of sense, by a kind of spurious reason, and is hardly real; which we beholding as in a dream, say of all existence that it must of necessity be in some place and occupy a space, but that what is neither in heaven nor in earth has no existence. . . .
> . . . And my verdict is that being and space and generation, these three, existed in their three ways before the heaven; and that the nurse of generation, moistened by water and inflamed by fire, and receiving the forms of earth and air, and experiencing all the affections which accompany these, presented a strange variety of appearances; and being full of powers which were neither similar nor equally balanced, was never in any part in a state of

equipoise, but swaying unevenly hither and thither, was shaken by them, and by its motion again shook them.[27]

This passage has given rise to much commentary over the centuries, but for my purposes here, I would note that one might think the relation between the first and second laws in a philosophically mythological fashion (as does Plato). The first law is very much in the mode of Plato's intelligible forms: nothing changes, it is timeless (energy is never lost, never changes as a totality); the second law is the law of change, agitation, violence, loss: entropy (time supplanting timelessness). But where is the "matrix" in which the second is (necessarily) generated out of the first (since the second is the movement of temporality, of coming after)?

Plato's myth involves a kind of sexual division, in which the chora, the space of generation, is a womb, "moistened by water and inflamed by fire"; it "receives" the "forms of earth and air," and then gives birth, shaken and shaking, "never in any part in a state of equipoise."

This is coded as a feminine space, in other words, passive but violent at the same time, shaken and shaking what it produces. But why should we accept this (obviously sexist) myth? Why should the chora be a void to be filled? And most notably, how does time arise through it if it is fully passive? Wouldn't it have to somehow produce time as well as phenomena if it is the mediator between timeless form and temporally bound things?

The passivity of the chora—space as womb—has been questioned by, among others, Rebekah Sheldon: "What would it look like to release the chora from this topographic suppression?"[28] Citing Deleuze and Guattari, as well as Foucault, Sheldon continues: "A resurgent, vitalized understanding of the 'sphere,' the 'support,' the 'chain . . . or system,' the 'moving substrate' in Foucault; the 'spatium' in Deleuze and Guattari; begins to suggest a way back to the chora in its activity, to inhuman reproductions, to an irruptive chora that exerts its own autonomous force" (213).

An active versus a passive chora; but why must it be either? If the chora somehow mediates between timelessness and change, one could conclude that it is both, and neither—that it, in other words, partakes of both things. It could be transgendered, if one wants to assign a gender to it at all. Plato seems to assume that the timeless forms are active (a contradiction?), and therefore that the chora must be passive, in order to produce the things perceived by the senses. But timeless things are perfectly still, while the objects of sense are, well, vibrant matter. Why then shouldn't the chora be perfectly still? Where is, precisely, the action of the chora? In its (seemingly) womb-like nature? Or is it an active agent that somehow transforms the objects of intellection into dynamic objects? Or is it neither—neither active nor passive, neither intellectual nor physical?

If we imagine a chora of energy rather than forms and mutable objects, we may think of it joining timelessness and time. It "isn't" anything—it's a myth. But it's a myth we somehow need—what, after all, links consciousness and matter? A myth, a representation, a metaphor, or a structure that is profoundly metaphorical. (To this day we think of ourselves as not just matter, but as "intelligent," "active," with a "will," etc., and nevertheless also somehow—and that's the mystery—tethered to dumb, passive matter, to our bodies, our meat.) Why not a chora linking the expenditure of energy (the second law) and the changelessness or mechanical repetition of energy (the first)? How, after all, are they conjoined? Generating one out of the other, but not necessarily in any order, and perhaps generating one in the other, repetitiously, endlessly, uniquely (who knows?).

Such a chora is, as Sheldon remarks, given to "inhuman reproductions." Indeed, if the first and second law morph into each other, in and out of time, then the human itself is not at stake; as with the "universe of things," we are dealing with some "thing" that escapes any attempt to grant it reality exclusively via the human.

The word "sustainable" would seem to be particularly inapt when it comes to an energetic chora. Sustainability, as we've seen, is time-centered: humans want (their) things to be sustained, they want to be sustained, in time, over a certain time (which can of course vary depending on context—but the longer the better). In this sustainability, perpetuity still means that things are in time.[29] The chora, however, rather than being temporal, would have to somehow conjoin time and timelessness, or movement as loss and perfect maintenance; in this sense it would be both an origin point of time (the progress of time) but by the same token that which puts sustainability to the test both in the mode of entropy (inevitable loss and degradation) and timelessness (that which can never change, that which always generates time). It would be the space of the inhumanity of sustainability, the point of emergence and loss of what is sustained or sustainable.

This would seem to be the *ne plus ultra* of first-order sustainability—it's the chora that somehow undergirds "what is," but this chora is both the origin of sustainability (coherent, directional time, presupposing continuity that is extendable or that extends itself) and its loss. Since there is no simple temporal relation between these two, one cannot in any sense say the chora itself is a mode of sustainability. It's rather the non-sense of sustainability. But perhaps there are other ways of thinking this most fundamental (non)sustainability. It's not just that there is sustainability, but not for us; there may also be sustainability for the chora, but not for us and not for it. The chora's sustainability might point to an escape from the correlationist sustainability that cannot posit a sustainability outside the human, but in that way it might point to an escape from sustainability itself.

Jacques Derrida, for his part, stresses the irreducible metaphoricity of the chora. What it "represents" is, in fact, a series of metaphors, a system; exiting from them is as impossible as exiting from language itself. Such a version may seem a variant of correlationism, but Derrida's point is well taken, in that irreducible metaphoricity, or tropicality (the irreducibility of tropes) is tied to a time that is irreducible to the demands of a humanized presence. Derrida notes:

> Thinking and translating here pass through [*traversent*] the same experience. . . . Whether it concerns the name of the chora itself ("space," "place," "placement," "region," "country") or what tradition calls figures— comparisons, images, metaphors—proposed by Timaeus himself ("mother," "wet nurse," "receptacle," "impression bearer" [*porte-empreinte*]), translations remain caught in networks of interpretation. They are induced by retrospective projections whose anachronism can always be suspected.[30]

Anachronism, in other words, goes hand in hand with thinking— knowing—the chora, since to know it is already to be trying to translate, compare, and interpret it. The chora is always "like" something else. It is fundamentally rhetorical. Derrida argues that this anachronism is inevitable, and not merely a symptom of sloppy thinking: the "thing" itself, the chora, is inseparable from networks of metaphors and systems of meaning. Our grasp of its meaning is always after the fact—belated. This leads Derrida to conclude:

> It's a matter, really, of a structure and not of some essence of the chora, since the question of essence no longer has any meaning in its context. How,

since it has no essence, will the chora maintain itself beyond its name? The chora is *anachronistic,* it "is" anachrony in being, or rather the anachrony of being. It anachronises being.[31]

Derrida inherits a neologism first coined by the critic Leon Daudet, writing, in 1922, of Charles Baudelaire: *L'anachronie* is a state of being "outside of one's time."[32] But Derrida is not writing of a person, but of a word: chora is not of its time because it always implies a translation, a metaphoric process that inserts a delay, a spacing, into what we might want to be its immediately graspable "meaning."

So the chora is not anachronistic in the way that, say, Union forces in the Civil War using AK-47s would be. "Anachrony" (and its verb, "anachronizing") indicates instead the temporal gap, the delay, inherent in the meaning of the word chora. The chora is this spacing, or rather its introduction into being itself, since the chora, presumably, "is" the between space between timelessness and time, neither one nor the other, and both at the same "time" (16). As soon as we try to say what it is and what it is not, we are back to the undecidability of time, the gap between being and appearance, the metaphoricity that introduces the temporalizing gap of language itself. It's a gap that indicates, reinforces, and separates meaning and being "themselves."

Now, I would argue that this anachrony of the chora, which is the very movement of a delaying time in being itself, introduces a kind of sustainability into what at first seems the impossibility of simple temporal progression. The energetic chora may be figured as the space between, the mutual invagination of, the first and second laws of thermodynamics—of the atemporal, or temporally repetitious law of the conservation of energy, and the temporalizing law of entropy. Sustainability at first would seem to be situated in and against the second law: it is the movement by which stuff does not degrade as fast as it might, either on a human scale (by and for humans) or, as Georges Bataille would put it, "on the scale of the universe." Sustainability is not the defeat of entropy, but its delay (as is life itself), even ideally (and impossibly) its indefinite delay. Indeed, life depends on and presupposes entropy: it is the continuous marshaling of energy resources, and the postponement in reproduction of their loss. As happens in the biosphere, it is entropy that plays itself out in delay (living things expend energy, but in and through the processes of appropriation and conservation). In the simplest sense, we could say that first-order sustainability is the tendency of things to—well, sustain themselves, irrespective of our wants and desires, irrespective of our timescales. But if time itself is deeply anthropocentric, and if unidirectional entropic energy is the "power to do work," then we might posit a more fundamental sustainability: in this case, time is not simply directional, but a gap, a space that does not lead any-where or "sustain" anything. This is the sustainability of the energetic chora, and its anachrony. It is the sustaining of time outside of time, the sustainability that both generates and is excluded, rejected: it sustains both sustaining and rejection, in the spacing of rhetoricity. This is a figurative process—one of doubling, repetition—that operates outside the demands of human agency.

In the *American Heritage Dictionary*'s definition of "to sustain," there is a nice contradiction between different senses of the word. Definition 5 reads: "To endure or withstand; bear up under: sustain hardships." Defini-tion 6, on the other hand, states: "To experience or suffer (loss or injury)."[33] (Can one sustain death?) And this is the sense, I think, and perhaps the most basic, of a first-order sustainability: not one of bearing up, or con-tinuing, or eternally returning to the same point (recovering what had seemed lost), but perhaps suffering, in the widest sense of the word. Not anthropomorphic suffering, but chora suffering. The chora, following Derrida, is anachronistic in the sense that it suffers a profound loss: that of the full synchronicity of its being, its presence to itself, temporally, con-ceptually, generically (in the sense that its genre and its gender, too, are in question: Active or passive? Temporal or atemporal? Deferred tempo-ral or atemporal?). A full synchronicity that it never possessed to lose (it is not simply "in" the time of loss). The chora sustains anachronism. Its injury is the loss of a coherent temporality, of a diachronic movement, or of a synchronic totality. Out of the energetic chora, time and energy are generated, but both are mere human constructs, after-meanings projected, anachronistic attributions of sense, the correlationist demand for ener-getic laws and useful work. As Feynman reminds us, energy is a no-thing, subject to our imposed / required measurements but resolutely resistant to our characterization—like the chora "itself." The chora sustains, in other words, a profound anachronism, a state in which time is always out of joint, invaginated in and against itself, in eternal recurrence, in movement forward, in movement forward in repetition, in repetition in movement backward. (How to distinguish between backward and forward in repeti-tion?) Vibrancy and stasis are not simply opposed within each other, they are in each other in anachronistic pockets, in the nontemporalized sustaining of these pockets.

This, I would argue, is the most fundamental sustainability, but we can't count on it to sustain anything in a simple linear or recurrent movement or narrative; it is not just the remaining of stuff without us ("to endure or withstand"—again, durability), satisfying as that fantasy or revelation might be. It is the point at which energy cannot be taken for granted, not because it "is" finitude, or not simply because it is finite, but because its very relation to a coherent, forward-moving time that nevertheless continuously mandates a return to the point from which it has sprung— the most fundamental component of sustainability—is open to a non-anthropomorphically wounding question. This questioning is the element of delay, of aftereffect, "loss or injury," metaphor, the movement that opens a space of nonsynchronicity within time, or opens a moment of time within nonsynchronicity. The chora is a mythical construct, inherited from Plato, and rewritten afterward. It is not a myth that resolves contradictions on a higher level; it is, instead, the fault line on which disparate times and energies interpenetrate, rub together, repulse, and are repulsed. The chora, then, is of language, but it is not simply a linguistic production resulting from human intention. Human intention may, indeed, only be its aftereffect.

Having reached this *Nullpunkt,* one can turn back, like Lot's wife, or Blanchot's Orpheus, and see what cannot be seen. It's the impossible to see, that which a correlationist frame both mandates and prohibits one from perceiving. A momentary escape from correlationism freezes in the inhuman, in the act of turning inside out, invaginating with the space of the unthinkable, the impossible. That is the chora, and its sustainability. It does not sustain a wound, an opening, in a phenomenological sense; it does not overcome a threat to its body. It sustains instead the noncorrelation, because the doubling of the two laws of thermodynamics, their impossible interpenetrations, their anachrony, is beyond the purview of interpretations, language, laws. From this point there is nowhere to go. Having sustained this most fundamental sustainability, one doubles it by sustaining its injury.

We move on. Who is this "we"? Mere characters in a Samuel Beckett play, linguistic shifters defined by (non)action: we can't go on, but we go on? Since we can't really gaze upon a chora, any more than we can look

at the sun, our gaze turns to what most flagrantly is not us, while reminding us, inescapably, of us (since that which is most human in us—the
Anthropocene—affirms our fundamental animality): animals. Animals are
the not-us we can look at and imagine really being not-us. And they are,
kind of, not-us, perhaps not as not-us as the energetic and temporalizing
chora, but at least we can see them and even talk to them. (And they never
answer, at least in any way we can be sure of.)[34] Animals are, then, the next
atemporal moment of first-order sustainability.

2 Animals, Scale, Death

Nowadays, it seems, it's hard to think about animals. It used to be easy: they were there, we ate them, we played with them, they were not us. True, they helped us (like dogs or cats), so we domesticated them; if they were of no help or use, we invented poisons to eradicate them. The philosopher Descartes thought we were special: we as humans were the *cogito,* the ability to think, to doubt, to be aware; animals were just glorified machines. We had consciousness, free will, language; they just ran around eating things, pooping, and dying; no history, no ideas, no self-awareness. No ability to reflect rationally. Whole tracts were written on why and how we were special: the philosopher Mortimer J. Adler had a book back in the 1960s titled *The Difference of Man and the Difference It Makes.*[1] Needless to say that difference was the difference between "man" and animals.

So lately it's gotten harder. Quite a few of Adler's pet differences have fallen. Above all, language and tool use. It turns out, on closer inspection, animals have both. Perhaps not just like us, but close enough. Do they have rights? Agency? Well, they can certainly suffer; that's the first question philosopher Peter Singer says we should consider: Can they suffer?[2] If they can, then they have rights too: the right not to suffer, the right to live what for them would amount to a good life. They are, in other words, sentient beings. Curiously, Singer is not concerned with animals as species: he is not concerned with whether an entire population of, say, wolves is suffering (if that's the word), if they are in the process of going extinct. Singer's only concern is with the individual sentient wolf: whether it suffers in any given situation. So the immorality of mechanized farming would lie in the massive amount of individual suffering of animals caused by it, not in the collective exploitation of animal populations. Considerations of animals' rights from this perspective are not entwined with ecological concerns. Animal members of an extinct species, after all, cannot suffer.

Animals, then, have rights, but species do not. Any given species from this perspective does not have the right to exist. A species cannot suffer; only an individual can. I think there's something troubling about this. In this kind of argumentation, at first we imagine that we are contradicting Adler and his human suprematism: we are not the only ones to have language, tools, rights; animals are "like us," therefore, and like us they have the right not to suffer. But they don't have the right to exist! Not as a species anyway. If an animal dies without suffering, the last of its species, then that's acceptable. Its individual rights have been maintained. And if we kill it, and it dies painlessly, without suffering through its anticipation of death, then that would, no doubt, be acceptable as well. For the ability to suffer is not confused, in Singer, with a self-awareness that would characterize the human.

Asking if animals suffer, then, does not entail the question of animals' self-reflexivity, whether or not they are capable of self-certainty. Recall that Descartes arrives at his "I think, therefore I exist" through a rigorous process of elimination, in which he incessantly asks himself: What do I know? What can I be certain of?[3] This question is also an autobiographical one: When I figure out what I can know, what I can be certain of, then I know what, and who, I am. I am my own consciousness, which is a consciousness of my doubt concerning what I can know. My doubt is my thought which is me. I am established, elaborated, through time and through the process of my doubt.

So I am my own autobiographical story; I face myself in the mirror, so to speak, I face myself as an other, the other of my thought, my doubt, which is me. Animals need not apply—they don't do this. They are not caught in the speculative–historical relation that is me, myself, and I . The philosopher Jacques Derrida complicates this model. He is certainly concerned with Singer's question: Do animals suffer? But Derrida would knock "Man" off his plinth by focusing precisely on the specular, autobiographical relation, which is also that of seduction and desire. Derrida meditates on being seen by his cat. But this specular relation also involves the philosopher's nakedness; there is the intimation that Derrida feels shame being naked in front of his cat. Human supremacists, of course, would say that this is absurd: the cat knows no shame, it's not human. It couldn't care less that the great philosopher is walking around naked under its gaze. But

Derrida links the feeling of shame, which entails specular and hence speculative doubling—I am ashamed in front of the other, in the mirrored relation between myself, naked, and the other, clothed, who sees me—and the
doubling animals undergo in their rituals of desire. He writes:

> Wherever reproduction functions by means of sexual coupling . . . well, then,
> one has to register some mirror effect—visual, oral, indeed olfactory—some
> hetero-narcissistic "self as other." Especially when . . . this hetero-narcissism
> is erotic . . . account has to be taken of the seductive pursuit without which
> there is no sexual experience, and no desire or choice of partner in general.[4]

Animals, just like people, then, are engaged in a speculative relation of
doubling, of autobiographical (self-)development through an other. They
do it not by reflecting on their own nakedness, of course, but in recognizing another receptive version of themselves in the other, in pursuing
that other, following it, desiring it. The animal too, it seems, has its own
mirror stage.

Derrida does not confront the simple question of the animal's suffering.
His version of animal doubling and desire situates the animal directly in
the same sphere of self-creation through self-reflection in time (the "mirror effect") so central to Descartes's effort at isolating human identity in
(autobiographical) certainty.

This is a new way of questioning "Man's" position high on the pedestal.
But here, too, as with Singer, there is an ecological blind spot. Once again,
the animal is seen as an *individual*. Before, it was the individual animal who
suffered. Now it is the individual animal who looks back. This new version
of animal/human shame is a feature of the age-old shame before a desiring other (now a cat): an other who is separate, identified or identifiable,
separate from his or her species, or community, or environment.

When the animal desires, it is one on one, just as when a human desires.
The human, too, tracks, follows, sniffs out the other, confronts it (him or
her) face-to-face, experiences arousal and its double, shame. When the
human/animal barrier breaks down, if it can ever be said to have existed,
it is as a doubling that doubles the mirroring of the desire relation. But the
animal as a member of a species existing in an environment, in an ecological niche, does not exist—other than perhaps as a sexual hunter.

This is the question that is avoided both by Singer and Derrida: How is
the human to respect the rights of the animal *as a member of a species* (and

not just as an individual characterized by a self-reflecting, or sentient aware-ness)? From an ecological perspective, one could say that the crucial ques-tion is not the suffering or self-constitution of a single individual, but the right of a species to exist. In such a scenario, the rights of animal individu-als will not be the same as the rights of human individuals. An example: the health of certain ecosystems (such as at Yellowstone Park) depends on the presence of wolves—of predators. It has been argued that the park has benefited greatly from the (controversial) lupine presence: wolves hunt, intimidate, and kill elk and coyote, among others. By cutting down the num-bers of those animals, and restricting their freedom of movement, wolves have ameliorated the larger environmental health of the park, and the col-lective health of any number of other species (plants, birds, and animals).[5]

So perhaps animal rights should be seen in the context of environmen-tal health, and the larger health of a species in an environment, rather than of an individual in isolation. But if we think of animal rights that way, the whole specular relation between human as autobiographical subject and animal as autobiographical subject (the scenario of the animal furthering his or her existence through the specular constitution of the self) tends to get lost. What is left?

There is another problem: not only is the autobiographical element set aside (we define ourselves through the other . . .), but the central ques-tion of debunking human exclusivity and superiority is lost as well. Ironi-cally, paying attention to ecological questions, such as the role of a species in a larger ecology, leads to a reassertion of the identity and superiority of the human: after all, it is the human who decides that the wolf will be re-introduced into Yellowstone, it is the human who is using the wolf to cull the elk herd, and so on. By bracketing the individuality of any given ani-mal we only reaffirm our species superiority—the right to decide for all other members of the ecosystem, whether it is to their benefit as individu-als or not.

I think one way to get around this problem is to see humans in ecologies not as the lord and master but as just one more element in an assemblage. Our managerial mastery can go only so far. We too are elements in a larger ecology, and not simply its (collective or individual) decision-maker. In a brilliant article, geographers Steve Hinchliffe and Sarah Whatmore make the point that cities are ecological space and not simply the product of the strategies of top-down human planners, with wildlife (of whatever sort) an irrelevant or secondary add-on. As they put it:

1. Cities are inhabited with and against the design of cities.
2. Cities are not simply inhabited but cohabited, in ways that are multiple and entangled and that disrupt established ethologies and ecologies.
3. Engaging with [various] inhabitants and becomings requires political and scientific experiments, relaxing the coordinates of presence and absence that are so dominant in scientific and legal conservation theory and so ungainly in practice.[6]

This last point is an important one: Hinchliffe and Whatmore single out the cases of several urban denizens, such as the water vole or the black redstart, which are very rare in British cities but that nevertheless, under the radar of human planners and ecologists, establish a "presence" that is never quite certain. Ecologies of place in this view entail not a characterization through simple presence or absence of species that can be determined by all-knowing human planners, but rather an element of "not-knowing" (111). The probable and improbable, in other words, condition not only a science of animal populations but also the very certainty of human subjectivity itself in "nature" (be it "wild" or "urban"). The sedentary planning authority sees its authority usurped by nomadic multitudes. The upshot is a recognition of the necessity of the freedom of all populations, "nonhuman" and "human," in their quest for a livable space within an ecological justice.[7] This model puts in question, then, the autonomy and visibility of both the animal and the human as subjectivities.

Chiara Certomà writes the following on Hinchliffe and Whatmore:

> Who is making the city? [Hinchliffe and Whatmore's] findings show that nonhumans are active agents in forging urban places, and, by converse, their life is constantly influenced by urban relations—even though their ecology might be completely different from the one observed in wild contexts. The result is a peculiar living space where ecologies become urban and cities become ecological.[8]

Of course, one could go on and speculate that the very difference between the "wild" and the "urban" is challenged by this kind of analysis. If indeed ecological space, and not just the city, entails "heterogeneous formations emerging from the interaction between multiple and disparate actors" (100), then such "actor-network" assemblages put in question a model in which such space is always ordered on *the scale of the human*, be it for the benefit

of all humans or, more likely, to the benefit of some and the detriment
of others (race- and class-based segregation, differential exposure to toxic
waste, etc.). Such a scale would entail not only the size of the human (the
human body, ecological space tailored to the human), but human responsibility for and simple presence within larger historical and indeed geological spaces. In this context, opposing city and country makes little sense. Or,
put another way, it's all city, with any given space on the planet an intersection of various networks of agency—that of people (and in and through
them, capital), to be sure, but also bacteria, insects (e.g., leaf-cutter ants),
animals who may or may not be there, toxic waste, all acting together, but
following different but occasionally intersecting and certainly conflicting
agendas.

This question of human agency—of will, of free will, of the consciousness behind or identifiable with free will—touches also any discussion of the
Anthropocene. If the Anthropocene is the first geological epoch formed
through the (inadvertent) action of conscious human activity, then in principle it is different from all other epochs that have come before. Can human
subjectivity be said to be the unique author of the Anthropocene? For Derek
Woods, in his article "Scale Critique for the Anthropocene," the question
is this: Can the human be said to apply, in its volition and presence, on all
temporal and spatial scales? Clearly not, he responds: "Certain scale differences constitute differences of kind rather than degree, and design principles must mutate to accommodate new constraints."[9] "Geometries of
space" act "as a constraint in architecture and engineering"; in the biological world, a scaled-up ant the size of an elephant would not be viable, for any
number of reasons (open circulatory system, different surface forces, etc.).
Woods stresses that there are "domains of scale," discrete breaks between
the operations of, say, ecosystems on the level of scale, both spatial and
temporal. There is no universal scale that can span, for example, the very
small and the very large. The human cannot be said to be the central causative agent in all the scales of space (and we might add, time).

This is a problem considered most memorably by Pascal: *la disproportion de l'homme*[10] involved the fact that the universe was infinitely large and
infinitely small—without boundaries—and "Man" was somehow suspended
between these two infinities, at home nowhere, out of proportion, so to
speak, with the farthest reaches of the cosmos on one hand and the inner
abyss of the atom on the other. There was no top or bottom, and "Man"
could nowhere find a place, a scale. For Pascal, writing in the seventeenth

century, just after the discoveries of the telescope and the microscope, scale disruption meant disruption of the human, of the place of the human in the world, and certainly of human mastery in relation to space and time. Facing the two infinities, humans in Pascal's analysis experienced terror, but above all boredom (*l'ennui*—displeasure, pain, boredom), which they hoped to forget by "diverting" themselves. Pascal invoked God to resolve this crisis, but today God has left the building, so to speak, and the recognition that "Man"—human volition, human consciousness—does not master, and in a sense is not at home in, the world—leads once again to the fear of "his" loss of mastery in an infinity of spaces and times.

A common and, we might say, non-Pascalian way of seeing things is that "Man" is "responsible for" the Anthropocene—that is, climate change, species loss, environmental degradation: a "consumer-cum-geoengineer, capable of customizing the earth. Through analogy, individual human intelligence becomes the subject of the Anthropocene" (137). Human subjectivity, in other words, spans all scales, determines the future (degradation) of the earth, bears responsibility for it, and for this reason bears responsibility, as a subject acting upon an object (nature) for the salvation of the earth as well. Thus the old nature/culture divide is inscribed in the universal scale of the overweening human. Paradoxically, the human would no longer be in disproportion if it were to be said (correctly) to be alone *responsible* for global warming. This would also imply that humanity, again exclusively on its own responsibility, is capable of working its own way out of the Anthropocene, pulling itself up by its own bootstraps.

Woods will have none of it: if we note that there are multiple scales involved, the Anthropocene then becomes much more than simply a product of human subjective will. As Woods puts it:

> The subject of the Anthropocene is not an individual or species-based "intelligence" that, without mutation, projects across scales to shape the matter of the Earth. . . . By contrast, scale critique shows that the subject of the Anthropocene is not the human species but modern terraforming assemblages. . . . When we take the concept of scale variance into account, we can describe these assemblages as the "subject" of the transformation now underway. (134, 138)

All "causal chains," in this view, do not lead "back to the embodied intelligence of *Homo sapiens*"; instead of this vertical chain, there are horizontal

relations between "humans, nonhuman species, and technics," all working together, or at cross purposes, all autonomous or semiautonomous
agents collaborating, or fighting, in assemblages. We are back in the city
of Hinchliffe and Whatmore, but this time it's the earth itself, and a geological epoch called the "present," which is a space–time locus of the interaction of many different agencies, some "present," some not so present,
some knowable, some lost in a cloud of unknowing.

It seems we have moved in the opposite direction from the world in
which humans pick and choose when it comes to establishing ecologies,
whether they be of national parks, cities, or the planet itself. Now "Man"
is just one more factor in a "terraforming assemblage." Global warming,
the catastrophe we all face with trepidation, is not simply the product of
one agent, nor is it amenable to solution by one agent capable of transcending all the discontinuous scales of the planet and the universe. The take-
away from Woods's article is that human reason, acting in and through the
nature/culture divide, is no longer capable of an authority, a responsibility, on the scale of the destruction or salvation of the earth. The most
optimistic reading would hold that "Man" needs to put "his" pride on the
shelf and work with all the other agents in the assemblage. But how to work
with them if the scale of interactions is *discontinuous*? How do humans
work as just one more member of a discontinuous assemblage? How will
the assemblage master its disproportion and get anything done, if the religious option is no longer available?

We no longer have the luxury of Pascal's fear of the silences of infinite space. In any case, we know now that space is not silent, that there's a
lot going on in it, and that we have to somehow figure out how to move
among the disproportions if we are to survive as a species. And, following
Hinchliffe and Whatmore, we must recognize the "not-knowing" associated
with these discontinuities. These are the stakes of the Anthropocene: we
are staring extinction in the face, and our vaunted reason and autonomy—
the very human exceptionalism put in question by Derrida—is put to the
test and found wanting. This is where the real scale disruption lies, one
could argue. The looming catastrophe is situated in the fissure between
our overwhelming knowledge and control—enough to wreck the planet—
and our perplexity as to how to go about saving it.[11] We are both omnipresent and absent from the scene, drifting from one position to the other.
Our disproportion might very well lie in this scale disruption between
the dominion of human reason and its impotence. But no one, Woods

included, is willing to accept a simple incapacity of "Man" on this score. We believe by making a calculated bet, then following blindly various strategies we are told will work. We never confront head-on our radical disproportion; instead we bet that a few simple gestures will overcome the problem and give us a good infinity, in conjunction with the good infinities of all the other actants in the assemblage: not so much an afterlife, but a grand infinity that traverses our existence, overcomes the time out of joint, and makes it all worthwhile. Future generations will thank us. But Pascal writes:

> [Man] feels his nothingness, his abandonment, his insufficiency, his dependency, his powerlessness, his void. . . . I have often said that all the misfortune of man comes from not knowing how to sit calmly in a room. (Sections 131, 139)

Is there more to this *desideratum* of sitting alone in a room and being happy with it? For our disproportion entails not just drifting somewhere between the crab nebula and the quark, between scientific mastery and ecological impotence; it is also the incomprehensible inner space of the assemblage, the linkages we can't fathom not just between timescales, but between the scales of radically different beings—living, dead, technological, animal, plant, mineral, generations long gone and those yet to come. Where do we situate our time in all the other times, how do we see a coordination between them, and how does that coordination allow us to posit a more beneficial strategy of sustainability than that authorized by the "humanity first" doctrine?

Woods seems confident that the master-subjectivity of the terraforming assemblages actually will terraform, and that it will all go better than through the other route, by which humans would somehow go it alone. But just as Pascal proposes two infinities, one good (God), one bad (the double infinity of space), so too we might imagine two assemblages, one good, one bad.

The good one, roughly comparable to Pascal's God, the good infinity that sets right the bad disproportion of the irreligious doubter (or the gambler who only puts money on the line), is that of the assemblage as posited by Woods. A larger conglomeration presumably can do things that the mystified category of the arbitrarily separated human cannot. Woods writes:

> The point of arguing that the subject of the Anthropocene is nonhuman is not to suggest that biological humans can have no influence over this

geological epoch. The point is to rewrite the epoch's causes in order to see what forms agency takes and which mediators entangle it. So long as the smooth zoom and the human/nature gap dominate writing on the Anthropocene, a scaled up, abstract notion of the human mystifies the agency of terraforming assemblages. (140)

So it still is a question of agency, even of subjectivity, but the clash of scale has been overcome and somehow the assemblage as a whole—which incorporates in some way the human—exercises a benign and progressive agency. The vision is a happy one, a good infinity of relations, all actants working together in a larger subjectivity to overcome the challenge of the Anthropocene. Subjectivity and objectivity are once again put in opposition, this time on a higher scale. God is gone, but this subjectivity (agency) comes after Him, putting all the pieces together and helping humans overcome the diversions of multiple and fruitless efforts to solve the problem of a planet dominated by—humans.

That's the good infinity. The bad infinity entails not being able to coordinate between the spatial and temporal scales of different agencies. Above all, the temporality of different agents—their timescales—differ radically. Each agent faces its own disproportion before the two infinities. *And no agent is definitively committed to work with any other.* Nobody's in charge, nobody can be in charge, and all one is left with is a series of unthought and unthinking alliances, played out on a horizontal field. As Ed Yong, in *I Contain Multitudes: The Microbes Within Us and a Grander View of Life,* writes:

A cut or bruise can split some of your cells apart and spill fragments of mitochondria into your blood—fragments that still keep some of their ancient bacterial character. When your immune system spots them, it mistakenly assumes that an infection is under way and mounts a strong defense. If the injury is severe, and enough mitochondria are released, the resulting bodywide inflammation can build into a lethal condition called systemic inflammatory response syndrome (SIRS). SIRS can be worse than the original injury. Absurdly, it's simply the result of a human body mistakenly overreacting to microbes that have been domesticated for over two billion years. Just as a weed is a flower in the wrong place, microbes might be invaluable in one organ but dangerous in another, or essential inside our cells but lethal outside them. "If you go immunosuppressed for a little bit, they'll kill you. When

you die, they'll eat you," says coral biologist Forest Rohwer. "They don't
care. It's not a nice relationship. It's just biology."

So the world of symbiosis is one in which our allies can disappoint us
and our enemies can rally to our side. It's a world where mutualisms shatter
for the matter of a few millimeters.[12]

We cannot survive without microbes and mitochondria, and they without
us, and yet things go wrong. The past is both remotely distant and yet is
ever with us; mitochondria are "us," they are in our cells, they fuel our
cells, but they are also strangers, as they were two billion years ago. Our
time is a hybrid time, or a disproportionate time of different agents, different agencies. Whatmore and Hinchliffe's city/cities, fragmented across
different scales (cosmic, urban, microscopic) may be exciting, but not necessarily peaceful or harmonious. In microscopic space mitochondria can
easily pass from "us" in the present to the hostile bacteria of two billion years
ago. Past generations and future generations come together in a moment
that refuses to be situated in one time, or one easily digested progression.
A moment of survival easily flips to the point of death: a critical threshold
or void erupts at the meeting of times. Heterogeneous times or epochs
violently interpenetrate. And if "our" genome survives another two billion years—all those future generations—it will be tracked by bacteria,
and mitochondria, always with and against us, our agency and theirs, in
our time and theirs.[13] Moreover, this lack of stasis is enfolded within (like
mitochondria) any promise of the sustainable. Ironically, the sustaining of
different generations of different species, things, machines, in different, conflicting or allied timescales, precludes the stability of any simple development of the generations of any given biont, let alone holobiont. It certainly
precludes any talk of a single "subjectivity of the Anthropocene," of whatever sort, be it human *or* assemblage.[14]

I would like now to return to the question of animals. I've argued that
Singer and Derrida seemed to miss the mark when considering animals
only as individuals, with whom we have a relation of either cruelty or salvation. We can abuse them, or we can spare their suffering. The crucial
question is indeed: Do they suffer? In other words, are they like us? We
want to spare, rightly enough, their suffering if they are like us in that they
suffer. That's Singer's line, anyway; Derrida's is less focused on suffering,
and more on desire: when we look into the face of the cat, when we look
into its eyes, and we are naked, do we experience shame? If we do, it's

because animals too have a mirroring relation with the other, mediated through desire. Our grand philosophical tradition that holds that we are vastly superior to animals crumbles when we think of animals as suffering, or desiring.

One could certainly identify this line of argument with that of Hinchliffe and Whatmore: human reason loses its dominion, and the grand overview of Reason loses its power, when it is noted that animals too can feel pain or identify with each other and, presumably, somehow with humans. Just as they work to make and unmake the city, using their tactics in and against our strategy, so too their modes of comportment and reaction, operating on levels that humans often can't even perceive, go to undermine "our" imperial and rational (and illusory) domain of urbanity and self-mastery.

But one could also argue that Singer and Derrida reestablish the scale of the human above all else. Animals are recognized as agents only if they are like us. We approach them as individuals. From Singer's perspective, we are willing to save an animal if we can identify with its suffering. And from Derrida's, we puzzle over what lies behind the animal's eyes only if we determine that, on some level, our shame intersects with its doubled sexual desiring and its mating rituals.

Our solution to this problem, so far, is not much more satisfying. If we consider populations instead of individual animals, we do so in order to protect ecologies, but ecologies only as human artifacts. We marvel at the way the introduction of wolves transforms the ecology of Yellowstone Park, but the new ecology is just as much a product of our will as the old. The animals are used by us to effect a certain result, a certain reconfiguration of "Nature" according to our practical or aesthetic desires. We no longer look an individual animal in the face, but we still are operating on an entirely human scale, as if what we do determines, and exhausts, the meaning, use, and even "intrinsic value" of a locale, an ecology.

Emmanuel Levinas is well known for his philosophy of the "face." The ethical relation is to be found in the "face-to-face"—and this would seem to return us to the issue we first encountered with Derrida: Can we somehow get away from the face, which individualizes and, one could argue, anthropomorphizes the other? Invoking Levinas would seem to go in precisely the wrong direction . . .

But there is more to the face in Levinas than a simple view of the material face of another human. For Levinas, the face is always associated with speech: "The attestation of oneself is possible only as a face, that is, as speech" (201). But why is speech associated with a face that is both the foundation of the ethical relation and, at the same time, infinitely distant? I think Levinas gives us a clue as to both the distance of the face and its status in relation to speech, when he writes:

> The knowledge that absorbs the Other is forthwith situated within the discourse I address to him. Speaking, rather than "letting be," solicits the Other. Speech cuts across vision. . . . In discourse the divergence that inevitably opens between the Other as my theme and the Other as my interlocutor, emancipated from the theme that seemed a moment to hold him, forthwith contests the meaning I ascribe to my interlocutor. The formal structure of language thereby announces the ethical inviolability of the Other, and, without any odor of the "numinous" or "holiness."[15]

Levinas, then, does not put much stock in the visual; otherness is not constituted by or in vision, of the face or anything else. The elevation of the face, its "most High" status, derives from the fact that there is a contestation between the Other as "my theme" and the Other as an interlocutor in its own right. In other words, the face, if we choose to call it that, is the independence of the other vis-à-vis my language; it is the fact that the interlocutor is not my language or characterization, my attempt to slice and dice, but rather is independence in the Other's own speech, in relation to the meaning I would impose. A rhetorical relation puts in question the integrity of my subjectivity as an expression of will. I, of course, can always try to interpret, and I do, the speech of the Other, but I can never own it or control it or totalize its meaning. It is, so to speak, infinitely distant from me, in its eluding of my grasp, my control, my interpretation. I can recognize that distance, or I can take the opposite tack and try to control it, own it, and thereby destroy it.

Levinas writes of a "disproportion" between "infinity and my powers"; we face the paradox that murder, even if carried out, is impossible. The face is weak, powerless; it exercises no control over me, but rather eludes my grasp, infinitely. It calls the world, and my own power, into question. Levinas writes:

> To kill is not to dominate but to annihilate; it is to renounce comprehension absolutely. Murder exercises a power over what escapes power. It is still a power, for the face expresses itself in the sensible, but already impotency,

because the face rends the sensible. . . . I can wish to kill only an existent absolutely independent, which exceeds my powers infinitely, and therefore does not oppose them but paralyzes the very power of power. The Other is the sole being I can wish to kill. (198)

The Other is alone an object of desire—to kill, that is—because it alone eludes my grasp, my control, infinitely. But because it does so completely, killing it is impossible, even if I commit murder. I have still not killed the Other, destroyed the face; all I have done is wipe out something I thought was mine. I have murdered my double, my phantom, what I thought was identical to me in the power of its opposition—but I have left untouched the Other. Against the Other, I can do nothing, even in my worst spasms of violence. As Levinas puts it:

> The impossibility of killing does not have a simply negative and formal sig-
> nification; the relation with infinity, the idea of infinity in us, conditions it
> positively. Infinity presents itself as a face in the ethical resistance that para-
> lyzes my powers and from the depths of defenseless eyes rises firm and abso-
> lute in its nudity and destitution. (199–200)

The Other is power-free, defenseless, and that, one could argue, and per-haps against Levinas, is its power. Its antipower power. Its power is to serve as the institution of the ethical; out of its "destitution" I recognize my own fundamental powerlessness, and respond to its "appeal." According to Levinas:

> The being that expresses itself imposes itself, but does so precisely by appeal-
> ing to me with its destitution and nudity—its hunger—without my being able
> to be deaf to that appeal. Thus in expression the being that imposes itself
> does not limit but promotes my freedom, by arousing my goodness. (200)

It all sounds very Sartrean: I attain my freedom through the recognition of the freedom of the other.[16] Nevertheless, there is a big assumption here, and it has to do with my goodness. Is my goodness so easily aroused? Writing after World War II, Levinas is certainly aware that many millions of murders could be and have been committed by those who would exer-cise their power over others; how exactly the destitution of the other is to bring about my goodness, my recognition that the Other's otherness both challenges me and "promotes my freedom," is not entirely clear. Perhaps it lies in the very recognition that those millions of murders were literally senseless; the tragedy of mass murder, its terrible pointlessness, is the proof—if any were needed—that the simple imposition of power over others is self-defeating. Freedom, in this sense, grows out of the recognition that the violence of trying to impose "the same" on the infinitely distant results not in the joy in mastery of those who would control but in the destruction of their own freedom. Freedom arises, as well, from the recognition of the destitution of the Other—and from my addressing that destitution, and attempting to remedy it, in an act arising not so much from planning and calculation as from my own hunger and nudity.

What has this to do with the Anthropocene? I could suggest that we can reinterpret Levinas by arguing that the face does not have to be literally a face, either of another person, or even of an animal. The face, after all, is Levinas's term for the Other as its speech. But here again we need not take speech in its most literal sense, as what someone says to me in a conversation. Speech can be any number of signs, or traces, left by an Other that I am in a position, or not (and this aleatory aspect is important), to decipher. And the "presence" of the Other is what is in question here. Assuming a simple presence to itself of the Other, a presence that can then fall, without difficulty, under my own power, is what the traces of the Other would preclude.

Here one could think back again to the example of the water voles or black redstarts cited in Hinchliffe and Whatmore's essay. The authors' point was that these animals, these denizens of the city, are not simply "present" and accounted for, by us, the human planners. Their presence is a matter of possibility, of conjecture, of might be and might have been; there is a "non-knowledge" that always accompanies a knowledge, a certainty, of the various nonhuman urban inhabitants. I would argue that our interpretation of their signs means necessarily that they are independent urban agents, and that the possibility of our interpretation depends on our recognition of their independence, their freedom, their radical distance. Just as the face in Levinas eludes our power and institutes an ethical relation of freedom that we then (at least try to) internalize, we could say that animals in Hinchliffe and Whatmore's city, by their very nonpresence, and through their indefinitely interpretable traces, instill in us a recognition of the impossibility of our own ecological power—that is, the impossibility of simply imposing human will and human subjectivity on other "actants."[17]

Recall that I noted that in thinking of animal populations rather than individual animals we risked simply imposing another anthropomorphic vision, another human-centered "strategy," on the collection of assemblages that we call the world. I would suggest now that this Levinasian way of looking at animal "Others" addresses that issue. Other populations cannot be totalized; they are elusive, challenging our notions of accounting, control, tasking, and eradication. We plan, they subvert. We propose our strategies, they work out their tactics. And in the best of all possible worlds, we come to affirm their speech, its powerless burrowing (as Kafka would say) under the certainties we bring to our understanding, and attempts at controlling, the world.

A consideration of Levinas will help us consider the workings, if you will, of the assemblages—animal, human, even technological and geological—put forward by Woods in his essay on scale critique. How do assemblages function? How do all the actors get together and work, without the establishment of an overarching subjectivity? Obviously, I can't speak for black redstarts and renewable power grids. That's the point. Just as I cannot speak for the Other—he / she / it is determined by its distance from me, its impoverished alienness to my linguistic and logical appropriation, and by its own speech, its own traces—so all the other agents of the assemblages we find ourselves a part of will (hopefully) respond if somehow we can hear them in their infinite remove. Therein lies our own freedom. If global climate change is to be addressed at all, it will be from within such assemblages.

There is another side to this: the impossibility of murder. Or destruction, on the grand scale. Perhaps we can use the word "sustainability" in the context of a world that implies the scale critique of which I've spoken, a critique that eschews the grand strategies of, by, and for "humans alone."

This may entail a sustainability that could serve as a measure of the impossibility of ecological destruction. Recall what Levinas says of killing: it is impossible within a frame of possibility. Black redstarts can be made extinct—as they already may be in Britain. From Levinas, however, we can derive this bizarre observation: *ecocide is impossible*. The more we destroy, the less we destroy. The more we make the earth in our image, the less we do so. There will always be one more ecology, though it might be not to our liking. The "world"[18] in its destitution and infinite distance has a deep sustainability that goes beyond, and indeed is even fostered by, human attempts at total control and eradication. The world sustains itself in the midst of human-scale destruction. The more humans, under the aegis of capital, take the world as mere raw material, the less influence they have.[19] They merely create the conditions for an ecological collapse, which is, as Hinchliffe and Whatmore might say, a city for any number of other agents to establish their own terrain and migration routes. The total exercise of human ecological power is also the complete loss of anything that could be called human freedom. The triumph of humans as grand strategists, dominating all ecological scale, their ultimate self-representation in Reason, may also be their eradication as tacticians in any ecological assemblage, and perhaps their subsequent eradication *tout court*.

Sustainability, then, may entail not only our face-to-face with the eco-logical Other but, what amounts to the same thing, the confrontation with death. In *Totality and Infinity,* Levinas considers the nature of time in our relation to death. Why are we afraid of death? Can we imagine our passage from life into death? He writes:

> Death is a menace that approaches me as a mystery; its secrecy determines it—it approaches without being able to be assumed, such that the time that separates me from my death dwindles and dwindles without end, involves a sort of last interval which my consciousness cannot traverse, and where a leap will somehow be produced from death to me. The last part of the route will be crossed without me; the time of death flows upstream; the I in its projection toward the future is overturned by a movement of imminence, pure menace, which comes to me from an absolute alterity. (235)

Two things stand out in this passage: First, the idea of the time that sepa-rates me from death as a kind of microscopic infinity, Zeno's paradox. It "dwindles and dwindles without end." There is no end, no death, in time, from my perspective. I can of course commit suicide, but I cannot reach out and actively grasp death and end time. Time will always flow, there will always be time, no matter how short the interval remains between my awareness of time (me, in other words) and my death. When death comes—and this is the second major point of the passage—it will not be my modification of time so that I can accede directly to death (since time is the continuation of life, of me), but rather of a death that reaches out to me, and to my time, penetrating it and nullifying it. This is another measure of my radical vulnerability.

Time is infinite, it always goes on, I cannot "experience" its end within time itself. I cannot do anything from within time to end its flow. Time is endless, even in the infinitely brief moment. My activity means nothing in the passage of time in relation to death. Like Pascal's space, Levinas's time presents the active human with a paradox: "he" is master, but in its dwindling—and presumably its expansion as well—time calls into question human mastery. Death is a reckoning that underscores the fact that humans are suspended between the extremes of time, mastering neither, in proportion with neither. Death is the mark of human temporal disproportion. It is the Other that demonstrates the lack of integrity of the human: the lack of temporal mastery is also the lack of any possibility of the mastery of the Other.

Levinas's *ennui*, not so much boredom as fear, can be said to be the recognition that time cannot be mastered, with the resultant passivity. Levinas writes:

> But imminence is at the same time menace and postponement. It pushes on, and it leaves time. To be temporal is both to be for death and to still have time, to be against death. In the way the menace affects me in imminence resides my being implicated by the menace, and the essence of fear. It is a relation with an instant whose exceptional character is due not to the fact that it is at the threshold of nothingness or of a rebirth, but to the fact that, in life, it is the impossibility of every possibility, the stroke of a total passivity alongside of which the passivity of the sensibility, which moves into activity, is but a distant imitation. Thus the fear for my being which is my relation with death is not the fear of nothingness, but the fear of violence—and thus it extends into the fear of the Other, of the absolutely unforeseeable. (235)

This is passivity before passivity, so to speak, and the passivity is such that the result is not false action—diversion—but terror before the encroachment of the Other. But this encroachment can only be in time, so that one remains "against death" as long as one is "in time."

Levinas, unlike Pascal, puts a happy face on this fear; the result is not the desire to lose oneself in diversions, or to end it all by opening oneself up to death, but rather to affirm the "desire of the Other," a "goodness liberated from the egoist gratification." Here, like the freedom we earlier saw in Levinas, which resulted from a recognition of the infinite distance of the Other, desire somehow overcomes the "threatened will" and appears as the "goodness whose meaning death cannot efface" (236).

If, however, the face of the Other is the face of an ecology beyond human desire, a new set of problems appears. We know we cannot kill the Other, and that indeed the menace of death is the Other. If we think back to the point made by the science writer Ed Yonge on the relation of the body to the micro-biome of which it is composed, we realize that the ecological Other is not only "in us" as our uncanny double, but that its Otherness has to do with the fact that death is not simply existential, but biological. Fear of the Other, and of the radical passivity that goes along with it, has to do not just with our desire to master the Other, the discourse of the Other, and the impossibility of doing that. Nor does it have to do with the fact that the Other threatens us with death, or embodies (or is) death. Rather, the problem is the incertitude of death, based on the fact that not only is the ecological Other in us, but we cannot even easily recognize the Otherness of the Other. The Other is not just like the black redstarts in Britain, whose "presence" can never be straightforwardly ascertained. It is like—it is—the mitochondria that mimics, that indeed is directly descended from, ancient bacteria that were incorporated, imperfectly, in the biology of cells, our cells, long before they were even the cells of an organism. The ecological end, the death of cells, bacteria, and viruses, of vast ecologies of organisms, is "us."

Time in this scenario is not only the lived time that never ends, which infinitely contracts as we are conscious of our passivity in relation to the coming radical alterity of death, and which cannot escape our active consciousness (that passivity is our activity). Time is also the infinite expansion in and out of our bodies that are not our bodies: "I" am a relation to an Other that is the radical distance of the ecological relations between my cells, the organelles that make up my cells, all the bacteria that reside in my body. These are not me, but work to keep me going, and the temporality of that Other that stretches back billions of years, but which telescopes into the instant in which I suffer because of (for example) an autoimmune disorder. My passivity beyond and before passivity is my knowledge of this condition, as well as my inability to master death in the sense that I cannot master all the relations between the organisms and residues of organisms that make me up, are me, but are not me at the same time. My unity, so to speak, is challenged not only by my inability to master in time a death that comes to me, penetrating my time from outside, but also by my inability to control a time that stretches back to the earliest time of my (animal) ancestors, and thus means that "I" am less a will or desire than I am a loose amalgamation of organisms, of animals, of ecologies, that may or may not consolidate to keep me in time, to keep me in an infinitely contracting time before death. The death before me as Other reaches out to me and is thus doubled by the death within me as Other; before death my time contracts infinitely, my activity is powerless, transforming into a radical vulnerability; within me the other time expands infinitely, or at least to the very unknowable beginnings of life itself, and to the inevitable but ungraspable end of life on earth, the end of all organic sustainabilities, and my activity blunders and dissipates before a host of suddenly unrelated or tentatively connected beings. Ecosystems in their mortality and unknowability that I face are also my death, and it terrifies me; ecosystems within me are also infinitely distant, the ultimate threat to my coherence, and their disruption—but certainly not their end (other sorts of organisms will inhabit me after my death). This terrifies me as well. Pascal: "The eternal silence of these infinite spaces terrifies me."

Levinas's passivity is beyond the active/passive divide: it is a kind of non-negative passivity, because it is incapable transforming itself into an activity through an act of will. Indeed it is the will itself that is completely passive before a death that cannot be inserted into lived time, the time of awareness and activity. That death is not only the radical independence of the Other as another simple agent (another "person" who speaks) before me, but the independence of all the animals, all the ecologies that I face both "within" and "outside" me. But once we go outside the active/passive divide, or we operate at its margins, performing a kind of proto-deconstruction of it, we can ask: What verb suffices to convey the sense of this passivity before passivity, this radical "destitution"? Don't verbs usually convey an action, something that is done? How can we even speak of this passivity when no verb exists in language—perhaps no verb can exist in any language—to convey what is "done" in this radical passivity? Could we say we "suffer" not passively, but as passivity before the Other? Would this correspond to the fear that rends us before the Other?

Perhaps we could leave Levinas's fear for a moment. To emphasize fear is still to stress the action of someone or something—me—experiencing fear. But this event (for lack of a better word) before death puts me into question to such an extent that what is there cannot even entail fear. Subjectivity, my own and all others, is "endlessly ruptured and interrupted by the demand of the other."[20] Conventional passivity does imply fear, of course. But this is not conventional passivity. And that kind of passivity might convey as its opposite, typically, suffering: to act is to do, to effect change, but to be passive is to suffer. But what if there is no scale-dominating "me" to do the suffering, to be passive?

Levinas's infinitely contracting time may presuppose a "me" for whom time passes—even before the executioner, time passes; even at the instant before the blade drops, time passes. It always passes for "me." It is always there, even when we know its radical finitude. The fact that we know that finitude means that it still passes.

But the ecological relation is different. The Other's radical alterity is not just before me or outside me, but in me, it *is* me. "I" am beside the point. "If you go immunosuppressed for a little bit, they'll kill you. When you die, they'll eat you. They don't care. It's not a nice relationship. It's just biology." My body attacks its own organelles. This radical passivity, some-how before and outside activity and passivity (my activity is irrelevant when it comes to a passivity that puts in question my momentary corporeal and psychic coherence, the existence of the "me") calls for a term outside the activity/passivity dyad. If I am my body, a simple battleground of var-ious animals and former animals pressed into service as something else, my passivity is not just my inability to control or know death. I can even attempt remediation, through a medical action, and it might be success-ful, for a time. But it doesn't get at the central problem, which is my fun-damental passivity in relation to all the combinations of agents that are distant from me, in my inability to "ascribe a meaning to them." It is the passivity of a constantly changing, transforming, expanding, and contract-ing ecology that escapes my definitive linguistic and conceptual control and coordination. The formulation "human self" is not adequate to describe this, nor is the notion of a coherent assemblage in which I function. Radical passivity comes to seem inadequate to describing it as well, to the extent that passivity still seems to require an agent being passive, no matter how primordial the passivity might "be." If there is a self mixed up in there, its only function is to recognize the awkward coordination of all the larger assemblages, "in" the body and "outside" it, all those ecologies, some flour-ishing, some subsisting, some dying, some locatable, some not. It's not a case, *pace* Woods, of somehow harnessing that assemblage or cooperating with for the good of all. That would simply mean taming the scale dis-parity and once again impossibly affirming a single agent, a subjectivity of assemblages. Rather, the self is its own disproportion in relation to all not-knowable assemblages.

If that's the case, the word, the verb, "suffers" may be inadequate as well. Suffering is what an agent *does*, when it's not able to exercise its agency. It is challenged in its agency. If there is no fear here, there is no suffering. And this is where we might consider another word, the contrary of Levinas's proto-passivity—a contrary that is not a simple contrary, but an alternative, an offshoot, a by-blow, maybe a supplement. Such a word would not imply the simple absence of action as a kind of deficiency, but freedom before the vulnerability of the Other. That word is "sustainability"—in the sense I mentioned in the preceding chapter: "To endure or withstand; to bear up under." Note that in this definition there is no definitive attribution of agency; no one is doing something, there "is" only "bearing up." But it doesn't imply sheer passivity either. The word does not have to have a human subject (Pluto could sustain a terrible asteroid strike, for example). It implies some temporality, a before and after, but not a temporality tied to the (dis)proportions of a human will or consciousness. This is the sustainability that counters that which cannot be countered, the radical neediness of organisms or ecologies of or in organisms when they come face to face with each other (and with death). It cannot simply eliminate that neediness, but it affirms if nothing else a momentary encounter, an instantaneous and perhaps unpremeditated act that confronts destitution, the nudity before the eventual dissolution—an act that in some way responds to the demand of the ecological Other.

And there might be a human there, not a self but an accretion, an appendage, a sidekick, who looks back for a moment and sees that its own assemblage is only a pile-up and looks forward to ruin and redemption. It is inseparable from an aggregation that it cannot simply use or that guarantees it anything, one that is momentarily taken up and defended before it is lost. It is there in the gap between things, larger and smaller, past and future, a mediation that is not a mediation, but an incomprehensible juncture-point. It is there (where?) not as master but as a kind of prisoner, always rejected, forever attuned to the dominion of the unknowability of a nongraspable larger ecology. That is its freedom, and the death it stares in the face; that is the unmasterable language (for a time, an infinitely contracting time) of the Other it sustains. But it may also be the freedom to act, if the act is a response to the Other's destitution, and an arousal of "goodness."[21]

Or, put another way, the ecological Other in its infinite distance also sustains . . .

3 Statues, Language, Machines

Stuff can stick around for a very long time: there are rocks on earth that have been dated back over four billion years.[1] Now that's sustainable. So if we want to talk about unqualified sustainability, we should first note that the most basic and unquestionable, and unquestioned, thing we can think about matter is that it is just there, and will be for a while, outside of our wants and needs. But wait—maybe we can join our worth as symbolically charged people, at least as we imagine it, to the indisputable permanence of solid materials. We can make statues. These are representations of us, of our beliefs, our value systems (personified), in materials so durable they will be around long after we are gone. By extension, our beliefs, our society even, will gain a kind of material–social sustainability through its attachment to statues. We can put statues up in cities as memorials; at strategic sites, statues will delineate a space saturated with our beliefs, in a way that guarantees those beliefs' endurance, as well as the endurance of the value of the site. Future generations will see the statues, appreciate them, and understand not only us, but what we stood for. The statues will act as value transmitters, assuring that our ideological needs will be met without compromising the ability of future generations to meet their own ideological needs, as determined by us.

The erection of statues in age-defying materials attempts to assure that any effort to remove a statue will be seen as a major, epochal, and transgressive event. The solidity of statues symbolizes the sustainability of not only a culture's beliefs, but its livelihood, its economic and ecological security, typically in an urban context. For that reason it would be very hard to tear down or destroy a statue without calling into question in some way the urban space it inaugurates, or at least the primary function of that space. And once the statue has inaugurated that space, the consecrated uses of the city space will in turn enforce the dominant position of the statue.[2]

Statues, then, are a way of conquering space and time; they are the imposition of a certain human scale and set of beliefs (political, cultural, racial) upon the time of generations and the space of urban cohesion and identity. A person is small, mortal. A statue is big, stops time and conquers space: the person, the observer, by identification necessarily takes on the qualities, the power, the serenity, of the statue. The material and its location makes this sustainability possible. The statue is a human that surpasses the human, but for all that it is inhuman, just metal or stone; it cannot think or move like a living human. The statue is—it incarnates in its representative function—the human that uses the world, uncritically. For the statue, in principle, there is no split between the human that, without reflection, drives the world (with discoveries, conquests, transcendent acts) and the world that is driven.

Permanence, however, is never assured. Great Mayan statues molder in rainforests, enigmatic remainders that challenge all interpretation. Ozymandias rules over the desert, forgotten; the partial ruin of his material is doubled by the emptiness of vast, sandy wastes. The nineteenth century certainly appreciated this: Maxime Du Camp, among others, carefully photographed endless desert wastes and the ruins of neglected Egyptian statues and temples, and sold the prints.[3] One could even argue that the nineteenth century had its ruin porn, centered on statues, just as we have ours today, devoted to our derelict cities.

Yet the material is not "mute." The resistance of stone or metal leads to a paradox, which is also a paradox of sustainability. Matter defies human action. It defies myths and human projects. Its own sustainability is merged with great difficulty with what we might call a more superficial, human sustainability. The statue's first-order sustainability, a "simple" one—metal and stone go on for millions or billions of years before and after "our" appearance—somehow contradicts the impermanence of the overlay of a human-oriented sustainability (the same culture will be necessary to sustain the same ecology, for generations), and negates it. Such a reflection is impossible in the sense that sheer matter can never easily be bent to human purposes; it can never simply represent. It can never speak in the unambiguous words we find completely satisfying. Yet represent it does, if nothing more than its ultimate resistance to representation. (And not just bronze and stone revel in their bad sustainability, their resistance to human sustainability; plastic does too, with a vengeance.) There is a profound disproportion between the self-sustaining of metal and stone and the short-term sustaining of civilizations and ideologies that would graft themselves onto statues. And yet that impossibility characterizes an aspect of first-level sustainability: its profound simplicity is also inseparable from a recognition—on the part of matter itself—that human (ecological, cultural) sustainability is never simple. First-order sustainability, in its recognition of the scale disruption that challenges the empire of human sustainability, is inseparable from reflection upon that challenge. Statues speak, and they tell us about the folly of an anthropocentric sustainability. They are the sacred icons above all of first-order sustainability. In their reflection, in their complicity with semiotic systems and languages, they find themselves identified with the human drive to self-sustain. But as sheer matter this complicity is difficult and awkward, and in the end, points away from the human, indeed points to the void of the human. Simple matter sustains, but its very recalcitrance presides over the loss or disfigurement of meaning. A lonely statue in a park or cemetery seems strange, bewildering: What were they thinking when they put that up?—let's ignore it and rollerblade around it. And fallen statues call attention to the very lack of grandeur of the worthies they were meant to celebrate. But the fall of the statue may be more important than the statue itself.

Some of these problems can be seen at work in Louis Aragon's surrealist novel, *Le Paysan de Paris* (1923; *Paris Peasant*). This is the great novel of the city and its passages, its arcades, the depiction of which inspired Walter Benjamin in his *Passagenarbeit*.[4] But beyond the passages there is a striking passage that depicts the "speech of the statue."

Paris in the 1920s—the later Third Republic—was clogged with statues. Statues seemed to sprout on every corner, leading to the coining of the term *Statuomanie*.[5] The Third Republic was an epoch of civic and urban celebrations, and statues were erected to serve as focal points for celebrations of both Right and Left. Just as the Right used the statue of Jeanne d'Arc on the rue des Pyramides and the statue of Strasbourg on the Place de La Concorde as pilgrimage points, so the Left erected a statue of Étienne Dolet, first publisher of Rabelais and champion of freedom of the press, on the Place Maubert, and one of the Chevalier de la Barre, victim of religious intolerance in the eighteenth century, near the Sacré-Cœur cathedral. The statue of Dolet was the endpoint of a procession celebrating freedom *from* religion.[6] The statue of the Chevalier de la Barre celebrated revolutionary religious disbelief in front of the cathedral built to celebrate the downfall of the Commune, during which the archbishop of Paris was executed.

It got so that there were statues everywhere, and some indeed were pretty bad. Aragon, as a surrealist and writer of the Left, mentions the Strasbourg statue, and the right-wing ceremony in which the poet Paul Déroulede ("the already decomposed corpse") laid a wreath, each year, commemorating the loss of Strasbourg to the Germans after the Franco-Prussian war.[7] Aragon, in fact, devotes a whole page to an inventory of many of the most egregious Parisian statues.[8]

Aragon's narrator rants against this situation in which soon it will be "scarcely possible to make one's way along the streets choked with statues, across the field of poses" (152). But the problem is not that there is simply a chaos of statues. The real problem lies in the fact that the statues seem to be summoning a "divine power who is both reckless summoner of entities and unfortunate victim of disproportion and dream" (152). It seems that while at first humans made statues devoted to the gods that ended up representing men, they now make statues and "what promptly emerges is a god." But what kind of god?

Statues embody a kind of *détournement,* not so much one carried out by human artists (as by the Situationists), but by the very materials of the statues themselves. Human ideals, after their embodiment in dense matter, are precisely the elements of "disproportion and dream" that end up as the only signified of the statue. Humans *are* disproportion and dream, but they take themselves to be carriers of higher secular principles. What the statue really "represents" is something quite different. It calls the humans' bluff.

> O vigor of a night embodied in bronze, black precipice of dead, sunken eyes, just above the ground, disqualification of reason by specters, willpower crumbled around these feet chained to their rock.
>
> I repeat: seeking to check this progress of the divine through space, this invasion of matter by the immaterial, man, with an eye-winking of consciousness of his destiny and his action, had undertaken to sculpt henceforth nothing but hideousness with hips of emptiness. (152)

The rationalists of the Third Republic attempt to "check the progress of the divine" and establish a solidity for themselves that is nevertheless taken from the divine and eternal charge of materials. And we learn that the statues, at first glance "simulacra of modern times," nevertheless ."derive from the very inoffensiveness of this garb a magical power unknown to Ephesus or Angkor. So true is this that in the end new religions are established in honor of the new idols" (152–53). The statues as idols generate, in spite of themselves, new religions.

This "divine" or "magical" power is the real charge of the statue, but it is not the official meaning that humans apply to it. "New religions" are the product of an "immaterial" in materials that is not the product of human will or meaning; the statues refute this very meaning through their power of material resistance. But how can divinity or magic be somehow behind (or responsible for) a meaning that is not the result of the signifying drives of humans themselves?

We are deep in surrealism here, a movement that finds "modern mythologies" on offer everywhere, but mythologies that contradict or simply ignore the official ideologies of bourgeois life. Divinity here is a strange thing, not just an immaterial movement through space, but a "vigor of night," a sacred, base charge that defies all merely human elevations.[9]

The statue now speaks. For fifty years it has stood in the park (in this case, Buttes-Chaumont, in Paris), and it is not happy. "It is high time that all these moving, laughing people who trickle through the landscape where I am for ever frozen should be plugged with lead." What's more, the statue tells us that the "idea" to which it is, or has been, devoted by its human makers is an inaccessible ideal. It both gestures toward the idea, and shows humans that they are remote from it. The statue is the living/dead refutation of what it is meant to embody.

> Man's idea! above the fields . . . man's idea appears, larger than nature, in the exemplary gesture of a sprinter or a king. At the feet of this idea man lives, his eyes upraised, without ever attaining identity with it, at the feet of this idea he rends himself and writes in agony, in the throes of the great abstract delirium called psychology.
>
> On the solemn oath of a statue, there is not a single activity in all the hundred thousand nooks and corners of space . . . which seems to me as ridiculous as psychology. (154)

And yet the idea frees itself, "finds nourishment in itself," floats free of the humans who would grasp it. It floats free thanks to the statue, who both gestures toward it and separates humans from it. They are rooted in the earth, the idea escapes on the wing (156–57), and between them there is matter, which signifies nothing, mute stuff which speaks only of its inability to connect people with the idea that flies away.

The idea twists in the wind, finding nourishment in itself, coming unmoored from the system it supposedly represents and indicating a divinity or mythology beyond the grasp and even the authorship of humans; it is the divinity of garrulous mute stones and metal. What's left behind is what the statue calls psychology. This is not so much psychology in the contemporary sense, but a positivism that would link what can only be known—empirical fact—to human mental and social life. Auguste Comte's model of positivism had as the highest science, the crown of the sciences, not physics, but sociology. A lay religion would be grounded in scientific fact, not faith, but its highest teaching, and the highest object of veneration, would be Man himself.[10]

Psychology in this view is the belief that the human mind is the ultimate subject and guarantor of science, and the ultimate object of scientific inquiry. Correlationism turns back on itself and studies itself and its origin as a solid scientific fact. The statue scoffs.

> Content with very little, man, when confronted by any abyss, learned to make use of these detours to map the brinks of the abyss, to forget the abyss and the torments of the infinite. Unshakeable human positivism: you never ask yourselves . . . what your phantom witnesses on their plinths engraved with famous names think of your trickery, positive or not. (155)

They don't think much. The statue turns against its own meaning, and knows itself not as a reference to the truth of psychology (thereby linking humans to their ideal) but as a blockage or cut between earth and sky, human rooted in dirt and the sky teeming with gods, demons, myths, and lies—all the aberrant ideals, all the aberrant meanings that humans have hatched and that have escaped human will. The statue impossibly reflects upon itself—in other words, only as sheer matter, as stone or bronze, as material blockage between fleeting ideal and barely covered abyss. That is the divinity that passes through it. The statue indicates itself as impossibility of indication, all the while pointing to the inaccessible ideal of the scientifically rooted mind as the ultimate arbiter of truth. It recycles itself as simple bronze, refusing its symbolic overlay; it recognizes the dumbness of its materials that could be repurposed for any symbolic use. It anticipates its later melting by enemy occupiers, eager to scrounge it and put it to other uses (mainly military).

The statue, meant to aid in the reflection of earth and sky, instead sunders it. Humanity would unite matter and mind, earth and gods, science and self-identity, in the reflection symbolized and made sustainable by the statue. But self-identity in matter-mind becomes, through the statue, a rude break, insults and jeers. One recalls the myth of Rousseau's *Pygmalion,* as recounted by the critic and theorist Paul de Man. The problem in Jean-Jacques Rousseau's text is that the fantasy of a unified self—the union of artist and stone in life—becomes simply a "cold" series of oppositions, an unresolvable "chain of (as)symetrical polarities: hot/cold, inside/outside, art/nature," and so on.[11] De Man goes on to note:

> The separation of the group work-author-reader from the consciousness of the protagonist indicates that we are no longer within a thematic context dominated by selfhood but in a figural representation of a structure of tropes. (186)

This separation is precisely what we see allegorized in Aragon's statue: the selfhood of the statue, reflecting on its unifying role (uniting its self with that of its creator, which in turn unites all of humanity as it reflects upon its union of general human consciousness and scientific truth in positivism) now cuts out, and the statue produces empty verbiage that reflects on the (literal) hollowness of its materialized self in relation to the larger program. Its reflection in turn is nothing more than the production of a series of tropes of separation, the jumble of all the ridiculous forms of human activity, indeed all the forms of "psychology" itself. ("One by one, the various psychologies were born"[155]). These forms or versions are now nothing but an endless metonymic series that results not in any kind of coherent human selfhood that a statue could embody, but an arbitrary collection of metaphors and metonymies that generate the statue's denunciation.

The fact is, however, that the trope-production could be anything: the statue denounces, but not because it wills, or has a will. It is no Galatea in relation to Aragon's Pygmalion. It has not come to life. It is still just matter. Rather, the denunciation, such as it is, is less thematic than it is the mere affirmation that the supposedly sustaining element—the statue—is just one more signifier in an endless chain. Affirmation in this sense is the same as denunciation: the very need to affirm itself calls out the insufficiency of a transcending and transcendent self (collective or individual). Such a self, beyond difference, would have no need to speak of difference, of hiatus between earth and sky, separation between self and other (or between statue and humanity).

Hence the "wing" that somehow floats over Aragon's statue, and to which it apostrophizes. The wing, at one point compared to an American flag—a flag that symbolizes the union of disparate elements in disunion—itself somehow causes "blessings" to

> rain down upon all owners of statues, the Italian vendors of plaster casts, the proprietors of wax museums, the executors of memorial monuments, the subscribers to patriotic mausoleums, the schoolboy modelers of funny figures, the kneaders of breadcrumbs, the New Zealanders who create with clusters of little pebbles huge fantastic birds. (157)

The wing is a metaphor for the generation not of statues in themselves but of their "owners," all the figures of responsibility who somehow curate or authorize statues or statue-like representations. The owner is not the statue, but is contiguous with it; the statue is not a statue, but a kind of statue, and a kind of reference. Each relation is different, each self–other relation is an absurd difference ("kneaders of breadcrumbs"?) from every other one.

A statue is both a metaphor and a metonymy. It's a metaphor in the sense that it transfers the qualities of one term that's represented to another—the form of a living man (Étienne Dolet) tied to the stake and about to burn, is transferred to cold and immovable bronze. But it's also a metonymy; the part (a man about to burn because he has been condemned for printing a forbidden book) represents a conceptual whole (the need for freedom of the press, Republican virtue). But as soon as one defamiliarizes the tropes, sees them as a senseless (surreal, in fact) series, each always generating another, never coalescing in a single signified or in a larger personal or social self, one ends up with just chunks of metal or stone somehow impossibly speaking for the dead. The statue is a specter that sees only specters. The dead here is not the dead Étienne Dolet, but the dead speaking self, that dead larger unification of dyads that comes to symbolize—and nothing more, since it's just one more symbol—the amalgam of social and personal coherence, triumphing over death.

And yet in a strange way—the way of zombies, of specters—the only generation of a self is as a dead one. It is the dead, parodic self of the machine. The trope of the speaking statue is that of prosopopoeia. In another essay, de Man writes of this trope, and of its links to autobiography:

> Prosopopoeia [is] the fiction of an apostrophe to an absent, deceased, or voice-less entity, which posits the possibility of the latter's reply and confers upon it the power of speech. Voice assumes mouth, eye, and finally face, a chain that is manifest in the etymology of the trope's name, prosopon poein, to confer a mask or a face [prosopon]. Prosopopoeia is the trope of autobiography, by which one's name . . . is made as intelligible and memorable as a face. Our topic deals with the giving and taking away of faces.[12]

The statue is the ultimate figure of prosopopoeia, in the sense that it speaks, but is dead, doubly: it represents a forever-dead person, and it is forever-dead material (metal or stone). De Man argues that all texts are in a sense autobiographical:

> The autobiographical moment happens as an alignment between the two subjects involved in the process of reading in which they determine each other by mutual reflexive substitution. The structure implies differentiation as well as similarity, since both depend on a substitutive exchange that constitutes the subject. This specular structure is interiorized in a text in which the author declares himself the subject of his own understanding, but this merely makes explicit the wider claim to authorship that takes place whenever a text is stated to be by someone. (70)

For de Man, the relation between self and other—between self and statue, Pygmalion and Galatea, as well as between self and text—is an autobiographical one. We have seen that already with Aragon's statue: the "substitutive exchange" that constitutes the subject is an autobiographical one in the sense that the statue in some sense was meant to convey to those who see it a social or existential totality—for, in the case of Étienne Dolet, the morality of the Third Republic. The self in that case, through the statue, constitutes itself through its specular other, the reason of the Republican polity. If that specularity is broken—as it is by Aragon's statue—the unified autobiographical subject is sundered; the radically foreign, the resistant material, is inserted into the space between doubles, and the statue spouts endless verbiage. This gap or disconnection is nevertheless also the space of signification, of the functioning of tropes, and, as de Man would have it, it is the space of prosopopoeia, the projection of the face onto the other, of language onto mute, cold matter.

The statue speaks, and in Aragon it speaks its inability to speak, its inability to serve as a good statue that unifies conclusively self and other, earth and sky, society and ideal. Rather it speaks the emptiness of the sheer trope, of the projection of life onto and into death. De Man writes of the "latent threat that inhabits prosopopoeia":

> By making the death [sic] speak, the symmetrical structure of the trope implies, by the same token, that the living are struck dumb, frozen in their own death. [There is, then, in the use of the trope] a sinister connotation that is not only the prefiguration of one's own mortality but our actual entry into the frozen world of the dead. (78)

The statue as autobiographical text deals us death in its incarnation of the trope of prosopopoeia; we see ourselves in the statue, and we are meant to see ourselves there, but the reversibility of the trope is such that we, specular doubles of the statue, receive its death. The myth of Pygmalion is reversed, and this reversal is contained in the "modern mythology" of the statue as Aragon presents it. His talking statue is nothing other than the death of the bourgeois, humanist subject, the arbiter and sustainer of the truth of Man.

One could even argue that if statues are figures of sustainability, authorizing the autobiographical permanence of an urban, political, and ecological order, then the overt prosopopoeia of the statue in Aragon is nothing less than the passage from a naive cultural sustainability—the permanence of the Republic—to another sustainability, one that excludes the mastery of the human and affirms merely the permanence of materials, of stone and metal. But it may not be as simple as that. After all, for de Man, the generation of death through autobiography is also the generation of language, of text—if the statue is dead, it is still talking, and if, by tropological reversal, we are dead, and we are talking, what is our language use? Is it somehow sustainable? In what way?

"The statue's speech" is a speech of severance, of severing: the statue denies its community with all other statues, it severs its links with obtuse humanity, and it severs the links of mankind with its ego ideal. But in so doing, its speech acts—the continuous stream of not-always rational insult—only manages to throw off more meaning. Meaning now is to be found not in positivism, but in its abeyance, in the affirmation of humanity's distance from its truth. This is just another truth. It is another representation of a state of affairs, and another form of self-knowledge, and the statue must continue in its insults, indefinitely, in order to yet again discredit humanity's, and its own, truth. Or vice versa: the discrediting and insulting always produces more truth, whose sole function is to perpetuate the insulting. The speech act is repeated indefinitely, and the production of a cognitive element (of self-knowledge) is only an aftereffect. This itself is a self-sustaining structure, but it is the structure of language as machine, not of human intention or self-knowledge (or statue self-knowledge, as the case may be). It goes on as long as the machine can be fueled.

De Man analyzes exactly this situation in Rousseau in the last chapter of *Allegories of Reading*, "Rousseau (Excuses)." Rousseau's *Confessions* include an incident in which Rousseau confesses his guilt in accusing another (a young woman on whom he has a crush, Marion) of stealing a ribbon, whereas he himself had stolen it. The guilt that has haunted him throughout his life, from de Man's perspective, is simply what has been produced by the performative function of language—excuse making itself. Rousseau's excuse is that he has impulsively accused Marion of the theft: he unthinkingly indulged in another speech act. The speech act (the performative), in other words, produces guilt (the constative) only to eliminate it, and so on to infinity (speech act produces guilt, which requires another speech act, and so on). As de Man notes:

> The text as body, with all its implications of substitutive tropes ultimately always retraceable to metaphor, is displaced by the text as machine and, in the process, it suffers the loss of the illusion of meaning. The deconstruction of the figural dimension is a process that takes place independently of any desire; as such it is not unconscious but mechanical, systematic in its performance but arbitrary in its principle, like a grammar. This threatens the autobiographical subject not as the loss of something that once was present and that it once possessed, but as a radical estrangement between the meaning and the performance of any text.[13]

The result of this is that meaning, the cognitive element of the text, is subordinate to and posterior to the purely "mechanical" process of textual generation ("grammar"). De Man writes: "We have to produce guilt . . . in order to make the excuse meaningful. Excuses generate the very guilt they exonerate, though always in excess or by default" (299).

The autobiographical body of the statue morphs into the textual machine. We could even argue that all statues are autobiographical, not simply through the trope of prosopopoeia, but through their necessary self-reference as to why they are representing something (the history of their genesis). The statue of Dolet had, at its plinth, another statue, supplementing Dolet's, of a mother instructing her daughter, and pointing to Dolet. The statue, in its pose, in its silent but supposed speech, has a double that refers to its action of reference, and to the necessary truth of this reference. And all the more so in the case of Dolet, the purveyor of truth in banned (and soon to be burned) books. Aragon's statue muses on its never-ending activity as destroyer of the truth of statues.

But if the body, and the statue's body, can be seen as the autobiographical text—the putting of a face on a name, or a name on a face—it can also be a machine. The autobiographical text, as de Man reminds us, is a machine, or it is a (performative) grammar, always doing something (excusing itself, asserting itself, insulting someone, or even itself); the grammar functions in a void, throwing off meaning but itself an impersonal function. It is "systematic in its performance but arbitrary in its principle."

Machine grammar's operation can seemingly continue indefinitely. This, we might say, is the (first-order) sustainability of grammar: it functions indefinitely, outside or against any human scale. Grammar is a purely formal function, disconnected from human desires and goals, or even human identity. As de Man writes of Rousseau:

> The cognition would have been the excuse, and this convergence [of cognition and excuse, constative and performative] is precisely what is no longer conceivable as soon as the metaphorical integrity of the text is put in question, as soon as the text is said not to be a figural body but a machine. (299)

But is this all we are left with? The reversibility of the trope suggests something more might be at stake. After all, at the end of "Autobiography as De-Facement" de Man notes:

> Death is a displaced name for a linguistic predicament, and the restoration of mortality by autobiography (the prosopopoeia of the voice and the name) deprives and disfigures to the precise extent that it restores.[14]

But note that de Man does state that it restores. The restoration of the death-bound self will be a back-projection of the self onto the figural body as machine. Subjectivity is the after-effect of the impersonal action of the trope. It's not much, but it's what we have. It is a self, which we can accept in bad faith, since we always know that it is as much linguistic predicament as it is a human identity. Not to operate in bad faith is to attempt to suspend entirely the trope of prosopopoeia, a futile gesture. Our linguistic predicament bizarrely generates human subjectivity at the very moment it reveals its fundamental dishonesty. The machine can only function as human to the extent we recognize that it is only a machine, that the human is lost in, devoured by, a relentless grammar that reduces the human to the refiguring of the lie. But recognizing that lie is also recognizing our human selves. One can recognize the lie, it seems, or one can recognize the self; both are inescapable. But how to recognize them both at the same time? Would there be a kind of alternation between the two? (More on this later.)

First-order sustainability, in this version, is the projection onto the dead or not-yet existent other of our own speech, in order to constitute ourselves. The ability of future generations to meet their own needs is our own meaning. We define ourselves, our own sustainable consciousness, through the needs, and no doubt wants, of future generations, onto whom we project our own face. They will say, with one voice: we can meet our own needs, thanks to the affirmation of sustainability by that shining generation now gone, now dead (our forefathers and mothers, who almost destroyed the planet). Future generations will create themselves through prosopopoeia, by projecting back onto us the speech of sustainability, which we will (according to other texts) have spoken. In first-order sustainability, we nevertheless recognize the fundamental lie of this operation, the textual machine operating behind the ideal of a self-aware sustainability. It's the sustainability of a logical or grammatical machine operating in a void.

And in all this, "we" will simply be illusory (but impossibly self-aware) aftereffects of grammar, functioning on its own. Grammar sustains itself, irrespective of our wants, desires, or timelines. Grammar in this sense is no different from the "machine" of nature itself, continuously running, and sustaining, itself, irrespective of our input, good or bad—even our inability to completely destroy it.

If all is machine, what exactly does the machine do? Metaphor, as we know, is "transfer," movement, projection onto another; but nomination is also separation, cutting one crudely delineated thing from another, comparing and identifying things based on the arbitrary selection of attributes, and self-identifying with those things.[15] The cut makes possible the identification of self and other, but it also renders it impossible. It destroys coherence. Aragon's statue separated, cut off, the fools who erected the statues from their absurd ideals, which they thought enabled them to constitute themselves. It was a severing machine. For Gilles Deleuze and Félix Guattari in *Anti-Oedipus,* the machine operates by imposing multiple dualities:

> A machine may be defined as a *system of interruptions* or breaks *[coupures]*). These breaks should in no way be considered as a separation from reality; rather, they operate along lines that vary according to whatever aspect of them we are considering. Every machine, in the first place, is related to a continual material flow *[hylè]* that it cuts into. It functions like a ham-slicing machine, removing portions from the associative flow: the anus and the flow of shit it cuts off, for instance; the mouth that cuts off not only the flow of milk but also the flow of air and sound; the penis that interrupts not only the flow of urine but also the flow of sperm. Each associative flow must be seen as an ideal thing, an endless flux, flowing from something not unlike the immense thigh of a pig.[16]

Like de Man's machine-grammar, Deleuze and Guattari's desiring machines operate on their own, independently of the transcendent signified, so to speak, and certainly independent of an overlording consciousness. All of the machines mentioned in this passage—ham-slicer, anus, mouth, penis— do not come together to constitute a coherent whole; rather each does its own thing, spinning off ever new series of severed elements, which can interact or interrelate in various ways. The machines constitute not elements of a larger entity, but rather devices that only sever the continuities churned out by other machines, thereby producing flows that are in turn interrupted by other machines: "Every machine functions as a break in the flow in relation to the machine to which it is connected, but at the same time is also a flow itself, or the production of a flow, in relation to the machine connected to it." (36) (This counterintuitive statement makes sense if one considers, for example, an oil refinery, which both receives an interrupted flow of oil, in turn interrupts it in various other ways, and then produces another flow for other machines to cut up [various pumps, automobile fuel lines, etc.].)

There is no hierarchy: rather than each machine pointing to a larger function or result that subsumes all, there is instead a chaos (or skein) of machines, each operating in relation to another, but not producing any one sense, or object. Flows reverse back into other machines; the human is not even a machine, but a body ("without organs," without interiority) with a variety of other machines arbitrarily attached to it.

In fact, for Deleuze and Guattari, there is no human, no anthropomorphic identity that can be separated from the multiplicity of desiring machines.

> We make no distinction between man and nature: the human essence of nature and the natural essence of man become one within nature in the form of production or industry, just as they do within the life of man as a species. Industry is then no longer considered from the extrinsic point of view of utility, but rather from the point of view of its fundamental identity with nature as production of man and by man. (4)

Without utility, the usual hierarchy between Man and nature dissipates; all is flow, and cutting; rather than useful production, all production is excess and in excess. What is produced by one machine, and is excessively disgorged, is taken up by another, treated (segmented, etc.) and is once again disgorged as that machine's excess. Nothing is retained "in order to" carry out some higher goal, some activity leading to an end.

Nevertheless the human does creep back into Deleuze and Guattari's account, just as the self manages to reappear in de Man's. Deleuze and Guattari go on to note:

> [Man is not] the king of creation, but rather . . . the being who is in intimate contact with the profound life of all forms or all types of beings, who is responsible for even the stars and animal life, and who ceaselessly plugs an organ-machine into an energy machine . . . : the eternal custodian of the machines of the universe. (4)

Man is not simply identifiable without distinction or difference with all the other machines of the universe. All is not homogeneous pap. It is segmented, and the prime segmentation is between Man and nature, with Man serving as "custodian." Man is not in opposition to creation, but relates to it, we are informed, as "producer-product" (5).

My purpose here is not to "call out" Deleuze and Guattari on some privileging of humanity, but to note that for them all is not simple homogeneous flux. Like de Man, Deleuze and Guattari need a placeholder to be established in relation to a kind of universal machine, if only to provide an articulation for that machine and provide a certain situatedness in relation to its operation. That placeholder is us, for want of anything else. The grammar of machine interaction needs an autobiographical subject, no matter how illusory or empty, in order for names to continue being given faces. That's how the machinery of grammar works. The universe of machines needs "Man" or something resembling it for machines to be represented, interpreted, and maintained as producing and segmenting flows that in turn resemble. This interpretation is Deleuze and Guattari's own theory of rhetoric, though they do not use the term.

> Every "object" presupposes the continuity of a flow; every flow, the fragmentation of an object. Doubtless each organ-machine interprets the entire world from the perspective of its own flux, *from the point of view of the energy that flows from it*: the eye interprets everything—speaking, understanding, shitting, fucking—in terms of seeing. (6; italics added)

Subjectivity returns, if empty: organ-machines are not just impersonal machines with a point of view (hence with a simulacrum of consciousness, even "intelligence"). Man-machines are privileged, in "intimate contact" with "the profound life of all forms." That intimacy has to do with interpretation. And as soon as interpretation arises, we have the custodian-function: that which interprets must classify, arrange, oversee (like the eye in Deleuze and Guattari's example), even if that classification is itself subject to further classification. Perhaps the reappearance of interpretation and a point of view—notably lacking in de Man, but nevertheless implicit as soon as we have any kind of self, if only a formal, textual projection—is tied here to "the point of view of the energy that flows from it." For energy, if we consider it for a minute, would seem somewhat eccentric to a uniform universe of flows.

Deleuze and Guattari like to get down and dirty, and when they speak of flows it's often yucky. But the flow in the above quote involves perhaps the mother of all flows, which is energy itself. And yet energy, as we've seen in earlier chapters, is not really a flow that can be pinpointed as easily as flowing stuff. To be sure, flowing oil from a spigot presents us with energy, at least if we refine and burn it. And machines are adept at plugging into each other and processing, cutting up, and passing on oil flows in order to facilitate its conversion into energy, through various fuels: kerosene, jet fuel, gasoline, and so on, as long as humans are supervising.[17] But energy is not a flow as such, it is not a "thing." It is a set of numbers, a constant when one kind of energy (say, chemical, in gasoline) is converted into another (say, kinetic, in the movement of a car). It does not have an "origin" in any one "source," but nevertheless one would have to say it starts somewhere. But does it? Who knows where? The chora? Where does energy "in itself" come from? It's a nonsense question (first law of thermodynamics). Energy is not a material flux, it may not have an origin outside of mythology (and where then does the chora come from?), and it cannot be indefinitely recycled through various segmenting machines (second law). Deleuze and Guattari's universe is one of an infinite regress of machines, a kind of Borgesian library of devices that transmit and retransmit (the first law). Nevertheless the energy that powers it is transmitted from somewhere and when it is used up, it dissipates (the second law). It starts somewhere, at least some arbitrary point that we know of—say, the sun, via ancient plant life, then oil and its processing into fuels—and it goes somewhere (as usable energy, at least, it is lost in entropy). Thus the unidirectional movement of energy runs against any endless dissemination of flows. In fact, we never are shown the fuel powering their desiring machines, or how the energy allowing them to do "work" is dissipated.

Deleuze and Guattari's model works against the "arrow of time." Time, if in question at all, would prove itself to be circular: the eternal return (a mechanical, Newtonian time). Yet by assigning the human some sort of role in relation to flows they seem to suggest that the point of view of the human is more than just one more point of view—that it is, instead, necessary, and not just because "we" happen to be human.

Of course from one perspective this is absurd. "Machines" do not need a "custodian." The custodian is precisely what makes conventional (second-order) sustainability seem so narrowly focused.[18] All of nature, considered as a machine or anything else, does not need to be sustained. That old desiring machine, the one who severs earth and sky, Aragon's statue, would have had a good laugh at that. Surely somewhere that statue would sniff out another statue, an allegorical representation of sustainability, in other words one devoted to sustainability as representation, as prosopopoeia, which it in turn could lure into a derisory and futile revolt against its own rhetorical function.

But do humans need a custodian? What would a custodian of humans be if machinic humans were themselves otherwise occupied? If humans were simply machines, indistinguishable from other machines (which themselves break down the difference machine/nature), how would they speak? What would they say? Jane Jacobs writes:

> What is the purpose of [human] life? For us, the answer will be clear, established, and for all practical purposes indisputable: the purpose of life is to produce and consume automobiles.[19]

This is a trope that, since Jacobs's struggles with Robert Moses over the role of cars in New York City back in the 1950s, has become commonplace. But it still packs its punch. Viewed as an *actant,* as Bruno Latour would say, the car has an enormous place in any potential parliament of things. It's not just in the parliament; it's the prime minister, and the queen giving the speech. It, and its fossil fuel footprint, dictates, as Jane Jacobs well knew, how we should live in cities, and how we should communicate with other humans—not much at all, in fact, since we mainly sit in cars. (We communicate mainly by our presence in certain cars, and not in others.) Are we *custodians* of our cars? One could argue that we are even less than that: a custodianship still implies some authority, some control over maintenance. But for most of us the "possession" of a car is not voluntary, and is not really even conscious: it is simply something we do because it is done, because the car must be "owned" and must be "driven." One could say, as Jacobs implies, that we are not even human, and that we are certainly less than the machines we service. If all of urban space is arranged for the car; if our jobs are devoted primarily to being able to afford cars; if our economy is determined by our ability to produce and sell cars; if our psychic lives are determined by the need to drive and be seen in cars; if we, as Ivan Illich maintains,[20] move just about walking speed even though we drive our cars everywhere (or *because* we drive our cars everywhere); and so on, then we could say that the cars are indeed the dominant life-form on the planet, and we are aphids to the cars' ants. Cars are the custodians of the planet. That's certainly how we would be seen by extraterrestrials, noting the dominance of certain organisms (or machine-organisms).

And one could go on in a similar vein with other machines. The point is this: if we are entirely subordinate to cars, are they as actants beings that somehow share in our (organic, sentient) "life," and that are necessarily subordinate (as the actants in a Latour's parliament, which is mediated and organized by humans),[21] or are we simply actants in a larger parliament of things dominated by the automobile? If the latter is the case, then we are simply adjuncts to machines. We are not so much cyborgs, mutant syntheses of humans and machine; rather, with the dominance of the car as mechanical life-form we're much closer to a world of the sort sketched out in the *Terminator* movies, where machines dominate, and humans are merely their slaves or victims (the eternal underdogs).

In this sense, we might speak of a reverse prosopopoeia, where humans speak as the ventriloquist dummies of cars. If in the de Manian model the dead statues (or texts) speak, as revivifications of rhetorical mechanisms, and if Aragon's dead statue spoke and denounced the illusion of statues that meaningfully speak, now we are purely mechanical artifacts that speak (and perhaps denounce) the truth of the dominance of machines, and specifically of the automobile. The trope has turned once again, and now the universe is a purely mechanical one, at best inhabited by machines that continue going about their jobs amid the ecological devastation.

In such a world there is no concern for energy or energy flows. The car as placeholder immediately gives way to an undifferentiated world of machines servicing machines. Machines simply process flows and don't concern themselves with where those flows, or the energy associated with them, come from. Custodial work involves filling the gas tank. If first-level sustainability is the sustainability of stuff regardless of whether we are "here" or not, managing perfectly well without us, then a world of cars where humans work to maintain cars and speak *as* cars, is merely a world of machinic first-level sustainability. The practical distinction between humans and machines is obliterated, and humans as a separate category are swallowed up by an ecology, a universe, of (in this case) machines. Humans *are* their cars, without distinction: they are what they drive, in the full accomplishment of the ready-to-hand. This universe of motorized humans will sustain itself perfectly until the usable energy resources run out, whenever that is, but this is of no real concern to any of the machines, human or nonhuman.

This is all well and good, or not, as one would perhaps prefer, but one might also, in this context, recall the Deleuze and Guattari quote cited above.

As soon as Deleuze and Guattari write of energy they start to concern themselves with "point of view": the "point of view" of the eye, for example, which determines what this "organ-machine" sees "from the perspective of its own flux." Here is point of view, beyond simple amorphous identification (human = car). Now we are in a zone where there is a concern for energy. A point of view, no matter how empty, turns its gaze on itself and sees energy expenditure. This is a big difference. The simple machine repetitions of grammar or anything else do not concern themselves with the sources of their energetic input or (for that reason) their long-term survival. The custodians now have slightly different concerns from those of their machines. They actually want things to keep going. They may even have some awareness of themselves, some "point of view." The autobiography of their intelligence will turn around their concern for energy inputs. They will, as they put it, "use" machines to do things in their own interest, and not those of their machines—even if that interest is defined largely by what their machines demand. (They have to "fix" their cars on occasion.)

Whether this kind of concern is an illusion or not is not at issue; after all, as de Man reminded us, the "restoration of mortality by autobiography . . . deprives and disfigures to the precise extent that it restores." De Man doesn't dwell on this, but mortality is a human concern, and not a worry a machine would have. In the aporia of prosopopoeia, the self is restored to the extent that it is deprived: we can take that to mean that deprivation has the upper hand (we see it as somehow definitive), or restoration does. It's necessary (but also impossible) to see the two simultaneously (*there is* figural anamorphosis). If you've been restored, as a self, as a human, you have to at least momentarily forget your deprivation of disfigurement—and, of course, vice versa. At a certain moment, the restored human rears its head, so to speak, or at least its disfigured face, and proclaims its self-restoration. The statue speaks, aping a human: that is its humanity. Such are the wonders of rhetoric, of speaking statues that ultimately, once again, take themselves to be human subjects (if only in their denunciation of humanity).

Once humans are back on the scene, back on the throne, so too is their custodial function. What are they custodians of? Cars, of course. But the relation now is completely different—or at least it can be seen as a reversal, a tropic reversal, in which now the human is separate and dominant (or sees itself as dominant, in any case). The human has a car, drives it, uses it, studies it (it is "present-at-hand"), *has to care for it.*

The relations are now reversed; the human is above all, but also in an awkward and painful position of responsibility. And for that very reason, the human, now dominating the machine, must be concerned with energy flows. The good old days of the ready-to-hand, the seamless "man-machine-nature" combine, are over. Humans, in order to meld with their machines, must be concerned with, worried about, the larger energy use patterns that they have created in and through their machines. Their subjectivity, inevitably tied to their intelligence, now has a job. Subjectivity reappears as the (self-)awareness of the machine in its relation to energy resources. A machine that has stopped working is a scary instance of entropy. The human, becoming self-aware, is now forced to think (think about machines; think technics). *This is the point of the genesis of second-level sustainability.* Machine-rhetoric generates subjectivity as an aftereffect of its functioning. Humans still self-identify with machines, but only in and through their difference. Their selfhood is generated through this difference. It might be illusory, but it is necessary for their self-positing. They use machines, machines don't use them. A nice fiction, as de Man would argue, and an autobiographical one, but a powerful one nonetheless. It includes the imperative not only to power the machine (and thus to power oneself), but to maintain the machine's power and efficacy (and with it, "nature's") into the indefinite future: sustainability.

One can think of the relation between the machine as human controlled and the human as machine as an anamorphosis: like the indistinguishable blur that takes shape as a skull (Hans Holbein the younger's *The Ambassadors* [1533])[22] when we position ourselves correctly—off to the side—so in this case, the relation between first- and second-order sustainabilities is one of perspective that nevertheless puts in question the very transcendence of the human and the validity of a human perspective.

Jean Paulhan, literary theorist and author of *The Flowers of Tarbes,* writes of "Terror" and "Maintenance" in language. Terror is the awareness of words, and the desire to do away with empty phrases: critics attack wordiness, and empty language that is so crude that it calls attention to itself. The opposite of Terror would be Maintenance (of meaning), language that effaces itself before the meanings that are conveyed. But how to attain this level of meaning?

Now the paradox of Terror and Maintenance, according to Paulhan, is that one can see this duality in a single text. There is a Terrorist side—when one can see only the words, the rhetorical devices, and so on—and there is a Maintainer side, when one sees past the words, so to speak, forgets them, and perceives the meaning. It's not just that some texts are wordy and without meaning, and others meaningful; depending on our perspective, a single text can be both "nothing but words" and "full of meaning" (depending on how it is read). In fact, when one writes and rereads what one has written, one passes from one level to the other, incessantly.

Rhetoric itself is both Terrorist and Maintaining. The anamorphosis of the text is nothing more than this passage, from one to the other, within a single text. One (a writer, a reader) is "prisoner" of the text—when one is aware only of "words"—and one can also be freed by it, grasping its meaning and moving on. Paulhan writes of attempting to read an ambiguous text:

> What else can the reader do, caught between two *equally* possible meanings, hesitating and feeling his way around these alternatives, but turn back to words, and question them again, and weigh them up? In the same way a tennis player, if he has just missed a shot, looks with surprise at a racket that is suddenly *separate* from him. And an incompetent workman becomes more distinctly aware of the tool he's using; a patient, of his body—to the point where he sees himself as being subjected to this body, to this tool, and as if he is their prisoner. What strikes us most about a language we only know a little is its methods and its tools, and about our own language, its ideas.[23]

What strikes one here is the notion of imprisonment; when one suddenly is aware of the tool used, it is because it isn't doing what it's supposed to do. It may be broken—as long as something works fine, we don't think about it. When it breaks, we are painfully aware of it. This Heideggerian argument (ready-to-hand/present-at-hand), with which Paulhan was no doubt familiar, is also quite applicable in the case of sustainability. If language is, as de Man argues, a machine, there is in fact little difference between Paulhan's and Heidegger's arguments. In either case the "anamorphosis of the line," as de Man calls it[24] (the anamorphoses of rhetoric), applies to any situation where we are imprisoned by or masters of the machine, aware of the machine in our alienation or "objectivity," or identical with it in our blissful self/machine-certitude. There is a fluid movement between one side and the other, but reading puts us between them, or impossibly outside them (outside the outside), on the knife-edge of their intersection—the impossible space of their conjunction.

Identity with the machine, or language, results in perfect work, perfect meaning, but an absence of awareness of the larger implications of that work or meaning. We share an identity with the object, with the language of the text, and through this in the end our own identity emerges. But our identity is seamlessly linked to the object and meaning: it is not different from us, or from what we understand. Our identity with machine or language results in our own identity, our awareness, being turned elsewhere: in our obliviousness we lose sight of the fact that we are other than the machine or the word. It is us, our consciousness, consciousness in/as machine, we are it. We think of nothing more than the activity we are carrying out, we are that activity. If through anamorphosis our perspective changes, we are aware of our dependence on the thing, the word, we realize we have to use it, *but it is not us*. Sometimes we analyze it and we do successfully get it to work; we are relieved. And other times it stays stuck, it stays infelicitous, and we are painfully aware of that. Tools are always with us, alongside us, pressed more or less successfully into service.

In the first case we are, then, the machine in our full identity with it, to the extent that we are ignorant of this identity. There is critical distance, but not for us. In the second case, in which we attempt to write ourselves back into the first by assigning ourself an identity, a consciousness, we understand ourselves as users, as potential masters, or victims, of the machine in our difference from it. This is not a dialectical (in-itself / for-itself) relation; rather the anamorphosis, the doubling, that we see here, as Paulhan realized, is merely itself the operation of the language-machine, doubling and inevitably (but necessarily) misrepresenting, through the generation of mortal self-consciousness in labor and meaning.

Neither of these perspectives is "true." It's certainly true that we cannot be significantly separated from the world and that, as machines, as animals, our own sustainability is small change, trivial on the cosmic scale. We are engulfed in the larger, first-order sustainability, that of nebulae and machines that function "without" us (including the grammar of our language itself). But in our identity with the machine, with the world, we are both completely absent in our transparency, and omnipresent in our immanence. This immanence is such that our world is the world, the two are coterminous, and the world can (and will) carry on perfectly well without the need for our intervention. There will always be plenty of oil. Nothing ever happens in this world because there is nothing we can do. The world is perfectly capable of sustaining itself, no regulations or custodians required.

We're along for the ride. The existence of the world is our world, our eluding of correlationism (the infinite sustainability of stuff) is in the end perfect correlationism (our things are us). Our omnipotence and omnipresence is our absence, and our complete irrelevance.

We can, however, also say that we are responsible for the machines we so painfully know, but are different from, and custodians of, our own machinehood in the larger ecolog(ies) of the planet. With these two kinds of reading, first and second order, figure and ground, on both sides of the anamorphosis of the line, there is a sustainability, and we are caught between the two. There is sustainability, but not for "us," not for a coherent community of subjectivities; but there is a sustainability that we must, and will, manage, for our autobiographic selves, the planet, the universe. The two sides of the skull, together, yet infinitely distant.

Our first-level sustainability is impersonal and eternal—or instantaneous. The two scales are confounded in non-anthropomorphic juxtaposition. We are machines among machines, animals among animals, caught in the larger energy flows of desire. All is deterritorialization. We are dead/ extinct, or happy, or both. We drive to work, work to drive. But once we set ourselves over against a machine, or an animal, use it, abuse it, fix it, lose it, we are its master, but also its slave. And so too with energy. Energy slaves are a feature of second-level sustainability. We are the masters of things, but we secretly identify with them. How many energy slaves are needed for a person's daily life in official America?[25] Hundreds, thousands. But it can get nasty: the slave can turn on us. The slave becomes the master, as Hegel well foresaw. How many humans are necessary for the contentment of all the energy slaves? We reterritorialize around our embattled humanity, struggling to meet the needs of the present without compromising the ability of future (human) generations to meet their own needs. It is our human duty to master those energy slaves that have called us into being. Every object is known through its embodied energy. We, too, are only embodied energy. Now we become aware of the price of oil, in all the senses of that term. We become aware of energy politics, of energy scarcity, of energy apocalypse in which a loss of cheap energy means the loss of our lives (seen as independent or autonomous entities). We recognize that controlling global warming means enforcing (on others, on ourselves) a voluntary/involuntary peak oil in which the flows are kept in the ground, if not used up. We recognize, in other words, *finitude*. Conservation, with its economic mechanisms and consequences, is suddenly an issue. Seeing our place in larger ecologies means that we become cognizant of our difference, that we are not just one more organism, but that we are humans. The machine is broken, language is weird and empty and mechanical, ecology is not-us and not a self-enclosed totality, but rather something that must be managed and conserved. The object stops withholding itself only to reveal its looming exhaustion.

We are at the side of Holbein's painting now, the skull has snapped into view. It's grinning at us, it's infinitely distant, and we have to do something about its mortality, its absence in visibility. That interpellation generating us is our self-awareness in the world and the recognition of the burden of our necessarily heroic and fictional autobiography. We have to somehow master temporal finitude—an impossible necessity for a machine ("us") that was perfectly happy doing nothing more than taking in flows, processing them, shitting them out, and driving.

Restricted Sustainability

4 Technocracy, Energy Economics, Utopia

In second-order (restricted) sustainability, the human now is at the center; the future is sustainable in that it assures the sustaining of the human as a self-conscious species; ecological balance is assured in order to make possible the indefinite continuation of the human species. Energy now is fully countable and usable, established *for* the human. Objects are characterized in terms of their energetic inputs (embodied energy, or "emergy"), and this determines not only how they are incorporated in engineering projects, but how they are given an accurate (economic) valuation as well. Humans are no longer simply unthinking conduits of energy, but *self-conscious* conduits.

But how to get there from here? There is a strong element of utopian thought in any conception of second-order sustainability. This has much to do with the fact that, up to now, no one, in my estimation at least, has convincingly demonstrated how sustainability can be squared with capitalism (see my comments on Jeffrey Sachs's book in the introduction). We could think of capitalist (growth-oriented) sustainability as "shallow," and another, oriented around resources as "natural capital," expendable and therefore worthy of conservation, as "deep." But that doesn't make things easier: we live, after all, in a time in which, in the immortal dictum of Fredric Jameson, it is easier to imagine the end of the world than the end of capitalism. This transition from capitalism to "something else" is even presupposed in the original Brundtland statement, which, as we've noted, stresses development and not growth. But if one excludes growth, one excludes capitalism. *Voilà le problème.* Capitalism is absolutely dependent on economic growth—it's the treadmill from which we, as subjects, interpellated by the dollar, can never escape. So how to transition to a "steady-state" economy,

a postcapitalist one, in effect, that foresees the end of growth, an equalization of the distribution of wealth while, at the same time, recognizing that,
for many in the world—for those in "first-world" countries—a radical dim-
inution of quantities of things consumed is an absolutely necessary?

This question has been posed for a long time, and has been the stuff
of many utopias, all the way from Thomas More and Charles Fourier to
Edward Bellamy and beyond. Fredric Jameson (again), in an astute essay
on utopias, has noted a fundamental difference between that genre of social
imagining and the political agenda of Marxism. Marxism, too, imagines
another world of social justice and economic security, *sans* growth. Utopias
from More on always seek to address moral issues: human tendencies to
selfishness, violence, lust, and so on are to be circumscribed and limited by
social (and even geographical and urban) reform. Marxism, though, according to Jameson, by focusing on specific economic structures of society, proposes something quite different:

> What is crucial in Marx is that his perspective does not include a concept of
> human nature; it is not essentialist or psychological; it does not posit funda-
> mental drives, passions or sins like acquisitiveness, the lust for power, greed
> or pride. Marx's is a structural diagnosis, and is perfectly consistent with con-
> temporary existential, constructivist or anti-foundationalist and postmodern
> convictions which rule out presuppositions as to some pre-existing human
> nature or essence.[1]

Now I would argue that much ecologically oriented sustainability thinking does the same thing, but no longer from the perspective of precisely
calculable economic value derived from labor power. Marx's "structural
diagnosis," his "science" derived from the calculability of the surplus value
contained in the commodities produced under capitalism—and that right-
fully should go back to the producers of that value, the proletariat—is transformed in rigorous sustainability theory into a "diagnosis" not of the value
of labor inputs, but of energetic inputs, derived not primarily from human
(muscle) labor, but from external and mechanical sources: fuels of all sorts,
as well as wind, solar, geothermal, and so on.[2]

This, then, would be a profound link between ecological sustainability
analysis and Marxist analysis. Both would envisage a "diagnosis" of value, as
grounding for society, in things other than psychology or morality. Marx,
of course, even conceived of his method of analysis as "scientific"—having

to do just with numbers, not with the soul, sin, human nature, inherent guilt, or freedom. And a more rigorous ecological take on things would also see relations as structurally determined, and therefore structurally fixable. Individual or collective morality as criteria for change would have nothing to do with economic and social transformation. For Marx, the growing inequality between classes leads to class conflict, and eventually to a final Revolution in which the proletariat comes to power. From a "deep" sustainability perspective, on the other hand, the final Revolution would have to do more with modes of consumption, tied with value based upon the inputs of "natural capital."

But for all this (implied) precise calculation, utopia always looms: the establishment of a sustainable human order, such as (*pace* Jameson) a Marxist/communist one, which (however they are to be defined) requires for implementation a profound *moral* reform.[3] Indeed, the implementation of such utopian reform is the crucial question of any second-order sustainability model as well. The structural analysis of energy inputs, from the perspective of second-order sustainability, ultimately entails the question: how to get people to consume less ("responsibly"), *as a moral imperative*? In the end, as we will see, scientific analysis is inseparable from an inner-directed moral practice. But how then to impose that practice from the outside?

The energeticist method of analysis goes well back into the nineteenth century. Attributing value to energetic inputs, rather than labor, can be traced back to thinkers like Wilhelm Ostwald and Frederick Soddy. Thorstein Veblen, originator of the term "conspicuous consumption," published a book late in his career entitled *Engineers and the Price System* (1921). And following in this line, focusing on both the centrality of energetic inputs and the centrality of engineers as directors, was Technocracy Inc.[4]

This social–technical movement arose out of contacts between Veblen and the rather mysterious Howard Scott in the late teens and early twenties. Scott was not a trained engineer but claimed to be one; he was joined by other genuine technical experts, such as M. King Hubbert, a petroleum engineer, and the mechanical engineer Walter Rautenstrauch. What these men (and they were all men) had in common was the belief that the current Price System[5] (they never used the inflammatory word "capitalism," though this is clearly what they had in mind) was doomed; it produced only waste, unemployment, economic crisis, and war. It had to be replaced by an economic system as rigorously and rationally run as a gigantic services company, like the telephone system (then AT&T, a monopoly). There was no reason, in their view, that the entire economy could not be as rationally coordinated as a corporation; all inputs and distributions could be directed and carried out by engineers, following engineering principles: rational planning was to be accompanied by a steady state of social harmony and freedom from exploitation and unemployment. Mechanical engineers, then, were no different from social engineers. Not least, the Technocrats foresaw the rational use, and conservation, of natural resources, which in their view made social justice possible. For a brief moment in late 1932 and early 1933, it seemed to many that Technocracy might provide a viable alternative not only to the current American political alternatives, but to the very structure of the (capitalist) economic system of the world.

Technocracy never positioned itself as a political party; instead it dubbed itself "Technocracy Inc.," a strange melding of social movement, political tendency, and corporate entity. Technocracy now was a *good* thing; when the world was finally freed of politicians and economists, engineers would be free to do their job, and the earth would finally be livable. Economic reform was not a moral issue, but a technical project. The most fundamental tenet of Technocracy, which seemed a moot point in the 1920s but became a rallying cry of the early 1930s, was that the money model was not only obsolete, but dangerous. Money itself was only possible because of the concept of property. Ownership is an arbitrary and relative act: one could buy and sell something without that thing changing in the slightest. Property, Hubbert concludes in his *Technocracy Study Course,* "consists not in a physical object, but it is a *mode of behavior* with respect to a physical object."[6]

Despite this relative nature of private property, "almost every item of physical equipment that can be monopolized is at the present time considered to be the private property of individuals or groups of individuals" (125). Everything that can be controlled or corralled is private.[7] For Hubbert at least, value in the Price System is derived not from, say, labor inputs, or even energetic inputs; as a function of private property, value always operates (or is operated) in relation to monopoly—someone controls the resources or products, and is willing to sell them. Value is therefore determined by scarcity. And scarcity is only possible in trade; what I have becomes more valuable when there is less of it, or less is available, and others want it. Prices, in other words, are inseparable from the quantity of products available; if there is too much of any one item (such as air), it becomes worthless as property, and cannot be traded for profit, no matter how necessary it might be.

Money, from this perspective, is a function of socially determined scarcity. It is created through debt—my inability to pay, in barter, for what I would like. If I want something and cannot immediately provide its equivalent, I can give instead a "debt certificate," which will serve to guarantee my providing not some equivalent in kind, but the ability on the part of the other party to acquire something else (128).

Debt is a function of scarcity, and money arises only when debt is incurred. If I have no way of paying for something, I can borrow, and in this way money, a sheer abstraction, is created out of nothing. One can of course assign a rare substance, such as gold, a special status as a "standard," but the gold itself is only of value because it has, apparently, a fairly constant status as rare commodity. Its value too is based on scarcity— the ultimate scarcity, from the perspective of a (now) obsolete Price System (129).[8]

It is not hard to see how this untethering of value from what could be called use value (although Hubbert doesn't use this term) can lead to economic crisis. A scarcity of money, of abstract tokens of value, can result in mass misery, even though there may be enormous quantities of needed and easily produced supplies. Hubbert claims, as did many others at the time, that the entire system was rigged to produce demand for items for which there was no real need, but which guaranteed a profit. When demand slackens, as it inevitably will, people are laid off, and they have no money to spend. Scarcity returns in another form: mass misery. During the Depression, to keep prices up, production of food needed to be curtailed, despite the fact that this led to mass starvation (165).

The economic system promoted by Technocracy Inc., rather than basing value on scarcity, would be based on energetic inputs. "Everything that moves does so only with a corresponding transformation of energy" (235).

Suppose . . . that a system of record-keeping be instituted whereby a consuming power be granted to this adult public-at-large in an amount exactly equal to this net remainder of energy available for the producing of goods and services to be consumed by this group. This equality can only be accomplished by stating the consuming power itself in denominations of energy. Thus, if there be available the means of producing goods and services at an expenditure of 100,000 kilogram-calories per person per day, each person would be granted an income, or consuming power, at a rate of 100,000 kilogram-calories per day. (236)

Since there would no longer be conspicuous consumption or mediated desire (functions of artificial scarcity), each person would need to work at most twenty hours a week, for perhaps twenty years of his or her life (236). Everyone would receive, keyed in to the total energy amount he or she is allocated for the year, a number of "energy certificates." These could not be hoarded or traded, only spent for the necessities of life. The author maintains that the amount allocated could meet the needs of survival of everyone, and indeed could produce overall general well-being. Hubbert stresses the necessary role of the Continental Control, the coordinating central government, which would direct the production of energy resources, their use in the production of goods and services, the distribution of energy certificates to the population, and the use by the population of the certificates to obtain the goods and services produced.[9] All waste is eliminated; the system runs at maximum efficiency, all the while producing more than enough for everyone, and along with that, an enormous amount of leisure time.

> The clearing of the Energy Certificates, tabulated in all the various ways we have indicated, gives precise information at all times on the state of consumption of every kind of commodity or service in all parts of the country. In addition to this there is also corresponding information on stocks of materials and rates of operation in every stage of every industrial flow line. . . .
>
> [Technocracy will make possible] (a) A high physical standard of living, (b) a high standard of public health, (c) a minimum of unnecessary labor, (d) a minimum of wastage of nonreplaceabale resources, (e) an educational system to train the entire younger generation indiscriminately as regards all considerations other than inherent ability—a Continental system of human conditioning. (240)

Such a mechanism is to be found in the physical cost of production, namely the energy degradation in the production of goods and services. Incomes can be granted in denomination of energy in such a manner that they cannot be lost, saved, stolen or given away. All adult incomes are to be made equal, though probably larger than the average ability to consume.

Such an organization has no precedence in any of the political forms. It is
neither a democracy, an aristocracy, a plutocracy, a dictatorship, nor any of
the other familiar political forms . . . It is, instead, a Technocracy, being built
along the technological lines of the job at hand. (241)

The "average ability to consume" is the rule by which people will live,
and happily at that: all their physical needs will be met. The system cannot function without accounting, and accounting cannot function if it is
not centrally directed and universally respected. On the surface, the Technocratic model is not utopian in the traditional sense because it does not
propose moral or psychological critique or reform. This, however, should
be nuanced: the Technocratic model might not directly criticize the morality (or lack thereof) of the human subject (this subject is, in principle, fully
rational), but it does attempt to rethink, and reform, a *morality of the object*.
Recall the earlier Technocratic critique: property does not characterize the
object, but a mode of behavior in relation to the object. It could be argued
that, just as fundamental to the Technocratic conception as are the abundance of energy and the finitude of materials is the characterization of the
object (as analyzed in Technocracy) as divorced from all social relations. Ultimately, it is the Price System that Technocracy would purge; in that sense,
Technocracy is indeed a utopia, but a utopia of the (correctly conceived)
object, not of the person. It is the object in the Price System that bears
the moral flaw, not people. The Technocratic object, on the other hand,
is in principle completely divorced from social relations; it has a heterogeneous existence, above and beyond any social desires or inequities. It is
only conceived as a relation of energy and materials. The object for this
reason enters into social relations in a purely mechanical manner, the way
a properly machined cog would enter into a properly engineered machine.
But in that way the object has been transformed, and has become morally
pure. A car is just a car, and if it can be engineered to last a long time, and
run twenty-four hours a day for maximum efficiency (through a leasing
system), then it is living up to its status as a natural object (253–54).[10] The
car goes from being an object of social division (I want what you have) to
one purified of everything but its sheer utility. In this way it becomes good,
and worthy of production.

There is a new, Technocratic morality based on scarcity. The Technocrat
recognizes that resources are finite, that there is indeed a production curve
indicating that things someday will run out. This is a purely technical and

potential scarcity; it is not an artificial one demanded by private property, but one inherent to Nature itself. This scarcity mandates quantification in production and distribution, and the equalization of distribution. Frugality is the norm, but fortunately, since the system can be rendered highly efficient, ultimately enough can be produced so that there is abundance for all. Frugality is redefined as abundance, in effect. Technocratic morality, then, is obviously that of the engineer; it's a morality that dare not speak its name. All of the object's desirability is gone, and it leads a monastic existence. The object is there only in its stockpiling and its consumption.

There is, however, a problem that cannot be thought within this system. If things are "nonreplaceable," what happens when the supplies of raw materials are exhausted? For the object is finite. Calculation will do no good when the object finally gets the better of technology and withdraws. Its scarcity then will have to do with real scarcity. There is no fleeing from the object. What is rational behavior before the fundamental finitude of the object? Is it total conservation, which nevertheless recognizes that conservation can only go so far? Or is it a loss of faith, a creeping realization that, if the object itself is fundamentally, and not arbitrarily, scarce, if it is doomed to a slow fadeout, then it should be enjoyed now, without concern for the consequences? Enjoy it in its abundance, its excess, and not worry about its disappearance, since disappear it will, either way? Of what use is frugality when nonreplaceability characterizes everything anyway? Questions of morality thus return—the very stuff of utopian analysis— and they return as problems of the morality of the human agent.

This is the unthought of Technocracy, and here it most clearly resembles its utopian predecessors. Just as More's *Utopia* never shows how the society came to be instituted, what the mechanisms were by which people were convinced to change their immoral ways, and so on, so too here Technocracy never makes clear how humanity is to wean itself from the artificially scarce object, private property. How is the new form of object valuation— valuation as nonvaluation, the object as energy inputs—to be established? How is the new moral imperative to be enforced? There is nothing about an internal police force of the Continental Control, but this is nevertheless a central question. Technocracy's answers are completely rational, and yet they will confront the irrational: the love of the scarce, the exotic, the object that embodies unjust social relations—relations of greed, lust, dominance. The desire to spend. Objects exude sexiness. How will pure reason triumph over these urges without force? There is a hidden violence in

Technocracy, a hidden coercion, a hidden call to force, that shows itself in the cold and relentless rhetoric Hubbert uses, over hundreds of pages, to display the rationality of his system. The stain of repressive violence is readable in the transparency of rational action.

Hubbert was perfectly aware of this problem, though he never explicitly wrote on it. It is clear because his position slowly changes from 1934 (the first publication of the *Technocracy Study Course*) to 1949, the year of the groundbreaking essay he published in *Science,* "Energy from Fossil Fuels." In the *Technocracy Study Course,* the author recognizes the finitude of resources, the fact that eventually their scarcity will cause real problems for society. "Hubbert's Curve," the bell-shaped curve of resource extraction that was to become famous later, when linked to "peak oil," makes its first appearance there. In 1934 there was a reassuring message:

> It is not intended to convey by the above calculations the impression that the leveling-off of our present growth curves is due as yet in any large measure to exhaustion or scarcity of resources. The resource limitations are cited only as an illustration of one of the many things that must eventually aid in producing this result. (102–3)

An ambiguous remark, to be sure. The "levelling-off of our present growth curves" refers to the recent collapse of growth in the economy during the worst years of the Depression. Hubbert nevertheless recognizes the unavoidability of long-term resource scarcity that will produce "this result" (the leveling-off of growth curves). Yet he does not dwell on it; this is the only reference to the danger of the nonrenewability of fossil and mineral resources in the *Technocracy Study Course.*

Why? While Hubbert (writing as Technocracy Inc.) suggests a complete recalibration of American politics and the economy, he cannot take the space to suggest ways in which the innate scarcity of materials will ultimately have to be addressed. The crisis of the depression overshadows the crisis of resource depletion. The latter is, however, suggested by the curve on page 101, and by "Curve II," the extension of the peak of the curve that continues at the same level without descending. This is a "type of growth which reaches a maximum, and thereafter remains constant. A familiar illustration of this type of growth is represented by water power" (101). Curve IV on the graph is fossil fuel; after the peak, it descends back down to the same level as that on the left, before the ascension to the peak started.

This distinction between curves will be followed through fifteen years later in the article "Energy from Fossil Fuels." In 1949, after the amped-up prosperity of the war years, and the surprising continuation of the boom after the war, it was no longer a question of a Technocratic regime that would completely reformulate the economy and end the Depression. (Although many argued that the New Deal, with its governmental control of pricing and resource allocation, was itself technocratic, with a small if not a large *T*.)[11] And yet a no-growth economy was clearly still on Hubbert's mind, as was the distinction between Curves II and IV from the 1934 graph. Curve II, after all, presupposes what today would be called a steady-state ("sustainable") economy based on renewables, without the growth model fundamental to the Price System and capitalism. Curve IV is the catastrophic future of total fossil fuel depletion. The 1949 article does not, however, dwell on reforms under Technocracy; it stresses instead the future, and the potential of scarcity of fundamental resources.

Objects and resources—the two are, after all, inseparable (one cannot make objects without resources)—are now scarce not because people make them so, but because they are scarce, period, and are liable to near total depletion. On page 108 of the *Science* article, Hubbert presents a new curve, scary in its temporal reach and apocalyptic implications. "Hubbert's Peak," with all its implications, makes its first appearance, and for the first time, there is the conjoining of the curve of fossil fuel production/consumption with the rise and fall of civilization.[12] Under the heading "Energy from Fossil Fuels"—also the title of the article—the extremely brief reign of these fuels is shown; from 40,000 years in the past, to 40,000 in the future, there is a tiny bell curve, a blip really, which indicates the brief rise and fall of human population, and civilization. On either side, it's flat. For a brief period of two or three hundred years human population tracks energy intake per capita; from the 10,000 calories of daily consumption throughout history, mankind has boosted its intake up to at least 129,000 calories, most of which is derived from coal, oil, and natural gas (105). Soon it will be over.

As in the 1934 graph, a renewable line flows directly from the peak, and does not dip—in other words, if renewables can fill in for fossil fuels, mankind's level of energy consumption (and population numbers) can hold steady, but not grow. Hubbert stresses primarily water power (107) and solar (109) as substitutes for fossil fuels. His argument, clearly enough, fully anticipates discussions of steady-state ecological economies, based on renewable energy, that have continued over the ensuing sixty years. But Hubbert's tone now is ominous.

By 1949, Technocracy Inc. had fallen into disrepute, and Hubbert himself had been severely criticized for his allegiance to an "undemocratic" movement.[13] But without Technocracy Inc., and above all without the critique of the Price System that projected human moral failing onto the object itself, there was only one strategy left: project moral failing back onto humanity. The transition to a renewable future is no longer simply rational and inevitable, as the Technocrats saw it; now it is a moral imperative whose challenge humans might fail. Hubbert writes of his two curves, the steady state and the resource decline:

> Again it is physically possible to maintain a high value, as indicated by Curve I, on a stable basis for an indefinite period of time from current energy sources, particularly direct and indirect solar radiation. It is also possible, however, that *through cultural degeneration* this curve may decline, as in Curve II, to the subsistence level of our agrarian ancestors. (108; emphasis added)

The Technocrat is still here, but he has become a pessimist. If the call to Technocracy failed in the 1930s, why should one believe that the appeal to switch to renewables will be any more successful? "Moral degeneration," the "sacred cow behavior of our agrarian and prescientific past" (109), threatens to overtake the rational control of our economy and resource utilization. Utopia morphs into dystopia. "The future of our civilization depends" on our ability to "evolve a culture more nearly in conformity with the limitations imposed on us by the basic properties of matter and energy."

Yes, but how, given this "degeneration"? That's a rather sinister word (and it's used twice in the article); it's something one might expect from a fascist screed, not from an urtext of contemporary theories of sustainability. The problem of enforcement of transition was always hidden in the Technocratic writings: the implication there, though, was that a purely rational system of economic coordination would be established through presumably peaceful means. But degeneration, the worship of sacred cows—primitive irrationality in other words—would seem to call for a more forceful approach. After all, even Curve I in the 1949 article would seem to call for a transition from artificial scarcity, and thus from the cult of the power and seduction of objects. How to implement that change at a time when the country is flush, the factories are humming, and the long-suffering workers (many of whom are war veterans) quite happy with their new cars and houses? Technocracy, in other words, now grapples not with the austerity of economic collapse but with the delirium of consumer culture at full tilt.

This talk of "degeneration" is not encouraging. And the question of, let's say, enforcement, has hung over discussions of steady-state, renewable economies ever since. If resources are limited, and planners have to plan for a future of increasing scarcity of resources, how do they spread the word, and get people to go along? How can they be compelled or coaxed, in an ethically acceptable way, to go along?

Hubbert's analysis of 1949, I would argue, sets the terms for all subsequent debate concerning what I call second-order sustainability. The specter of Technocracy, or of a later-version, culturally and environmentally pessimistic Technocracy, hovers over all. Time is linear: history is focused solely on the fate of humanity, and humanity is defined by caloric and resource consumption. Humanity is set in a subject–object relation with all that surrounds it: inside, there is us, our needs, our morality, good or bad, our will, up to the task or not, our overwhelming but largely unexplained need (imperative?) to survive as a species. We (as humans) are the scale of the universe. Our morality is defined by that need, and by how we engage this world that is at our disposal. Outside, there is the world of resources and objects, living and inert, quantifiable, waiting for our grasp, yet fragile, susceptible to entropy, depletion, ecocide. And of course nowadays there is climate (and the awareness of climate as a problem), which is the response writ large to how we use and overuse resources. How to make humanity conform to this world of resources?

The Anthropocene, the term used today as shorthand for this crisis, is the overwhelming threat of time run amok, the sudden acceleration of species die-off and climate change, all taking place under the aegis of the human. But time for us humans should be easily measured, and passing at a steady pace, one linked to orderly production and consumption under stable conditions. Our time, the time of available and usable objects—and the time of our children, and grandchildren too. But the Anthropocene poses another time: one that teasingly starts out on our scale (just the last few hundred years) but quickly juts way out beyond that scale, pushing us back into the dreaded zone of disproportion. How to restore the human scale? Once again this is the realm of utopia: how to reform our behavior, and become truly moral beings?

Many theorists see a healthy environment as a kind of resource base, irrespective of the question of fossil fuels. This is explicit in the notion of "natural capital," a theory worked out by Herman Daly, Robert Costanza, Dieter Helm, and others.[14] The idea is simple enough: "services" and the "natural systems" providing them are both necessary to the functioning of our economy; their value should therefore be quantified. Among "services" of this sort are water supplies, erosion control, soil formation, nutrient cycling, pollination, biological control, refugia (habitat for resident and transient populations), food production, and many other things.[15] Thus natural capital (trees, minerals, ecosystems and their capabilities) can be considered to produce quantifiable valuation, along with manufactured capital (machines and buildings) and human capital (physical bodies and their capabilities) (254). Costanza et al. continue:

> We can consider the general class of natural capital as essential to human welfare. Zero natural capital implies zero human welfare because it is not feasible to substitute, in total, purely "non-natural" capital for natural capital. (255)

A prime example of the irreplaceability of natural capital and services is the effort of the creators of "Biosphere II" to create a kind of artificial ecology that would produce all needed ecological services, but under human design and direction. The effort was a notorious failure (255).

The upshot of this, then, is that it is incumbent upon humanity to preserve and protect larger and smaller ecosystems for the simple reason that they provide irreplaceable services (for us). But how to quantify those services? There's the rub:

> A large part of the contributions to human welfare by ecosystem services are of a purely public goods nature. They accrue directly to humans without passing through the money economy at all. In many cases people are not even aware of them. (257)

The danger is that the cost of using natural services tends to be "externalized"—that is, not recognized at all, because it is eliminated from accounting systems, which recognize only machine or human capital. By destroying ocean ecologies, and not including the cost of, say, restoring healthy ecologies in the cost of fish, one externalizes the value produced by the ocean, and renders it invisible. As Constanza et al. remark:

> If ecosystem services were actually paid for, in terms of their value contribu-
> tion to the global economy, the global Price System would be very different
> from what it is today. The price of commodities using ecosystem services
> directly or indirectly would be much greater. . . . World GNP would be very
> different in both magnitude and composition if it adequately incorporated
> the value of ecosystem services. (259)

The externalized cost of natural systems—the value of the services they
provide—must be internalized; the alternative would be the lack of accounting leading to the degradation, and eventual total loss, of these services.
If natural capital is not valued, if it is seen as just a freebie provided by
mother nature, it will be quickly used up: the externalized cost will be
passed on to future generations, who will have to live without the services
provided (if they can), thereby paying a higher price.

This is not so far from the Technocrats, then, or at least from the tweaking Hubbert provided (in 1949) after the demise of Technocracy Inc. as
a political force. The Technocrats, with their energy certificates, foresaw
the need for a precise calculation of all the inputs. The "natural capital"
argument also attempts to imagine how to internalize the value of ecosystem services in the economy. Paradoxically, given the difficulty of attributing a number to these services,[16] the only way to attribute a value may be
to write a dystopian fiction of total depletion, imagining the magnitude
of the cost of the absence of ecosystem services. The internalization of
externalized value depends for this reason ultimately not on quantification, but on terrifying narrative. The sublime enters into the cold calculations of second-order sustainability.

Continuing the argument a bit further, one could see the valuing of
natural inputs by carefully managing their depletion. Here's the problem:
resources may be nonreplaceable, but they must be used. Their drawdown
is inescapable, but also definitive. There is no way to sustain them. The
best that can be done is carefully to husband these forms of natural capital,
entering them into our energy certificate style of accounting, all the while
anticipating a day in which they no longer will be available. The utopia of
Technocratic sustainability meets the dystopia of resource depletion. Or,
to put a slightly more optimistic spin on things, the depletable resources
will have to be managed properly until renewables will finally replace fossil
fuels. And such management would entail the proper accounting of natural
capital. This was Hubbert's hope in 1949, and it is still with us today.

The dream of Technocracy in its 1934 version—wealth through restraint, and a careful accounting of available and limited resources—becomes, by the early 2000s, a dire warning and a call to arms. Hubbert's curve is now seen not as an interesting factoid justifying more exact energy accounting, but rather as the ominous predictor of societal collapse. Once again the object's fundamental scarcity, and not its fictitious scarcity in the "Price System," is the culprit. Hubbert's Peak exponent Richard Heinberg, in *Powerdown: Options and Actions for a Post-Carbon World,* puts it this way:

> If humankind is to avoid ruthless competition for dwindling energy resources, coordinated efforts toward cooperation and conservation will be needed: . . . Industrialized societies would have to forego further conventional economic growth in favor of a costly transition to alternative energy sources. All nations would have to make efforts to limit per-capita resource usage. . . . Everyone—especially those in rich, industrial nations—would have to undertake a change in lifestyle in the direction of more modest material goals more slowly achieved. (87–88)

The emphasis here is on "costly transition," but this was implied by Constanza et al. as well: if natural capital were (somehow) properly valued, the "price of commodities" in such a world would be "much greater." And the ultimate price is not only a "change in lifestyle" (downward), but a "relocalization"; with cheap fossil fuels gone, globalization as well becomes a thing of the past.

Heinberg rewrites Hubbert[17] without ever noting the un- (or post?) democratic tendencies of Technocracy Inc., epitomized in the purely technical determinations and impositions of the Continental Control. In the *Oil Depletion Protocol,* Heinberg imagines a way of saving the world from the economic chaos of steadily depleting oil supplies. One can indeed imagine the recessions, depressions, wars, and other chaos that would follow from the relentless increase in the price of oil. But Heinberg, unlike the later Hubbert, does not see a magic bullet in wind or solar, let alone nuclear. In his estimation, things are too far gone for that; there is not even enough oil left to make an easy transition to a renewable energy economy possible, following the tried-and-true tactics of the "debt" system. To be sure, the economy that produces more money through debt is the culprit; currency must be grounded in energy inputs.[18] But beyond this Hubbertian motif of economic transformation there is now an even stricter discipline:

it is not enough to transition; there must be sacrifice, some accommodation to the stark fact of fossil fuel shortfall.

Simple rationing on a national basis will not be enough, nor will laws requiring less consumption accompanied by arbitrary price increases. What is needed is a coherent global procedure—the Protocol—that will progressively limit oil consumption by tying availability to consumers to the ever-lessening quantities available in a rational, predictable, and reassuring way. This most rigorous of theories for the recognition and accommodation of "peak oil" requires a concerted worldwide effort to stave off economic crisis by progressively limiting fossil fuel resources in an equitable way.

Such a Protocol was first suggested by the oil geologist Colin Campbell (it is also known as the Uppsala Protocol). As Heinberg puts it in his *Oil Depletion Protocol*:

> [Campbell] has suggested a formula based on depletion rates that would work as follows: importers would reduce their imports by the world oil depletion rate, while producing countries would reduce their rate of production by the national depletion rate. (77–78)

The depletion rate, in other words, would also be "the amount by which production would be reduced each year" (78). This would assure a steady way down, so to speak, allowing a predictable and declining recovery rate of fuel resources from known deposits. As Heinberg puts it, Campbell's formula is "non-arbitrary, intuitively graspable by the layperson, and within the range of percentages that would likely be negotiable in any case" (79). Such a formula, one could add, would discourage speculation, hoarding, and unequal resource distribution, which would hurt poorer countries.

While the recent debate about peak oil seems to have switched from depletion to consumption (the idea being that there must be a kind of voluntary peak oil, a cessation of extraction, if the worst consequences of global climate change are to be avoided), the concept of the finitude of resources in general remains a central one. The basic thesis of *The Limits to Growth*—that all the world's resources are facing imminent depletion—is fundamental to any "natural capital" theory, and so Heinberg's concern with an Oil Protocol could be transferred to the depletion rate of any physical resource. The problems with such a Protocol, then, would remain constant across the domain of mineral and organic resources.

Nevertheless, it's significant that Heinberg, following Hubbert, imagines not only the calculated management of scarce resources in decline, but also a currency tied to energy inputs. If one assumes that energy resources are the first among equals—since without them no other resource use would even be possible—then any currency will have to be linked to them.

Just as the Technocrats had their energy certificates, so Heinberg's *Protocol* foresees "Tradable Energy Quotas." These, in coordination with the Protocol, as a "segment of the [national] Petroleum Budget," would be "issued as an unconditional entitlement to all adults and divided equally among them" (129). Interestingly, these quota units, accessed through a "petro-card or direct debit" (130) could be bought or sold; those needing or wanting more petroleum resources could pay those who used less.

The interesting thing here is that these Tradable Energy Quotas would then evidently not replace currency outright. And yet one is led to wonder . . . given this indirect form of rationing, and the fact that these tradable units are pegged to fossil fuels in such a way that they track the fuels availability in the economy as a whole, how could they not serve as a form of currency? One sees why the Technocrats were loathe to allow the trading, investing, and saving of energy certificates. How to prevent the development of a black market, the production of artificial scarcity? This was precisely the kind of problem the Protocol was meant to eliminate: by doing away with arbitrarily imposed rationing, the economy would be rendered stable. But the very possibility of trading makes likely hoarding, speculating, cheating, counterfeiting, and so on.

So the specter of a black market, of gaming the system, remains. And remember that this is a carefully calculated system whereby austerity will be imposed: people will be required, each year, to consume less. Progressively, they will give up their big cars, then their cars, then their mopeds . . . they will give up their transatlantic travel, then their continental travel, finally their local travel. It is not hard to imagine how this would go down.[19] The Technocrats, at least, imagined a Continental Control that would coordinate everything with precision. Heinberg's "Secretariat" (80–81) coordinates trade and austerity measures between economies, but it is not clear, as with the Continental Control, that it has entirely replaced democratic institutions.

The nagging question, then, is: How to enforce this austerity? The rhetorical gambit of Technocracy was to present the change in lifestyle as an increase not only of equality (equalized distribution of wealth) but of wealth itself. And yet under the Continental Control consumers would no longer be, well, consumers. Cars and razor blades would last forever, and there would no longer be competitive displays of luxury. Perhaps this is logical enough, given the transition from the object as conventionally scarce to the object as genuinely scarce. But the problem is still noticeable in Heinberg's more recent powerdown eco-state. And, as with Hubbert, somewhere in Heinberg's future there would have to be an authority—a police force—that would enforce the new, more restrained, modes of consumption. But, as with the Technocrats, nothing is said of it. Everyone, seeing reason, happily makes the transition. Outside, the equivalent of a global Continental Control, the Secretariat, imposing its will through sheer expertise, and with little apparent reference to local democracy; inside, the silence of the text, the easy acquiescence of the world as it enters the era of the Protocol, imposed by the police?

The "middle class," not only in the United States but worldwide, including the growing numbers of newly wealthy people in China, India, and elsewhere, will, under the persuasive sway of Heinberg's prose, give up their cars, their vacation homes, their plane flights to tourist destinations around the world? Never has rhetoric borne such a weighty eco-burden. Who, on the other hand, or what agency, will *require* them, or force them, to stop all this nonsense and consume responsibly? The hole in the text, in 1934, as in 1949, as in 2004, is the external agency, the state or local enforcement powers, that will enforce the necessary ecological awareness. Accounting for natural capital, compared to this, seems relatively easy.

The deep conflict here between the affirmation of a society without money (or money based on a rationally controlled energy resource) and the necessity and unspeakability of an external policing force indicates, one could argue, an almost textbook instance of a utopia. Certainly since the earliest utopias—Thomas More's, for example—money has been eliminated or downgraded, because it is the root of all evil. The object itself, in its reality, in its inevitability, takes pride of place: what can be known, worked, fashioned into useful objects—or, in the case of the Technocrats or "natural capital" people, what can be counted in its expenditure or depletion. In the case of the police force, what's interesting is not so much the specter of fascism as is the void of the unthought, suspended between external force and social autonomy. Does one need a police or not? Can self-government suffice? This un-thought, according to Louis Marin, is precisely what marks the utopia: it is a way of overcoming, in fiction, an unresolvable political contradiction.[20]

In a way, perhaps surprisingly, Heinberg himself admits this. Not of course that he is in any sense officially writing a utopia (his narrative stance is that of a rigorous prognosticator, not a whimsical fabulist), but rather that he is torn between imagining a world governed through one or a number of central authorities, and a world of autonomous, local, self-governing units. This is a question, or "nasty paradox," as Heinberg calls it, of scale:

> As fossil fuels become less available, globalization . . . will contract; ultimately, only a policy of re-localization will permit the survival of a functional social order. . . . However, in the interim it will also be necessary for existing national governments to take forceful and effective charge of their economies in such a way as to preserve social order while reversing the trend of industrial growth. (*Powerdown*, 102)

This qualm, it should be noted, is a concern in 2004; by 2006, it is glossed over completely. By that point, in *The Oil Depletion Protocol,* the local drops out. But this has not eliminated the "paradox" of scale. In fact, the future of human life as Heinberg conceives it is torn between these scales—the global and the local—and the dark space between them characterizes his utopia (in Marin's sense). It is an abstract space in which the police are either external, a force or authority needed only to get the ball rolling, or it is fully local, where the police are internalized as a moral imperative.

It seems it's hard to affirm Hubbert without ending up back in Technocracy. Heinberg, citing Hubbert, affirms (in his book *Peak Everything*) not only the peak resources graph first shown in the *Technocracy Study Course,* but also the crypto-critique of capitalism—a critique that (apparently) dare not speak its name—by noting the impossibility of the debt economy and what amounts to the critique of the Price System. And Heinberg imagines an eco-technocratic future in which the question of enforcement lingers. In that, too, he directly follows his Technocratic predecessors.

Robert Costanza, whom I've already discussed as an associate of the ecological economist Herman Daly and an exponent of "natural capital," has proposed a way around this problem. Rather than somehow imposing a sustainable and low-carbon intensity lifestyle from the outside, he instead proposes—as recounted in his article "Visions of Alternative (Unpredictable)

Futures and Their Use in Policy Analysis"—that citizens themselves be induced to make the right choice, freely.[21] He would ask them to consider four possible retrospective views of life in a future resource-constrained civilization: "Star Trek," "Mad Max," "Big Government," and "Ecotopia." Of the four, three are Costanza's version of popular contemporary fictions; one (Big Government) is a version of a fiction propagated by fear-mongering presidential administrations of recent years. Fully exposed to the implications of the alternative futures, people will presumably make the right choice. These "visions" will offer citizens the possible alternatives, and he believes they will make the right choice, without a Continental Control telling them what to do.

The Star Trek sci-fi scenario, following the TV show of that title, assumes that all resource and energetic problems will be taken care of, magically it seems, by sudden and wholly successful technological fixes. Fun, but highly unlikely. Mad Max assumes the opposite: nothing will work, or be done, and with no change in consumption patterns resource availability will peter out, population will go into decline, and everyone will end up living in postmodern paleolithic conditions of the sort purportedly shown in the dystopian film of that title. Big Government assumes that government will have intervened and solved our future resource, pollution, and climate change crises through a series of semi-successful techno-fixes (such as "warm fusion"), accompanied by awkward political accommodation:

> Warm fusion's slowness in coming on line was balanced with high taxes on fossil energy to counteract the greenhouse effect and stimulate renewable energy technologies. Global CO_2 emissions were brought to 1990 levels by 2005 [Costanza's article dates from 2000] and kept there through 2030 with connected government effort and high taxes, after which the new fusion reactors, along with new, cheaper photovoltaics, gradually eliminated the need for fossil fuels. (7)

The point here is that without changes in consumption patterns and values, big government and loopy sounding techno-fixes will have made life sort of livable in the future, but with eco-catastrophes ("Hurricane John" has wiped out New Orleans in 2010) and a fall in the population. (Actually this version of a tepid Green New Deal sounds pretty good from the perspective of [the real] 2021, given the other options most people now consider likely . . .)

The correct choice, it seems clear, and the most acceptable vision, is that of Ecotopia. This is a vision not of current consumption patterns mediated by more government action and techno-fantasy optimism, but rather of a society that has changed its values completely. People, after all, really want "self-esteem" and not a "fancy car," "serenity" and not "drugs" (3). Here is what happened in this future:

> The slogan for the new future became "Sustainability, equality, efficiency!" The longer form of these principles was embedded in the revised constitutions of many countries as the three goals:
>
> 1. Ensure that the scale of human activities within the biosphere is ecologically sustainable;
> 2. Distribute resources and property rights fairly; within the current generation of humans, between this and future generations, and between humans and other species;
> 3. Efficiently allocate resources (as constrained and defined by 1 and 2), including both marketed and non marketed resources (especially ecosystem services). (8)

Well, at least we know we're getting a heaping helping of "sustainability" here—the echo of Brundtland is clear enough. This is also another version of the Technocratic future: with less consumption and waste, we will not have to work so much: "By 2050, the work week had shortened in most countries to 20 hours or less and most 'full time' jobs became shared between two or three people." Even better, "rather than taking consumptive vacations far from home, [people] began to pursue more community actives (such as participatory music and sports) and public service (such as day care and elder care)" (8).

Costanza aims to convince us that these visions will be properly interpreted by the public when it fills out a survey. And, sure enough, when groups of college students (presumably taking his class) and internet users are exposed to the four visions, they pick the right one: Ecotopia (11). One is led to assume that when the entire American public is exposed to these futures, perhaps through a similar survey/referendum, they too will pick the right one. No constraint needed!

Without meaning to seem too cynical—after all, Constanza's version of ecotopia would be a big improvement over the current regime—one could point out that these visions share a strange parasitic relationship with popular narratives: TV shows, a popular novel, a political meme. Does narrative lend itself so easily to utopian/dystopian appropriation as a marketing tool for sustainability reform?

Narrative is subtle and slippery; it cannot be appropriated, one could argue, simply by signaling a few themes that everyone is supposed to know. I'll pass on *Mad Max* and *Star Trek;* these are multiple and often subtle narratives that may well propose a lot more (with a lot more complexity) than Constanza is ready to notice. Instead I'll focus on *Ecotopia,* the memorable novel of 1975 by Ernest Callenbach.

Callenbach set himself the task of imagining what a society would be like if "stable-state" reforms (in 1975 the word "sustainability" was not yet in vogue) really were implemented. As in many classic utopias, there is an isolated territory elaborating its own rules and practices, cut off from interference from all other states. In good utopian style, a traveler from our world, William Weston, gets through the nearly impenetrable border and sets about exploring this very foreign domain.

As in Technocracy Inc.'s model, economic life is based not on inflation, debt, and growth, but on a kind of universally accepted poverty: wealth is precisely calibrated to what the earth can produce, and money is what one uses to get by on. The population is slightly shrinking; technology itself is based on biodegradable plastics and the small-scale production of DIY living environments; energy production is based on renewable, geothermal heat sources (Ecotopia, after all, is Cascadia—Northern California, Oregon, and Washington—with its geysers and hot springs). Taxation is set up so that there is little accumulation of wealth, and workers share in the ownership and direction of enterprises. The question, as one expects in a utopian fiction, is how exactly the transformation was effected from the doomed world of greed and resource exploitation to a long-range economy of small-scale entrepreneurship and organization. As the narrator puts it:

> In economic terms, Ecotopia was forced [after its secession from the United States] to isolate its economy from the competition of harder-working peoples. Serious dislocations plagued their industry for years. There was a drop in Gross National Product by more than a third. But the profoundest implications of the decreased work week were philosophical and ecological: mankind, the Ecotopians assumed, was not meant for production, as the 19th and early 20th centuries had believed. Instead, humans were meant to take

their modest place in a seamless, stable-state web of living organisms, disturbing that web as little as possible. (43–44)

As in Heinberg, here too there is (at least initially) a larger government that knows how to organize, direct, and even terrorize, contrasted with the ultimate ideal of the local. The Ecotopian government was not beyond, "at the time of secession," either mining or at least spreading the rumor that it had mined "major [US] eastern cities with atomic weapons, which [it] had constructed in secret or seized from weapons research laboratories" (45).

Idealism and *realpolitik:* Callenbach's world is poised on the tightrope between utopia and dystopia, the one in which crunchy hippies live and flourish, and the one that cuts itself off, terrorizes its neighbors, and isolates recalcitrant citizens. The unthought of violence, applied from the outside or above, seems about as prominent as the new morality that Ecotopians themselves have formulated and integrated into their lives.

If workers work only twenty hours a week—that magic number again—the question remains: What do they do with the rest of their time? The "Ritual War Games," in which young men drink, fight, and try to kill one another, are one option. Fighting with "sharp obsidian blades," the lines of opponents rush each other, parry, fall back, and attack once again. At one point, Weston misses the action but is told that "a warrior had slipped on the grass during one of the rushes, and an opponent had seized the chance and managed to run a spear entirely through his shoulder" (72).

This man apparently survives; others do not ("something like 50 young men die in the games each year" [74]). The point seems to be that the mass violence of modern societies—the endless death of wars, car crashes, murder by firearm—has been concentrated in Ecotopia down to this one ritual. Everyone participates enthusiastically—both fighters and their fans—and the few deaths that occur are memorialized and celebrated. The young wounded man tells Weston, "I feel like a man. . . . Once more I have survived" (73). This "abhorrent spectacle," Weston goes on, "is a semireligious rite. . . . It may have antecedents in the institution of bullfighting, in football, in the Mass" (75). Those who do survive are celebrated when they return to their community, family, or "tribe." Indeed in the story the death of the young man leads to a sense of closeness on the part of his community.

Callenbach's narrative thrust here is, I believe, not so much against those who would have a starry-eyed ideal of the sustainable future as it is a warning concerning the very notion of a history-less and timeless regime in which *there is nothing left to do*. What's left when the world is on a steady-state run to infinity and you only have to work for twenty hours a week? Of course you can try to make the work more meaningful, as in Harold Loeb's *Life in a Technocracy*, or you can even slack off and do nothing as you prepare for your life as an artist *(Ecotopia)*. But the larger point is that history and violent change is finished; even art and creative activity in general will be beside the point because everything will already have been accomplished.[22]

This is the point where the Absolute Knowledge at the End of History is either faced or avoided. Constanza too imagines his Ecotopia—but he does not read Callenbach's closely enough. In Costanza's utopia, unlike Callenbach's, there is nothing more to "do" in the larger sense, but that's not a problem: one can always engage in "participatory music and sports" (8). There's plenty of that in Callenbach's vision as well, but the resurgence of violence, authorized by a central authority, demonstrates a simple idea: the drive to violence, to competition, to sacrificial murder, cannot simply be eliminated, replaced by the inevitable group music sessions or friendly sports. It all finds its way back in; the violent degeneracy of Mad Max erupts out of a perfectly closed utopia. The tendency to expend, to destroy, in the name of something or nothing, cannot be eliminated by the shortening of the work week or replacement of competitive capitalism with friendly DIY.

What is a society in which one no longer needs to work long and difficult hours to support one's family, or to change the world for the better (because it is already perfect)? Where one is, in essence, free to play? One could argue that the underside of such a place is still a "world of pain" to the extent that not everyone is a talented musician or athlete—that such a world would be one of terrible inequality and shame (as is the world of tweets and elusive "likes") just as much as one of amusement in freedom and equality. But let's look at the positive side: it would be *fun* (let's assume) to spend most of one's time playing music (no matter how badly) and competing in sports (no matter how dangerously or unsuccessfully).

The End of History means that nothing new can happen. It is the realization of reason in the world. For Hegel, the final phase before the end was Protestantism; but even that was limited, even that introduced an element of the irrational, since above reason there was still God. Barry Cooper, paraphrasing Hegel's *Philosophy of History* in his book *The End of History*, puts it this way:

Protestantism had affirmed the principle of subjectivity as the means by which harmony and recognition, *Befreiung* and *Befriedegung,* would be attained. But it still maintained a belief that the secular was inferior to a "Beyond." . . . Spirit [, however,] had gained the level of Thought and so demanded that the external World be as reasonable as the thinking Subject. Belief in miracles gave way to experimental science and technology, and right and morality were no longer understood as founded on God's command but rather resulted from man's will, actual practice, and universalist political interests. (118)

Or, in a more contemporary mode, one might say that the meaning of value is no longer found in intangible or transcendent meanings (gold, price, customary scarcity through mediated desire), but in the rational, measurable world of embodied energy. Once this changeover has been accomplished, Spirit is now accomplished in Thought, the world is fully rational in its circulations of energy, labor, and value, and nothing more needs to be done—except live. The scientific understanding of the world grounds both economy and politics, since politics now is only the transparent alignment of the rational understanding of the world's physical systems and human needs and wants: Ecotopia.

There is only one nagging question: at the End of History what is there to do? What is the status of all that music and gaming? The French Hegelian philosopher Alexandre Kojève, in a famous footnote to his *Introduction à la lecture de Hegel (Introduction to the reading of Hegel),* notes that discourse itself characterizes the human—but that at the End of History, since discourse is that of change, of the violence and productivity of historical transformation, of the triumph of the slave over the master, there will be no more discourse, and humans will be essentially mute (436). Of course they will continue to speak and write, to do their jobs and live, but the essential language, that of the negation-production of real work (and real revolution), will end.

What happens to the violence of history at its end? That was the great question that puzzled Kojève, and toward the end of his life, he had an idea: after traveling to Japan (1959), he decided that the negativity that was left over, after the end of history and discourse, would manifest itself in useless, formal activities (the supposed specialty of the Japanese), such as flower arrangements, or, more to the point, Kamikaze raids. From this perspective, society would not fall into a kind of mutism, or second animality.[23] It would remain truly, senselessly, violent.

Violence abides as heterogeneous but indispensable to closed econo-mies of value and energy; in fact, one could say that there are two vio-lences, one from within, one from without. The first is the violence noted by Callenbach and Kojève: the violence that resides within history, that cannot be extirpated at its end, in the steady-state economy, and that, un-employed, a leftover, erupts in empty practices. This violence continues in and through not only the end of slavery but the end of fossil fuels as well (enslaved people replaced by energy slaves): it morphs into the insatiable will to consume. Useless acts risk leading the way to pointless consump-tion, which in turn mandates a violence that will restrain it, imposed from without: the violence wielded by the Continental Control, by Heinberg's protocol and Secretariat, even by the government of Ecotopia and its vari-ous mechanisms of enforcement. How else does one control spending, among those who are used to, or are tempted by, the fossil fuel fiesta? The object, as Hubbert would remind us, is scarce not just by custom but by the laws of physics. The danger of inappropriate spending must be made appropriate, transformed into placid art or music. But even pointless activ-ity is a risk, a reminder that in the end there are always things that give pleasure, that cannot be fully accounted for, that will elude evaluations and grades. This very risk of condemnation and violent rejection will call forth guilty pleasure and provocation, and the cycle will continue. Inner and outer violence are doubles, each invoking the other.[24]

The implied violence of all constructive social organization doubles the quantified and fundamentally scarce object. It is subjects who are at that object's disposal, and it is the object's regime, in the end, that always threatens violence. Subjects are interpellated by the object, nominated by it, interrogated, classified, counted, and perhaps (the ultimate threat) eliminated. The subject–object combine is a function of the larger energy regime. The population is now the standing reserve, the bare life. The object as *emergy* is subject to relations of consumption and disposal in rela-tions of utility. And so are we (as subjects) in a world permanently free of degeneration.

This externality/internality of violence is the specter that haunts eco-technocracy. Sustainability—free, peaceful, in total mastery of inputs and outputs, of the economy of freedom and dignity—depends on a violence, internal and external, it can never fully extirpate. Second-order sustain-ability in this iteration, at least, is a creature of the violence (expenditure, waste, delirious and sadistic ritual) it must forcefully exile from itself in order to maintain its integrity as history-free ecotopia. The perfect circle of the closed ecological economy, of the mastered finitude of fossil fuels, the identical instant of plenitude always recurring, coming around again, can only be maintained thanks to a violence that hovers outside that circle, and whose exile is mandated from within it, guaranteeing the integrity of the now while rendering its coherence doubtful.

5 Solar Architecture, Sadism, Heterogeneity

There is a congruence between second-order sustainability theory and technocracy, whether we use a capital "T" or not. The object itself, and not just its social implementation, is profoundly limited: it is scarce not in an artificial way, the way of capitalism and the Price System, but in the most basic way: supplies of materials are finite, the object always marks itself as depletable from the very first moment of its incorporation into an economy of use and sense. Hence the need for control, calculation; indeed the specter of constraint is inseparable from any social model that recognizes the larger implications of material scarcity. People in a "steady-state" economy will fully accept the changes that austerity mandates; if not, the system will not, cannot, recognize their resistance. It will resist their resistance. Such use of force—how else could we make sure sustainability is sustained?—will necessarily be imposed from the outside: outside the individual will of someone who might be tempted to consume irrationally, to value, to recognize objects as socially *desirable,* and partial as well, outside of their utility. The rare thing, charged with explosive force, that risks destroying society as much as uniting it . . .

If external violence is implied, but largely unmentionable, so too is internal violence. As we saw in Callenbach's *Ecotopia,* violence risks returning because there is, inherent to social life, an irremediable force. Callenbach's narrator even calls it "sacrificial"; it may very well be the violence that motivates society, renews it, gives it its charge—or it may be a movement that degrades and brings it down. The risk and splendor of games, of festivals and ritual, all put forward an energy that cannot be easily subordinated to rational rule-making and discipline. The "artificially" scarce (but

unavoidable) object might very well return in the shock of glorious degradation. It will be the task of technocracy to counter this urge to spend.

I would like to shift our focus now from the United States to Europe,
and a peculiarly European variant of eco-technocracy. Sustainability in
Europe passes by way of the city. In Europe, one lives and consumes in
a city. Urban life and sociability are one and the same—there's a long tradition of thinking the meaning of social, economic, and esthetic life in
relation to urban space: Georg Simmel, Charles Baudelaire, the surrealists,
the situationists, Walter Benjamin, the list goes on to encompass an enormous amount of European thinking on modernity. But when it comes to
social life, economic, political, and social reform, and the city as mechanism
of sustainability, one name, however, stands out: Charles-Édouard Jeanneret,
aka Le Corbusier.

Le Corbusier a prophet of sustainability? For many, that's a ridiculous
thought: after all, the Swiss architect was a technician, a prophet of the
house as a "machine for living," a techno-freak who thought the city could
be scraped and rebuilt from the ground up, with a special focus of technically superb built units—housing, offices, factories—made from high energy
intensity concrete. Cities would turn their back on "nature" and rise into
the sky: the green space below would subsist only as an accoutrement of
the technically accomplished social and urban structure above.[1]

But we've seen that technical sophistication, technocracy, and a certain sustainability are hardly at odds, either in the early twentieth century
or among theorists today. What's important is that, in his city designs,
which evolved from the 1920s into the 1960s, Le Corbusier was always concerned with the maximum efficiency of *the use of the sun*. True, there are
inefficient cars circling in his cities, and he might even have foreseen the
constant rebuilding of city structures, carbon footprint be damned. But Le
Corbusier, like the activists of Technocracy Inc., was concerned above all
with grounding his society very precisely in renewable energy. He doesn't
talk much about money (let alone energy credits), but his city, if it is a
machine, is above all a solar machine, devoted to conserving precious resources and extending energetic efficiency.[2] Indeed, for Le Corbusier, the
city, like humans or any other animals, is nothing more than a way of properly channeling and thus conserving energy.[3] Le Corbusier was connected
with an avant-garde group in the 1920s, called "Plans."[4] All could be planned,
had to be planned, to preserve the world from the chaos into which it was
threatening to fall.

Le Corbusier was certainly not a "paper architect"—the *Unité d'habitation* of Marseille was built, as were the administrative buildings of Chandigarh, in India[5]—but his city truly comes to life on the page. His cities are ultimately written, and drawn: they are narratives, sketches, plans.

Le Corbusier's artwork is total and totalizing: every possible contingency is foreseen and every unpleasantness deflected. His cities are written and drawn by the hand of the master. At every moment we sense his presence behind the word: he it is who tells us what is wrong with the current city—its congestion, its dirt, its inefficiency and squalor. And he, too, provides us with illustrations, drawn in his own hand. His sketches, his handwriting, marvelously convey the plan of an old city center, a cathedral and its placement, the path of the sun across the sky, the structure of trees in relation to the architecture that he proposes. And the presence of giant housing blocks rising from the space of the transformed city.

As architect, as master, he is in touch with a deeper stratum—not just materials, but with a privileged way of accessing them. He sketches a nautilus shell, and its connection to a mathematical curve, and writes:

> The law of numbers is inscribed in natural works [*oeuvres naturelles*].
>
> Man, a product of the universe, carries in himself the mark of numbers.
>
> He discovers them, he expresses them, he uses them to direct his enterprises. Laws are inscribed in mechanics and in the calculation of the resistance of materials.[6]

Laws, numbers: the master has privileged access to the unchanging basis of things, to the profound relations between matter and law. Hence architecture and cities too, via this access to the law of number, will excel as art: they will be in harmony with the ratios, the golden mean, the "Modulor" that governs the harmony of the relations of all physical things. And the politics tied to this law of numbers will be equally precise, equally definitive. The inhabitants of the city will find their happiness in relation to this material and quantifiable law.

Le Corbusier's sketches, "in his hand," are not impressionistic; they are quite precise, and his architectural drawings feature straight lines, perspectives stretching to infinity. This is the law of the city: to be seen. The planner separates, as he must, different urban spaces: delivery lanes below, walkways above. The delivery lanes make possible the quick arrival of people and provisions to their destinations: they assure that motorized transport never gets stuck in some urban irrationality, never leads to time-wasting congestion. Roads, multilane freeways, are always free, always open, always guarantee maximum urban efficiency. Above these, however, or beside them, connected to the green spaces opened up by the tower blocks that dominate Le Corbusier's urban space, there are walkways that give access to shopping areas, cafés, schools. Urban space exists in a static and well-proportioned harmony. City space is not about surprise: there is only *one* psyche and *one* geography in Le Corbusier's psychogeography. I do, I see, what has been prepared for me, what has been programmed. I exercise, I go to my job, I receive my friends, I go to the café, I play sports, all in preplanned fashion. Alienation has been eliminated through numbers. If this visual life is in harmony with the laws of numbers, of materials, then there is nothing else: the architect-urbanist is not just someone providing a neutral structure, something to be used and forgotten, or contested and ironized, but rather a philosopher who provides the very meaning of life.

Thus the sketch "A Contemporary City," in *Urbanisme* (translated as *The City of To-Morrow*).[7] The caption tells us, among other things: "We are in the center of the city, the point of greatest density of population and traffic; there is any amount of room for both." In the distance, skyscraper housing blocks; on the right, below, a highway with cars; in the foreground, a café terrace, providing the perfect perspective to view the towers, the surrounding green area with trees; on a café table, a teapot and several cups; another table has a carafe and a water glass. In the sky, decoratively frozen, several biplanes, one seemingly headed, Icarus-like, down to earth. And yet we notice that this drawing does perfect justice to the scene, because it is the *only* perspective possible. It depicts the traffic and yet we see no movement. There can be no movement; it is transcended in a larger stasis. What's more, there are (despite the "greatest density") no people in the drawing. In fact, there are practically never people in Le Corbusier drawings, except of course for the Gumby-like Modulor figure of perfect human proportion who shows up in his own little proportion-boxes (was there ever a Modulor woman?). People are absent not because they are peripheral, or dispensable, but because they *are* the city, in its permanent configuration. The observer is on *this side* of the scene, never depicted. In this iconoclasm, the human is the autobiographical subject of the urban: Le Corbusier himself, in the perfect stasis of contemplation of self through contemplation of city, alone in his room. Meditation is only a subset of the technological.

Le Corbusier's narratives of life in the radiant city also project this time-lessness, this absolute of perspective. Here the cessation of time touches its corollary, the instantaneous. Nothing involves delay, any annoying separation of moments that could interrupt the perfect perspective, the perfect harmony of individuals, thanks to the urbanist. Le Corbusier is, above all, a narrator. The Radiant City is, finally, a story: the story of how we move and live, and can finally rest, in the city. It's a strange story, however, since Le Corbusier's narrative is one of absence of delay—in other words, the absence of the temporality necessary to all narrative.

Imagine, Le Corbusier suggests, life in one of the tower blocks he proposes, and in its surrounding green spaces. In *The City of To-Morrow,* Le Corbusier contrasts the city of today with what is to come. He writes of the angry and coercive concierge one has to deal with nowadays, the noise in the apartment, the impossibility of having parties for fear of bothering others, of trying to exercise in one's room because it's inconvenient to go to the health club. And it gets worse:

> As for food, your maid goes to the local store and wastes a lot of time, and everything is very expensive. As for your car, the garage is ten minutes away, and if it is raining you reach home soaked, in spite of having a car. And your children have to be taken to the Park to play: that is, if they have a nurse-maid or governess. (214)

Le Corbusier goes on to ask: "What if we could at one step wipe out all these difficulties?" and concludes: if only we could *"by order bring about freedom"* (214; emphasis in original).

Domestic Taylorism defeats bourgeois *anomie*. The agony of everyday life comes down to *waste:* wasted effort, wasted time. "Freedom" is the redefinition of one's life as a narrative in which, paradoxically, there is no waste, because time does not pass. The leisure of the leisure class is inseparable from instantaneity. Delay as such, the gap between desire and its fulfillment, the gap between the consciousness and its wants, the free will and its exercise, is eliminated. Such a freedom would abolish narrative because it would exit from time and exist in a kind of glorious present. Or, conversely, a not-narrative of freedom would somehow be elaborated in the absence of the passage of time.

We learn that, in the Radiant City, "grouping 660 flats" in a "block of closed cell-like elements" will facilitate the organization of life: freedom through order. On the ground floor would be "commissariat, the restaurant service, domestic service and laundering" (217). This pseudomilitary organization, rather than breeding the boredom ("hurry up and wait") of the army, instead leads to the immediate satisfaction of needs:

> The kitchen would be capable of supplying meals of a simple or elaborate sort at all hours. If you desired to bring some friends back to supper round about midnight, say after the theatre, a mere telephone call is all that is needed for you to find the table laid and waiting for you—with a servant who is not sulking, as he happens to have just come on for the night shift. An experienced hotel manager, a specialist with a staff of specialists, would organize and see to the whole domestic economy of the block. (217, 220)

The all-important dinner after the theatre is now organized along factory lines, and the sullen servant has been replaced, through the miracle of correct architectural organization, by one who is happy at his or her job. We have gone to a posthistorical realm, thanks to correct (solar) architecture, one where social tensions have been effectively done away with, and for this reason revolution is made obsolete.[8] The question of time in sustainability, the problem of the present and the indefinite continuation of the same, has been solved: things are sustained indefinitely at the end of history simply because there is no more time. That scalar problem is resolved: perpetual sustainability is also the timelessness of the instant, indefinitely repeated. Change, if such a thing were imaginable, would entail only the repetitious reestablishment (the eternal return) of the same.

At this point, Le Corbusier's words and sketches join: the not-narrative is inseparable from the not-sketch, the sketch that represents the absence of any living (and moving) urban inhabitants. The stain of the individual (will, project) has been removed from the perfect and perfectly closed system. All that is left is the figure of Le Corbusier himself, artist and technician, the last man hidden in the perfect plan, self-awareness as the seen. Art as technics triumphs, on the other hand, because without will and drift, without slackers to cause problems, total aesthetic organization—what Le Corbusier calls "freedom"—is for the first time possible. Le Corbusier still needs at least the idea of functioning bodies in his cities, but stripped of the delay represented by unfulfilled desires and irrational urges.

In all this, Le Corbusier elaborates the most sophisticated version yet of a technically perfected aesthetics, society, and ecology (given his cities' supreme eco-efficiency). If that perfection involves a certain subtraction, then so be it. Nothing happens in his world, or everything happens immediately, without happening, without resonance: the world—that is, cities—are perfect spectacles without anyone there. Le Corbusier's cities are perpetual motion machines in which there is no motion; when all motion is to be found in the repetition of the same, motion itself is lost in synchronicity. Delay is scarcity and dirt; with the fullness of the absence of time, via urban technology, a plenitude is attained.

But what grounds the technical for Le Corbusier? In the absence of so many institutions of civil society—Le Corbusier's cities seem to lack any third space: city halls, pool halls, fora, beer gardens—what motivates the hypothetical Corbusian citizen besides wanting a quick meal? What is he or she supposed to do all the time? And what is the city as "machine for living" supposed to do?

Instantaneity, it would seem, depends on the sun.

In the early 1940s, under the occupation, Le Corbusier journeyed to the French fascist capital, Vichy, to try to convince the authorities—going all the way up to Marshall Pétain himself—of the values of his radical model of urban renewal. He was met with utter indifference.[9] Along the way, he wrote a book with a fellow French corporatist, François de Pierrefeu, entitled *La maison des hommes* (The house of man). This is a fascinating book, not only for its political complexity but also for the questions it poses concerning authorship. If indeed we can take de Pierrefeu's argument as essentially representing Le Corbusier's—as Simon Richards, for example, does[10]—then we can follow the crucial step that Le Corbusier takes from a critique of contemporary life to the ultimate valorization of the sun.

De Pierrefeu–Le Corbusier stresses that the current economic order is engaged in "over-consumption"—that no respect is shown for the natural resources of the earth, and this leads to humans "weighing down on the earth":

> Oil, coal, minerals flow from the flanks of the earth in streams that will never run out. All discretion has been abolished vis-à-vis mother nature; more than abolished, derided. . . . The dogma of the day is *the wastage of a cosmic reserve,* one irreplaceable and given one time only.[11]

So far, we have a kind of proto-peak oil theory,[12] which is promptly tied to
another kind of over-consumption—that of what nowadays we would call
commodities, or rather commodity fetishes. De Pierrefeu notes

> how false needs, artificially aroused, show a tendency to cause each other to
> multiply, which industry, operating in an additive manner, will only be able
> to satisfy in an ever-more minimal way. From this, there will be disappoint-
> ment, furor, and revolt. Until the nature of things, in the end, gets revenge,
> as it did in America in 1929. (34)

False needs—again, the American Technocrats couldn't have put it better.
Where today is the "spiritual house" in this world of "imposed dreams"?
"Divertissements" (diversions), as Pascal would call them? Certainly not in
the urban "palace of mirages," which the author(s) associate with the current "Modern city," since the latter,

> [chasing] away the *sun,* also chased away the invisible radiance *[rayonnement]*
> of which it is the instrument and symbol, both of the morals of society and
> of the heart of the citizens. (39–40; italics in original)

De Pierrefeu–Le Corbusier would ground liberation from (bad) modernity
in the revision of current modes of energy consumption and in the reconstruction of the city by the planner. For today's city, the bad, pre-Corbu
city, is a mirage of false consumption, and it is *dark;* the essay suggests a
reciprocal causative link between these two. The darkness of illusion is
doubled by the darkness of the city, its congestion and blockage of sunlight. The darkness of the ignorant self in the city is the stain on the sun:
it is the negation of the very principle of sustainable energy, the analog of
the darkness caused by the airborne residue of fossil fuel consumption.
Since we are inattentive to things, since we waste them, since we misuse
them by taking them to be the source of real happiness, we are inattentive to
the origin of real health, hence urban decay, which in turn only reinforces
our delusions and immoral habits. We ourselves have created this blockage: if we are transformers of the sun, we alone, of all animals, are also the
nontransformers of the sun, its blockers.

The sun is "instrument and symbol," and for this reason, the sun is both
the origin and end of human, and of all life. Freeing ourselves from "false
dreams" means building the city and restoring its "principal and key," which

is the sun: "the 24-hour cycle," and the "radiation of the day" (40). The radiant city is not just a metaphor: it is indeed radiant, since the tower blocks designed by Le Corbusier are set at angles that allow for maximum sunlight. The sun is the central factor in what today we would call an ecologically oriented architecture: one attentive to "natural" rhythms and natural energy sources. But the sun is more than this: it takes on a kind of existential originality, in that it serves not just a practical function in life in and outside of buildings—but it also defines man. De Pierrefeu and Le Corbusier write:

> The reestablishment of fruitful labor, and a happier labor, imperatively demand the *radiance of the sun*. From the point of view of physics, the living being is nothing other than "a transformer of solar energy," in the apt formula of Dr. Pierre Winter, and of all the many forms of this energy, it is light, from the infrared to the ultraviolet, which constitutes its most indispensable nutrient. He absorbs it directly by the skin, through millions of papillae, tuned to the luminous vibrations like little precision tuners. He absorbs it directly through food—vegetables and meat—which are veritable "stores" of light. Darkness, the sick light of cities, broken up by smoke and dust, are the very power of tuberculosis, rickets, and neurasthenia. (44–46; emphasis in original)

Dr. Pierre Winter is also quoted in *Destin de Paris,* where the same point is made, with the additional statement by Le Corbusier: "The sun in every room, all year. Consequently, no windows facing north."[13] There is one crucial difference between the two passages, however; in *Destin de Paris,* Winter himself is directly quoted:

> The human being *[l'être humain]* is only a transformer of solar energy; life is only a circulation of this energy; light is one of our fundamental nutrients [aliments]. (We absorb it through our skin, we tap into it every day in these "reserves of light" constituted by the majority of vegetable and animal nutrients" (Dr. Pierre Winter, fifth CIAM congress, Paris 1937). (15)

De Pierrefeu and Le Corbusier in *La Maison des Hommes* write of the "living being" as solar transformer; Winter, however, writes of "human beings" as doing the transforming. Certainly the paraphrase of Winter is appropriate, because humans are, after all, living beings; yet Winter's own stress on humans in *Destin de Paris* is decisive.[14] It establishes a contrast between, on the one hand, all natural systems, dependent as they are on sunlight, and human beings in particular: it stresses the privileged link between the human as a natural system and the larger role of the sun. It puts the city, locus of the human, at the center of the relation between the sun and the ecology in which we thrive. The city of solar architecture is the differentiating space, the articulation point between simple nature and the human in all its complexity.

And yet there is something here that goes against the human. The fact is that man is "only" a "transformer" of energy; the metaphor here is of a device, the transformer, that changes the voltage of electricity (the transformer) in order to get a job done. Here the transformer is the human, electricity is solar light, and the job done is survival. The word "only" stresses the fact that everything that all humans do—all their grandiose accomplishments—is reducible to a mere transformation of energy, and that, in the end, our authors suggest that this role of and for the human is itself not even human: after all, *all* living beings do it. They transform, they are transformers. And, presumably, they are transformed. And if humans block solar energy in their dark cities, they alone are the creatures who block their own nature as transformers.

This is a revealing transformation: from human to all living beings. The transformation of solar energy cannot be seen as an exclusively anthropocentric gesture. In fact, the ironic mode of Winter's original statement already stresses this kinship between humans and life in general, and the relative insignificance of the human: all we do is transform energy. But we alone as humans tend to block it. Hierarchies are reversed: humans are not the authors but passive transformers, whether they know it or not. The solar expresses itself in the human, by transforming itself, but it does so in all other living beings as well. At best the human can be like all other creatures; at worst, it will try to block and deny solar energy. The human is potentially nothing more than the stain, the opacity, that blocks solar energy. Humans have to build cities, in order to most effectively transform solar energy; they have to do consciously what all other creatures do unconsciously. Their cities are solar transformers, that is their purpose: the furthering of human life through the intensification of the solar in cities.[15] But cities are also the embodiment of the human tendency to block the solar, humans acting against their own interests as living beings.

It's not, then, just a case of the solar becoming conscious of itself in the human. The book—Le Corbusier's book, his narrative—is necessary to transform humans into proper transformers, by showing them how to transform the city. The human must become a *conscious* solar transformer. Where the human really distinguishes itself—is unique—is not in the simple transformation of solar energy, but in the resistance to solar transformation, and to the eventual, necessarily conscious, undoing of this blockage through the reading of Le Corbusier. Solar consciousness is an aftereffect of blockage. The human is limitation, not plenitude, the irrational production of scarcity and dirt, the production of narrative delay (the sulky servants, the wait for dinner), but then also the conscious overcoming of this limitation. Humans unconsciously produce darkness, delay, and consequently, consciously, enable light. Solarity is an aftereffect of the human production of dirt. Sunlight for humans (unlike animals) is thus a technical construct of consciousness—and ultimately of Le Corbusier's consciousness.

Le Corbusier's solar utopian stasis embraces solitude and willed alienation. The model for this in Le Corbusier is, as Simon Richards has pointed out, Pascal.[16] It was Pascal who lamented all the world's "diversions," the need for the distractions that keep us from going crazy. Pascal's solution is to argue the necessity of the rejection of all *divertissements* that block us from God. We must turn from the world, sit alone in our rooms. "I have often said that the sole cause of man's unhappiness is that he does not know how to sit quietly in his room."[17]

The problem with this, of course, is that focusing on oneself in one's room can itself become a diversion. What's needed is the ability to isolate oneself and then isolate oneself from oneself. Thus Pascal could write:

> We must love a being who is within us but is not our own self . . . and is both ourselves and not ourselves. . . . True conversion consists of self-annihilation before the universal being.[18]

Richards stresses that Le Corbusier ultimately values in his city not the gregariousness of city life, but rather solitude. What can at first seem like an antiurban critique of the city—in effect, Le Corbusier redesigns the city in order to deurbanize it, because he profoundly distrusts city life in general[19]—goes on to reveal itself instead as a method for deriving a kind of higher spirituality through a new kind of alienated city living. But it all depends on how one defines alienation. For Le Corbusier, in effect, the point of the urban "machine for living" is to make it possible to live a modern life, all the while withdrawing from the world and annihilating oneself. All the services that would be provided in the city, the ultimate conveniences, have a larger purpose: they make Pascalian withdrawal from the world and human life itself possible. Hence Le Corbusier could write:

> And since leisure will require a man to spend more time in his room (Pascal's *desideratum*), a new concept of home will arise; an extension of the idea of home to take in the sun, all space and nature's green.[20]

The city turns the darkened, withdrawn Pascal into a motionless solar transformer. Withdrawal itself is solarized. A (non)society of Pascals living in *unités d'habitation,* in their cells, remains and flourishes. The mystical state of self-abstraction that Le Corbusier advocates is essentially godless, or, more accurately, the place of God in Pascal is taken in Le Corbusier by sun, space, and green. It is at this point that we start to see the logic of Le Corbusier's sun worship. The sun is less a plenitude than a movement of self-abstraction and self-abnegation. The technically superb appointments of the city and its dwellings make possible this meditation on, and before, the sun. The perfection of the city effaces itself, so to speak, before the "self-annihilation" of the solar subject, but it is nevertheless necessary. Meditation depends entirely on, and is a function of, the technical–solar orientation of urban architectural practice. The human as highest point of sustainability, ensconced as the nodal point of solar urbanism, is also a point of the technically grounded annihilation of human will. If the individual human will darkens, serves as a spot darkening solar self-presence, Pascalian meditation overcomes this stain of particularity, and lets the sunshine in.[21]

It's important to recall that, in Pascal, withdrawals from "diversions" are also a way of saving oneself from the "disproportion of man." If to be human is to be lost between the infinitely small and the infinitely large, then to lose oneself in diversions is one mode of forgetting. One hunts, plays cards, chases all the small and meaningless victories in life whose only value is to allow one to forget. But in withdrawing, sitting alone in one's room, what does one gain? Withdrawal is not affirmation of the self; it is loss of an unsuccessful effort to lose the self. One engages in the famous "wager," one bets on the existence of God (there is nothing, really, to lose), and on the promise of "infinity." If loss of self somewhere between the two infinities is bad, then self-loss in the good infinity of God is the only option.

One bets on God: Pascal's wager assumes that everyone would be willing to lose some momentary diversions on earth for the possibility of gain-
ing infinite happiness. You like to gamble, stave off boredom playing cards,
shooting dice? Well, I've got a bet you can't refuse . . . It's a clearheaded
decision, one doubled by another: in order to bet on God, one has to conquer one's passions. One follows the path of reason—betting on God—
by inculcating one's own belief in Him, not by convincing oneself of His
existence through unconvincing rational argument, but by going through
the motions, and making oneself stupid (*bête,* mindless like an animal):

> You want to arrive at faith, and you don't know the way. You want to cure
> yourself of infidelity, and you demand the remedy. Learn from those who
> have been tied up like you and who now wager all their possessions *[tout leur*
> *bien].* These are people who know the road that you want to follow and who
> are cured of an affliction *[un mal]* that you want to cure. Follow the road they
> have started on: it is by acting as if they believed, using holy water, having
> masses said, etc. Naturally that will make you believe and make you stupid
> *[vous abêtira].* (Brunschvicq, 233; my translation)[22]

Hence Le Corbusier's wager: by building the rational city, by inhabiting
rationality and betting on the sun, one strips away all other details of belief,
and one lives, presumably happily. Act as if you believe in the sun, and you
will believe. Do it blindly, like an animal: there's nothing to lose. Don't
confuse this act with any personal idiosyncrasies; your self is in the wager,
nothing more. All the old beliefs are associated with the dirt, the complica-
tions of the old city and old ideologies. Accept Le Corbusier's city, act, live
in it, and you will attain the enlightenment of the rational economy. And
you will channel energy efficiently, effortlessly, like an animal. What is the
content of that enlightenment? What do we learn? Certainly not leisure,
happiness, comfort. Much as in Pascal, where the theological content is
empty—reduced to simple physical motions—in Le Corbusier the content
of social and even spiritual life is emptied, and affirmed exclusively as withdrawal from the world. But at least the payoff of Pascal's wager was (the
good) infinity; in Le Corbusier we have only the repetitious return to rationality. At best we have tautology: I make the rational bet on withdrawal into
the *Ville Radieuse* in order to attain rationality (urban life à la Le Corbusier).
This is the law of Le Corbusier's sustainability: sustaining oneself in order to
sustain oneself sustaining. Infinite sustainability: the instantaneous shock of

the wager, repeated indefinitely, devoid of all content, *bête*. This is the nomination of the Pascalian / Corbusian self at the top of the tower, the pyramid: the empty sovereign subjectivity speaks, nominates itself as the final term of the motionless city. Le Corbusier writes his event-less autobiography in the final (but also initial) act of urban prosopopoeia.

What, then, of this rationality, this law of withdrawal to attain the law of rationality? Le Corbusier invokes Pascal, but we can also invoke Kant: in the *Critique of Practical Reason* it is Kant who formulates a devotion to a higher moral law that is *without content*. In Kant as well, the subject is emptied out, follows not a desire, not an inner inclination, not endless rationalization, but simply a formal law upon which human life must be based:

> We are indeed legislating members of a kingdom of morals possible through freedom and presented to us by practical reason for our respect . . .
>
> With this, however, the possibility of such a command as *Love God above all and your neighbor as yourself* agrees quite well. For as a command it does demand respect for a law that *orders love*, and does not leave it to one's discretionary choice to make this love one's principle. But love for God as inclination (pathological love) is impossible; for he is not an object of the senses. The same love toward human beings is indeed possible, but cannot be commanded; for no human being has it within his power to love someone merely on someone's order.[23]

Kant responds to Pascal: the ultimate moral law to which one must accede, and to which one must attempt to conform, is empty. Just as belief, love of, or at least submission to, God is nothing more than going through the motions, here the moral law does not even entail love. Kant rightly notes that one cannot be commanded to love: so loving God is an empty love, at least by human standards. It is not particular to my own personal belief. It is just being in perfect conformity with the law, hoping that if one does that successfully one will be saved (or the salvation is in the repetition itself). This is another version of the wager, without even the freedom to not wager. Here you are quite certain to fail if you do not wager—to fall short of the law, to violate it. But if the wager is successful—if you do manage to do the right thing, to fulfill the law—the result will not be belief, or some melding with the infinite. Instead all you will have is formal love of God, which is nothing more than following the law.

The critic Slavoj Žižek has noted the psychoanalytic implications of the paradox of this law. As he puts it,

> We run into the (form of) Law *at the precise point where the representation is lacking* (namely, the representation of an a priori object that could act as the impetus of our will). The form of moral Law is thus not simply the form of a certain content—its mediation with its content is far more paradoxical: it is so to speak the form *supplanting, holding the place of the missing content*. The structure is here again that of the Möbius band: form is not a simple reverse of content; we encounter it when we progress far enough on the side of content itself.[24]

When we progress far enough on the side of form we run into content. The content is the everlasting twisting of the form, or vice versa. In the case of the Kantian moral imperative, the subject inevitably splits, becoming on the one hand the "subject of the enunciated" (embodiment of the symbolic mandate, the empty Law) and on the other hand the "subject of enunciation" (the subject that expresses itself) that inevitably resists identification with the Law, because it is particular (233). The subject is, alas, separate from the Law, always attempting to conform to it—even though the Law is formulated only in relation to (as a control over) subjectivity.[25] This is the "pathology" of resistant subjectivity. This subject of enunciation then becomes, as Žižek puts it, the "object within the subject," the always heterogeneous bit out of conformity with the empty imperative, the point at which the subjectivity in and of the Möbius band "smears" into a moment of objective resistance (231).

This object is in principle lacking in Kant: the subject always conforms, far from any pathology. It is, after all, its duty, which has been internalized. Žižek notes, however, that the French psychoanalyst Jacques Lacan reads Kant against himself, through the Marquis de Sade. Kant and Sade[26] would seem to have little in common, but both figures, in fact, posit a Law, a superego, a subjectivity that inevitably splits and becomes an object. Žižek writes:

> Behind . . . the Law in its neutral, pacifying and solemn side, there is always a side of the object which announces an obscene mischievousness. . . . And that is why Sade is to be taken as the truth of Kant: this object whose experience is avoided by Kant emerges in Sade's work, in the guise of the executioner, the agent who practices his "sadistic" activity on the victim.

> The Sadeian executioner has nothing whatsoever to do with pleasure: his activity is *the stricto sensu* ethical, behind any "pathological" motive, he only fulfills his duty. . . . The executioner works for the enjoyment of the Other, not for his own: he becomes a sole instrument of the Other's will. (233–34)

One is never good enough, one never can live up to the law, and this law reincarnates itself as a subjectivity that turns on itself, becoming an object that harshly imposes itself. This could be registered as a personification, since the sadistic object is also, as Žižek notes, the superego (236): the subject, in attempting to conform to the empty Law, reincarnates as an external object, the "objet petit a," which turns against the subject and is personified as a torturer. Subjects and objects change places, and the subjectified object that oppresses is, like an unwanted statue with a powerful independent will, a terrible imposition upon a now broken and objectified subject. Žižek, coming from the former Yugoslavia, naturally thinks in terms of the Communist Party, which is internalized as a kind of never satisfied, sadistic superego, an inner relentless object to every tortured subject who attempts to act according to its will, an overwhelming subject to which every subject, trying to incarnate its truth, is nothing more than a pitiful and crushed object.

Le Corbusier is no Stalin, but (as one would say of two historical epochs) the two rhyme. The empty ideal to which one devotes oneself in Le Corbusier is a harsh master, a stern superego, in the sense that it affirms the necessity of loyalty to the empty ideal of perfect efficiency, and the melding of subject and object in the meditation of a subject alone in an architecturally perfect room. This is the moral law, the soul, of Le Corbusier's sustainability. Nothing is lost, everything is reappropriated, recycled, forever, without diversions, in a timeless time. But this solar law is sadistic; one can never be sustainable enough. Le Corbusier's text admits this, inadvertently, when it makes clear that one withdraws into one's room both to conform to Pascal's *desideratum* and, at the same time, because one wants to live efficiently and be able to have guests over after the theater, with a nice snack. The purity of Pascal is always interrupted by, tormented by, a bourgeois diversion, and by the technological considerations that frame it and would (in spite of everything) perpetuate it. Le Corbusier himself can never be Pascalian enough; the theater always disrupts meditation in the cell, and meditation always flees the theater. There is a little sadistic torturer always there in the background, reminding the inhabitant of the *Ville*

Radieuse that he or she could withdraw even further into the machine for living and more fully conform to the solar law. Conforming to this absolute law of sustainability is an infinite task: one's inevitably inefficient bourgeois subjectivity sees to that. How can one ever be sure that one's carbon footprint is small enough, that the infinity of calculations needed to assure one's conformity to the law has been carried out sufficiently, and correctly?[27]

Self-laceration, then, is perhaps the eternal mode of a second-order sustainability. But there may be more to it than that. There is something parasitical about this sadistic superego that incarnates the empty moral law. This object of disruption and torture is heterogeneous to the smooth functioning of the circularity of the Möbius sustainability strip. The sun has its law, but the incarnation of that law gives the lie to the perfect circularity of its operation. This can be seen as the origin of self-torture, the nightmare of the green *Heautontimoroumenos*. But in good Möbius strip fashion, the pure "subjectivity of the enunciated" might very well reverse itself into a "subjectivity of enunciation," a heterogeneity, that is more liberating than oppressive.

One can certainly frame the heterogeneity of the solar control as a negative—the *jouissance* of the Other, working through the sadist, invoked and feared again and again by the victim. But as the Möbius strip turns, the sheer homogeneity of the strip—its endless, featureless surface, mutates. Žižek notes:

> Lacan's point in "Kant avec Sade" is, however, that this wiping out of all "pathological" objects, this reduction to the pure form, produces of itself a new, unheard-of kind of object. . . . What Lacan does is to repeat the inversion proper to the Möbius band on the level of the form itself: *if we progress far enough on the surface of the pure form, we come across a non-formal "stain" of enjoyment which smears the form*—the very renunciation of "pathological" enjoyment (the wiping out of all "pathological" content) brings about a certain surplus-enjoyment. (231)

The empty Kantian form, renouncing all pathology, all content, twists around itself, smears, and produces, in the very process of eliminating, pathological self-certainty, self-enjoyment, a new subjectivity and a new self-enjoyment. In its perfect conformity to itself, to its own formal demands, the law enunciates a heterogeneous element. That element, of sadistic pleasure, of a stain on pure form, of opacity or resistance, of the self as particularized perspective, is the unrecoverable element necessary to the functioning of the form. It is the edge outside the anamorphosis of subject-object, inside and outside. In other words, that stain both grounds the seamless entity—the entity evidently cannot close or seal itself without it (after all, it always requires a willed decision, *bête* as it will be)—and at the same time is radically heterogeneous to it: it cannot be assimilated to the pure form of the law.[28]

A similar movement can be found in Derrida's famous essay "White Mythology." There, too, the seamless coherence of metaphorical structures that govern philosophy can be seen to be founded in the brilliance, and truth value, of the sun. The sun is essential to the coherent functioning of the meaning systems that ground sense; and yet the sun, as origin of meaning in a nature that transcends human (self-)fashioning, is both heterogeneous to human systems—it founds them—and is itself caught up in metaphor. Its heterogeneity to the system (as truth of nature) is essential to, and a guarantee of, the system's functioning. And yet it itself is always caught up in a round of metaphor; its heterogeneity to the system is violated by its own homogeneity. Or its heterogeneity to the system violates the repetitive series, the homogeneity of terms. Derrida writes, in "White Mythology":

> If the sun is already and always metaphorical, it is no longer simply natural. It is already, always, a chandelier *[un lustre],* one could say an artificial construction if one could still accredit this meaning when nature has disappeared. For if the sun is no longer natural, what remains of the natural in nature? (300)

The stain of metaphoricity renders opaque the perfect self-transparency of the truth-value of the sun. The sun masters the set of all metaphors only to the extent that it is just another metaphor—thereby obscuring the very absolute truth it would generate (or sow). Le Corbusier's sun is similarly double: it generates the truth of nature and life of Le Corbusier's architecture—that is, of all architecture—and renders it eternally sustainable through the perfect circulation of equivalent energy inputs. Yet, at the same time, the perfect summation of the truth—Pascalian meditation as a refutation, in life, of the bad infinite in nature—is stained, so to speak, by the pathology of personal comfort and facile convenience. Solar truth is just one more lifestyle, one more affirmation of a subjectivity lost in spatial and temporal disproportion, one more moment of the city as diversion, of man as delayed polluter and not apostle of sustainability.

The sun both produces truth and loses itself in its own labyrinth of truthy but truthless metaphors. It is absolute origin and guarantee, and just another reject.[29] It is the circulation of transparent truth, and one more deviant metaphor that calls attention to itself, that says "I," that sits just outside the overall system of inner and outer, truth and falsehood. There is, we could say, an endlessly circulating band, an architecture of metaphor necessary to the erection of the truth of architecture and life. But the loss, at the same time, of the sun as the grounding of all metaphor inserts a darkness into the edifice of life and law, life as law. The lofty establishment of the homogeneous formal structures topples, if only momentarily, but incessantly, into a maze of senses and forms without any necessary truth or grounding. The transcendent heterogeneity of the sun becomes an abased heterogeneity of a solar deviance, "mere" metaphor. There is always something else, some diversion, something that drifts, that serves to break the timeless homogeneity of time, that serves to extend the proliferation of arbitrary or wayward or pathological meanings. There is always a smirking waiter who risks being a little bit late, and the accompanying bet on a rigorous and mindless *(bête)* wager on renunciation.

The machine (of the law, of architecture) in its perfect functioning produces heterogeneous elements, stains, that interfere with the sheer mechanical self-presencing of signifying systems. This is how it runs. The machine expresses itself in an unauthorized way; it always says the wrong thing. Tucking oneself into a perfect solar edifice and attaining a perfect natural proportion—the *desideratum*—is fundamentally empty, an emptiness that will always return as boredom, frustration, the demand for some necessarily repressed bourgeois kink (or as the resistant awareness of the mechanism itself and the sadistic forgetting of meditation).

There are two heterogeneities: first, the solar as guarantee of the smooth and totalizing movement of the signifying, technical chain, the perfectly smooth form of the Möbius strip.[30] Here the sun is the founding member, so to speak, and the ultimate signified: truth, light, life, the perfect circulation of energy, sustainability under the sign of exchangeability—intellectual, physical, and moral recycling without remainder.

But this sun is doubled by the second, indicated (for us at least) by Derrida: this sun's mastery of the chain is doubled by the fact that it can never fully rise above it. It is always just one more metaphor. As such, the sun is

just a stain in the Möbius strip, the nonprivileged instantiation of a deleterious time (its privilege in the system is to register its lack of privilege). No
metaphor can ever convey its signified with complete integrity; there is
always a drift between signifier and signified, between the tropes guaranteeing, but also disrupting, the smooth functioning of the system. The perfect
objectivity of the system can only be capped by a drifter, a dissolute resister.

This is what Georges Bataille, polymath and friend of both Lacan and Le
Corbusier, had in mind when he posited, in his 1933/34 article "The Psychological Structure of Fascism," a double system of heterogeneity. This heterogeneity was contrasted with a homogeneity that characterized, significantly,
both social structure and the very nature of objects. Bataille writes:

> Production is the basis of a social *homogeneity*. *Homogeneous* society is pro-
> ductive society, namely, useful society. Every useless element is excluded,
> not from all of society, but from the *homogeneous* part. In this part, each ele-
> ment must be useful to another without the *homogeneous* activity ever being
> able to attain the form of activity *valid in itself*. A useful activity has a com-
> mon denominator with another useful activity, but not with *activity for itself*.
>
> The common denominator, the foundation of social *homogeneity* and of
> the activity arising from it, is money, namely the calculable equivalent of the
> different products of collective activity. Money serves to measure all work
> and makes man a function of measurable products.[31]

Bataille goes on to note that a physical reality corresponds to this homogeneity: "Homogeneous reality presents itself with the abstract and neutral
aspect of strictly defined and identified objects (basically, it is the specific
reality of solid objects)" (143).

Homogeneity, in Bataille's sense, follows the model of what I call second-
order sustainability: society defined by its production of useful things, every
activity serves another, all relations are calculable, all objects are stable,
predictable, useful, and presumably worthy of conservation and reuse (since
they would serve the production and conservation of other objects). The
reciprocity of society and the stability of objects lead to a world in which
accounts balance and time is measured through the steady production and
reproduction of the material world.

Money, interestingly, appears here not as the measure of artificially limited consumer objects (the Price System of the Technocrats), but as a measure that equalizes all goods, services, and (presumably) ecological inputs.

It is the abstracting and mediating fiction that renders everything equivalent, its ideal being something like the Technocrats' energy certificates.

Such a system, however, needs a heterogeneous element to justify it, to enable it to work. In the world of perfect homogeneity, nothing has value in and of itself, for itself. There are no higher values justifying the system, guaranteeing its significations (146). Thus its dependence on "imperative forces"—that is, forces heterogeneous to the smooth workings of everyday life but which, in one way or another, guarantee and legitimate them. This is the domain of religion, religious ritual, solar (monotheistic) worship, God himself. Bataille's overarching point is that, in an era of the "death of God," there is a kind of imperative heterogeneity crisis: heterogeneity today, the violent force exterior to everyday exchange but violently maintaining it, in the absence of God, falls to fascism. The bourgeois world in its crisis demonstrates the fact that homogeneity cannot function without a heterogeneous element. Fascist leaders are heterogeneous; like the military caste, they do no work, indeed they seem to have contempt for the everyday, peaceful activities of the bourgeois. They cynically explain that they are "stable geniuses" precisely because they are evidently neither stable nor possessed of genius in any conventional sense. They are outside (and they would argue above) the norms and laws that regulate homogeneous social structures and their laws. In their deviance, they are unconditioned, sovereign agents of foundation. That is their appeal: the scary or thrilling excitement generated by the leader, the mass hallucinations he incites, no matter how grotesque they might appear to outsiders, justify the existence of those who follow. And yet a large fraction, if not the majority, of the bourgeoisie invokes and reveres the leader precisely because it believes that he will somehow maintain them in their homogeneity.

Heterogeneity of this type is, according to Bataille, a "differentiated sadistic activity" (146). Sadism emerges because the fundamental irrationality of the heterogeneous power must maintain itself not just by maintaining homogeneity, but by violently repressing, with pleasure, another aspect of heterogeneity: its subversive side, its double. Bataille, following Émile Durkheim and Marcel Mauss, argues that the sacred—the totality of heterogeneous acts and objects—is in fact double, with an elevated, "right hand" side which (like God or the fascist leader) guarantees and affirms social coherence, and a "left hand" side of elements that are socially unredeemable, subversive, and repulsive. The pure and the impure (144).

My point here would be that Žižek's analysis of the Kant/Sade dyad posits a superego that is, precisely, heterogeneous in the imperative sense. It is the conscience that, sadistically, maintains against the impure stain of individuality ferocious negative judgments.

From this it is apparent that Le Corbusier's solar city as well is, from Bataille's perspective, erected under the aegis of an imperative heterogeneity, and certainly a sadistic one: the sun. The sun of philosophy and the cult of truth—the "elevated conception . . . the poetic meaning of mathematical serenity and spiritual elevation,"[32] that is, the sun that guarantees the smooth functioning of the erect homogeneous world (and its restricted economy)—is also the sun of a sadistic political imperative, what we might call sadistic sustainability. The sun is just one more term, one more metaphor in the chain, yet it can only enforce its heterogeneity, its radical separation, through repressive and differentiating (discriminating) violence. This is not to argue that Le Corbusier was necessarily an adept of, say, the fascist tendencies of Vichy, or even of the Nazis, whose swastika has its origins in sun symbolism.[33] Le Corbusier's model of sustainability, however, is inseparable from the Kantian law, the empty law that circulates, that prohibits all pathology in the very act of enabling it, indeed of generating it. The point at which the law establishes itself, enunciates itself, is the point of its own heterogeneity to itself and the system of which it is a part. It must turn on that heterogeneity with sadistic force, with the highest degree of constraint. All decay in the city must be extirpated, all inefficient diversion must be incessantly razed.

The imperative of the sun, and all it excludes, are fundamental to Le Corbusier's theory. And yet the sun needs the darkness; not merely physical congestion but the "base sacred," the heterogeneity that is the opposite number of solar elevation. Bataille writes of heterogeneous elements:

> The *heterogeneous* world includes everything resulting from *unproductive* expenditure (sacred things themselves form part of this whole). This consists of everything rejected by *homogeneous* society as waste or as superior transcendent value. Included are the waste products of the human body and certain analogous matter (trash, vermin, etc.); the parts of the body; persons, words, or acts having a suggestive erotic value; . . . the numerous elements or social forms that *homogeneous* society is powerless to assimilate: mobs, the warrior, aristocratic and impoverished classes. (142; emphasis in original)

Bataille goes on to note that, as opposed to the stable (and abstractly measurable) stability of homogeneous objects, heterogeneous "reality is that
of a force or a shock. It presents itself as a charge, as a value, passing from
one object to another" (143). This characterization follows Durkheim, who
noted the "charge" of sacred objects in *The Elementary Forms of the Religious
Life*.[34] The important thing to note is that this is not a purely "subjective"
characterization—Bataille notes the "objective" nature of "erotic activity."
But one could argue that the heterogeneous exits from the opposition sub-
jective/objective, in that that opposition is itself part of the homogeneous
universe of measurable, stable things, scientific calculation, and Cartesian
subjectivity. It is the "pathological" smear that Lacan has noted in the subjectivity that falls from the ethical system: a sovereign (unconditioned) element in thrall to no leader or economic–cultural hierarchy, in revolt against
the sadism of the closed system that would try to incorporate it. As the
fascist shock troops are sent into the city to guard the sacred and repressive
precincts, under orders of imperative heterogeneity (the grotesque, crimi-
nal leader), the base heterogeneous forces struggle against them, dancing
and displaying themselves in their profound nudity, all the while braving
tear gas, clubs, bullets.

If Le Corbusier's city is a homogeneous apparatus guaranteed by the
imperative heterogeneity of the sun, one could note *another* city, one of
erotically charged, cursed objects ("waste products") and the darkness of
descent (or the fall). This city does not simply enable the repetitious foundation of Le Corbusier's, through its incessant and violent rejection. The
sun's objectification of the "subject of enunciation," the inevitable stain
that embodies but resists the law, entails another urban subjectivity, one
in cellular distortion, turning against the larger architectonic organism.
The sun incarnates a subject that always falls, falls out in heterogeneous
squalor and revolt. This filthy city, readable in and against Le Corbusier's
radiant city, is, however, not simply its opposite, inefficient and unsus-
tainable, where Le Corbusier's is radiant and sustainable. It has its own
drifting ecology. If Le Corbusier's is principally human, with perhaps a
few domesticated animals (which we never really see),[35] this other city,
Bataille's, we can call it for short, is one of creatures and objects whose force
undermines the erection of science, mathematics, and the law. Bataille has
a whole bestiary and museum of oddities, including big toes, rotten suns,
moles, pineal eyes, and many others.[36] These are the urban denizens of a
city that itself is heterogeneous, a labyrinth rather than a pristine tower or

pyramid: a labyrinth of aberrant and virulent metaphors from which the sun can never fully extricate itself. This entails another urban ecology. Bataille writes:

> The disproportion, the absence of any common measure between various human entities [is], in some sort, one of the aspects of the general dispro-portion between man and nature.[37]

So-called nature is a *general* disproportion; the human is in disproportion with itself ("between various human entities") and thus a disproportion-ate element—"man"—is in disproportion with everything else, which is in disproportion with itself as well. Disproportion all the way down. And when Bataille considers this disproportion, he often uses urban terms:

> Reason is a sick machine when it is forced to represent a passerby, a paving stone, a shop, as nothing, and the supposed endless linkage of causes as a totality that nullifies its parts.[38]

A general heterogeneity of urban events: all the peculiarities of the city are what we overlook when we make scientifically verifiable statements about congregated life or the universe—when we make the city speak with one voice. Unassimilable details are forgotten in the larger abstraction of the whole. The city for Bataille is, instead, this "constellation," as he calls it, of elements of "aggressive fragmentation."

Bataille has turned the Kantian law inside out, so to speak; instead of a tyrannical and empty imperative—the command to love God somehow minus the pathology of the individual—we now have the pathology, in all its revolting versions, along with the virulent death of God. We only have the deviance of the instance of the law, the point at which the application of the law cannot fit into a larger totality. There are just powerful fetish objects, charged with the force of the sacred: the force of the reject, in other words, around which social groups might form and de-form—to experi-ence the shock collectively—but nothing that leads back to the higher law, the higher synthesis, the higher ventriloquized edifice. The sadism of the law, of imperative heterogeneity, is in periodic eclipse as base heterogene-ity erupts out of it.

The sun doubled, now "rotten," is caught in the drift of particular senses, of minimal differences, of momentary street sightings, of bad metaphors.

The heterogeneous object in its charge is always for that reason "symbolic" in Bataille's sense, a labyrinth of "irrational and particular symbols."[39] This is the maze that Denis Hollier notes as a figure of Bataille's writing. With the master metaphor brought low, without technocratic determinism, charged objects are uncontrolled, unclassifiable symbols. Hollier states:

> The labyrinth does not hold still, but because of its unbounded nature breaks open lexical prisons, prevents any word from finding a resting place ever, from resting in some arrested meaning, forces them into metamorphoses.[40]

Now imagine the labyrinth as a city whose minimal, senseless, and obsessive events, animals, people, constantly meet, interpenetrate, transform. Their movement is one of a metaphoric drift, uncontrollable, referring always to a master metaphor constantly shifting in its abasement and hence lacking all mastery. This city does not "exist." Its reality cannot be verified. Its lack of existence does not mean, though, that there is a "real" existence out there somewhere, a world of technical perfection, of which it falls short. The cursed city is a material one, but of a matter and animality that carries the charge of the sacred, a charge whose stability is menaced by its deviant symbolism, its symbolism as sheer unincorporable materiality. Rodolphe Gasché writes, on Bataille:

> [The] exterior is the absolute outside, whose contrary is not an interior (and which, moreover, has no contrary; that's why it's called matter); reason, radically disproportionate to it, is that which, through its restricted operations, produces the difference between inside and outside.[41]

Radical exteriority is not only outside of reason, but outside the outside / inside opposition. This outside of the outside is situated at the heart, the innermost interiority, of the labyrinth, of the city Le Corbusier must exclude in order to constitute his own in its perfection and atemporality. Its temporality, however, is so excessive that it cannot be controlled or, indeed, generated, through exclusion. Dirt, the heterogeneity of repugnant matter, is outside the relation impurity / cleanliness.

The two cities have differing relations to time: the return of the mechanical and the entropy of the return. If Le Corbusier's time is one of a rigorous sadistic (solar) production, conservation, measurement, and reuse, with the goal an elusive no-time in which nothing happens to disturb the perfect proportion (and repetition) of production and reproduction, the other city, Bataille's, is one of a time that progresses, but in a circular or unknowable, labyrinthine, way. It progresses around itself, back to itself, from itself, again and again, with difference, and facing mortality. In Nietzsche's *Gay Science* the "ignorance of the future"—which is cherished—is doubled by the affirmation of the eternal return, where we suppose the opposite—that everything we have known and will know will come back again, that if the future could be known, it would be affirmed—forever. Nietzsche characterizes the eternal return through the repetition of great, but also minimal and disconnected objects—"even this spider in the moonlight between the trees, and even this moment and I myself."[42] How to affirm this time of the fragment, without affirming mere complacency? How to imagine the eternal return outside the comforting orbit of the solar order?

The base heterogeneous, the explosive fragment, is affirmed in its repetition, or it is not affirmed at all. Nietzsche phrases this as a personal choice—there is almost a joyous uplift in saying yes to the *return as fall.* Bataille, however, writes not of personal affirmation but of urban crisis and fall. The Obelisk in the Place de la Concorde is, for Bataille, the site of the revelation of the return.[43] The Obelisk is the urban summit leading not to eternity or self-certainty, but to the repetitious fall into time. Bataille writes:

> TIME is unleashed in the "death" of the One whose eternity gave Being an immutable foundation. And the audacious act that represents the "return" at the summit of the rending agony only wrests from the dead God his *total* strength, in order to give it to the deleterious absurdity of TIME.[44]

But what of this affirmation of a different mortal time, no longer the calculation of the cyclical production processes of knowable stuff, or the perfect mechanical return of the first law of thermodynamics? If there is a return, it is inseparable from a "deleterious absurdity" of a time that both returns and opens to a future that defies cyclical perfection. And how can one write of a *sustainability* of this return? How are sustainability and eternal conjoined, in a labyrinth of urban detours?

6 Anamorphoses of the Future

Both the Technocrats and Le Corbusier posited a future of peace and plenty, with the careful coordination of energy inputs and resource circulation. Human culture would reach its endless end given the absence of constraints—temporal and material—that weighed down populations under the conditions of arbitrarily and unjustly imposed fiscal and urban regimes.

Ernst Jünger, a German officer and veteran of World War I, had a very different vision of technocracy. Jünger had miraculously survived four years in the trenches, and was wounded a number of times. While most veteran-authors who had gone through the war's harrowing violence turned resolutely toward pacifism—Wilfred Owen, Henri Barbusse, Eric Maria Remarque (even Louis-Ferdinand Céline) come to mind—Jünger's reaction was quite the opposite: he championed the war experience as an "inner experience," one that put soldiers into intimate contact with the true foundations of life. In works of the 1920s like *Storm of Steel* and *Copse 125*, he recounted not just the horrifying and destructive elements of war, but (according to him, at least) its power of transporting men (and his world was resolutely masculine) to another, virtually mystical, plane of human existence. What had broken most other soldiers seemed somehow to invigorate Jünger.

After recounting his personal experiences on the front as an officer (and recipient of the Pour le Mérite, Prussia's highest military award), Jünger wrote and published, in the early 1930s, a number of works sketching out his conception of the future of society (among them, *The Worker: Dominion and Form* [1932]; *On Pain* [1934]). Whereas the Technocrats and Le Corbusier blamed an inefficient and incoherent capitalist economy and built world for the crisis of civilization following World War I, Jünger blamed bourgeois individuality itself. The war for him was not "about" anything, least of all the crisis of capitalism or the struggle for dominance of one group of empires over another. Rather, it was an indication of the emergence of a world after the decline of interiority, individualism, and humanism. The war revealed that human life itself found its meaning not in stability or security, but in the undergoing of a radical regimentation and discipline, a state in which the regularization of technology came to be inseparable from work, creation, life, and death.

> In the liberal world, what one considered a "good" face was, properly speaking, a delicate face—nervous, pliant, changing, and open to the most diverse kinds of influences. By contrast, the disciplined face is resolute; . . . One immediately notices by every kind of rigorous training how the imposition of firm and impersonal rules and regulations is reflected in the hardening of the face.[1]

This personal and cultural regimentation is inseparable from a more profound experience, one in which the individual connects with what Jünger calls, in his essay *The Worker,* the "elemental." This is a dimension of experience beyond the bourgeois, for whom it is "irrational and thus the absolutely immoral."[2] The deep stratum of life, a Nietzschean "proximity of death, fire, and blood with health as had never been experienced before" (33) is revealed in the trenches. While romantics protest through inner resistance, the new "space" entails danger, which had been banished to the "outermost frontiers"; it now "seems to flow with greater speed back toward the centers" (33).

The embrace of the elemental takes place through the technological: war *is* the elemental as an expenditure of energy, with war itself the product of technological reason.[3] Risk, hardship, pain, the violent explosions and gruesome dismemberments that rock the millions of trench inhabitants are only possible because of technological progress. Technology ultimately reveals its truth and asserts its value not by facilitating "better living," but because it releases the human from the bonds of individuality. In *On Pain,* Jünger writes:

> Recently, a story circulated in the newspapers about a new torpedo that the Japanese navy is apparently developing. This weapon has an astounding

feature. It is no longer guided mechanically but by a human device—to be precise, by a human being at the helm, who is locked into a tiny compartment and regarded as a technical component of the torpedo as well as its actual intelligence.

The idea behind this peculiar organic construction drives the logic of the technical world a small step forward by transforming man in an unprecedented way into one of its component parts. (18)

Jünger is evidently taken aback by this removal of "all potential for good luck" in warfare, but he is also fascinated by this culmination of what is implicit in his outlook: the complete melding of man and machine, which calibrates itself—in sport, in warfare, even in entertainment—in, against, and through technological devices. The object—the tool—and the human are one: Jünger's version of the cyborg. The larger meaning of this synthesis is always the accomplishment of the human via the facing of death, in and through technology. Or, perhaps, the accomplishment of technology, in and through the mortal human.

The postwar (and posthistorical) world foreseen by Jünger, which, he argues, is (in 1932) already upon us, is one in which production, mechanization, development, and warfare are inseparable. This is not, he is at pains to stress, a political or economic future; democracy, communism, capitalism, all are irrelevant in a future in which all that counts are production, destruction, and the completion of humanity through its involvement in this process. His metonym for this process is "The Worker," although it is clear that this term is not to be understood in the communist or socialist sense. The worker encompasses all who make this future what it is: workers who make things, to be sure, but also the engineers and managers who supervise the processes, and the warriors without whom it would all be pointless. The truth of life is to be found not only in the battlefield, but in the entire war economy: management, centrally coordinated production of goods, services, and munitions, as well as combat and death. For Jünger the economy *was* the war economy. There might be a momentary hiatus, but "peace" was only a moment of recovery before the inevitable and necessary return to war.[4]

But who is this "worker"? It is, one could argue, finally, a figure of speech. It is a way of gathering together the various meanings of warfare / society as Jünger imagines it. It is a form *(Gestalt)*. In *The Worker,* he writes:

> By form we indicate a supreme meaning-giving reality. Its manifestations
> are important as symbols, representations, imprints of this reality. The form
> is a whole embracing more than the sum of its parts. We name this more,
> totality. (189)

Reality is defined by what it does: it gives meaning. It is a semiological
mechanism, and it is paradoxically "more than the sum of its parts"—as
any sign-generating system would be, engaging in the infinite permuta-
tions of syntactical linkages, representations, and speech acts. But through
that meaning-process, this always "more," there is "totality." Totality of
what? We might answer: a totality of the impossibility of totalization, of
summing up.

But this is not simply the infinite sign generation and reflection system
of a postmodern novel. At least Jünger doesn't take it for that. Form entails
the overcoming of contradictions, but not through their resolution in a
purely formal sense. Form and force are linked:

> A real force utilizes the surplus that it has at its disposal not to circumvent
> contradictions, but to pass straight through them. It will gain recognition
> not because it basks in feelings of superiority from the high vantage point of
> an illusory whole, but because it strives to seek the whole in battle. . . . The
> relationship to form reveals itself in surplus, in excess, a relationship that, in
> temporal terms, is experienced as a relationship to the future.
>
>   This surplus is what appears as inner certainty on this side of the battle
> zone and, after trial, as dominion on the other. (50)

The meaning-giving matrix (if that's the word) of the worker (as form) is
doubled by excess and a relationship to the future. It is inseparable from
this violence. Somehow, in this technocratic future, this world of guns and
butter (but mainly guns), of material and war materiel production, we have
to imagine a kind of inner violence that motivates, drives, and destroys. A
Heraclitean violence? Not only is life fully in and of technology, of peace
(production of useful goods) and war (production of destructive goods),
but technology is in and of both meaning giving and destroying. Meaning,
life, production, destruction are one; the world of measurement and creation is inseparable from the world of measurement and destruction.

Violence is repetitive. The worker *is* repetition, mechanical reproduction,
in itself. That's why the question of "why"—why war when you could have

a planned, peaceful society?—seems misplaced. If technology is by nature repetitive, the same turning of the same wheel a seemingly infinite number of times, then the transformations of workers, warriors, machines, images of machines, ensures a kind of eternal return of violence in the process of production in which energy is maximized. Perhaps recalling the jurist (and Jünger's friend) Carl Schmitt's work, there will and must always be an enemy, but the enemy will only be another "typus" of the worker.

Any technocratic system worthy of the name will define itself not only in relation to a form, but to an object. But what of the problem of energy measurement, conservation, and maximization so characteristic of other technocracies? For Jünger, the object of utility and the object of destruction are never separable, and the object of utility itself, in its indefinite reproduction, is itself destructive. The object expresses this in total mobilization and war. An economy that manufactures great quantities of stuff, and the primacy of stuff itself, destroys the primacy of individual consciousness. Writing in *The Worker* of the idealistic young student-soldiers slaughtered early in World War I, Jünger writes:

> But the sensations of the heart and the systems of the intellect can be denied, while an object is irrefutable—and one such object is the machine gun. . . .
>
> The bearers of an idea, having however become a prettier copy remote from the original images, will be brought down by matter, the mother of things. But this contact endows them, by mythical law, with new forces. What dies, what falls away, is the individual as the representative of weakened and doomed orders. (68)

The sentimentality associated with idealistic self-sacrifice early in the war—student-recruits supposedly sang the German national anthem as they charged forward ("singers of the hill of sacrifice"), to be mowed down by British machine guns—will ultimately be endowed with a ruthless movement that has nothing to do with individual idealism.[5] It is contact with the violent object—the machine gun—that transforms the Worker into a new type. This type is affirmed by death, pursued "by attack" (98).[6] The object is violent in its form (in Jünger's sense).

The technological object's form entails the intensification of energy linked to, and responsible for, complete cultural transformation in total mobilization. In *The Worker,* this mobilization entails a saturation of space via the proper utilization of energy:

One holds power insofar as one represents the form of the Worker and thus gains access to the dimension of totality associated with this form. To this distinction [between the army as vehicle of personal independence and the military as collective power] corresponds a distinction in armaments; and, in fact, we observe an influx of energies indicative of the presence of a new kind of space. . . .

Just as the offensive no longer seeks to reach the fronts in the old sense of the word, but rather works, with various and not only specifically military resources, to reach the depths of space, with its systems and populations, so its specific countermeasures no longer rely merely on the army, but on the planned organization of energy as a whole. (185)

Jünger here would seem to be rejecting a vision of the militarization of the universe, but in fact he is merely arguing that military organization has progressed from that of the army alone winning battles to "energy as a whole." All of life, in other words all organization of energy, will be disciplined along military–technical lines, essentially saturating space, with its "systems and populations." The entire earth will become subject to larger military–industrial strategy, with no space outside its energy. It's a closed circle: energy will be planned, organized, but planning and organization themselves will be functions of energy, and its total mobilization.

Space will be closed: not just the space of the world, but the space of history. The circularity of violence-production will be enclosed in the physical space of the globe—its extension to every available nook and cranny—but cultural and social space will contain the energy, the violence, that drives it on. It is not a question of the establishment of a posthistory through the domestication of violence (permanent peace), but the establishment of a liberation of violence in history through the internalization of a space of conflict.[7]

This, then, is a temporality of eternal return, a kind of sustainability of the human population, absent the individual, in the mechanical reproduction of war. People, populations, demand rearmament (in Jünger's view), since the peaceful world of the contented individual is only one of alienating stagnation. This putative Nietzschean vision nevertheless calls forth a kind of claustrophobia: even though we are meant to think of a larger canvas than that of the battlefield alone, one imagines the incessant instances of energy in its constructive–destructive cycles as one of the tightly closed world of trench and bunker. If the Brundtland vision of sustainability is a world at peace endlessly reproducing itself in a historical and cultural stasis, Jünger's is one of a world at war that repetitively affirms itself in the violence of reproduction and death: sustainability in service to the patently nonsustainable. The peaceful Brundtland world eliminates constraint by presenting an eminently reasonable future of constrained production and consumption that no one—at least no reasonable person—could refuse. Jünger's world, on the other hand, seemingly eliminates constraint by positing a world without individual will in which no one could possibly refuse because of the individual's absorption in a general will of production and consumption. The perpetual and violent mechanized consumption of energy is at the heart of Jünger's vision; it is, finally, his entire vision. The question of the finitude of energy resources is subsumed by the totalizing esthetics of violence.

In this plenitude of energy, Jünger is able to find a totality behind the Heraclitean conflict driving his world. But it is easy enough to associate this with a larger aestheticism: the aestheticization of politics condemned by so many appears in Jünger, as it does in many other fascist or protofascist authors. The Worker becomes a machine, inseparable from work and violence, and yet as a totality this *Gestalt* entails a transport into a realm of the modernist sublime on the part of society as a whole. What appears to be a world of conflict is only one of collective unanimity in the joy of shock. It is not far from the parade ground to parades, celebrations, rallies—all full-throated anticipations of the glamor of death.

The (very unorthodox) Marxist critic Walter Benjamin, writing at the same time in Germany (and later, in exile, in France) as Jünger, also had a theory of mechanical repetition, and reproduction. Benjamin's valorization of the machine, and of repetition, is similar to, but also very different from, that of Jünger. Benjamin, too, notes the decline of what he calls the "aura," the cultic aspect of the traditional work of art—the aesthetic and sacred object—that marks the era of bourgeois individualism and capitalist industrialization. Like Jünger, Benjamin is all for this decline, but unlike Jünger, he situates it specifically in the context of class conflict, or at least of the political and social rise of the proletariat. Benjamin, like Jünger, clearly sees the decline of romanticism, and no doubt of bourgeois individualism, linked to the rise of the machine, but his machine, his object, is a movie camera (and projector), not a machine gun.[8] Hence in his essay "The Work of Art in the Age of Technological Reproducibility" (1935), he can write:

What withers in the age of the technological reproducibility of the work of art is the latter's aura. This process is symptomatic; its significance extends far beyond the realm of art. *It might be stated as a general formula that the technology of reproduction detaches the reproduced object from the realm of tradition. By replicating the work many times over, it substitutes a mass existence for a unique existence. And in permitting the reproduction to reach the recipient in his or her own situation, it actualizes that which is reproduced.* These two processes lead to a massive upheaval in the domain of objects handed down from the past—a shattering of tradition which is the reverse side of the present crisis and renewal of humanity.[9]

If "aura" is the vibe of the traditional art object—an object wreathed in respect, distance, tradition, and sacred ritual—the destruction of aura is the dissemination of the object and its loss of authenticity and interiority. It becomes near, an object not of respect or awe but of critical perception and analysis.

The obvious example is the photographic image, or the volatilization of that image in successive shots, in film. The photographed/filmed object is represented close up, it is slowed down, speeded up, seen in all its aspects. Its mystery is gone; it is with us here and now, as an object of pleasure and use.

Benjamin does not stop at the object producing and/or represented in multiple images, however. History is also a process of reproduction and repetition. But history itself can be wreathed in an aura: that would be the idea that historical processes inevitably lead to a happy conclusion, that history is a nice story that ends once and for all in a new and comforting (albeit perhaps repetitious) endpoint. In "On the Concept of History" (1940), Benjamin writes:

Universal history has no armature. Its procedure is additive: it musters a mass of data to fill the homogeneous, empty time. Materialist historiography, on the other hand, is based on a constructive principle. Thinking involves not only the movement of thoughts, but their arrest as well. . . . The historical materialist approaches a historical object only where it confronts him as a monad. In this structure it recognizes the sign of a messianic arrest of happening, or (to put it differently) a revolutionary chance in the fight for the oppressed past. He takes cognizance of it in order to blast a specific era out of the homogeneous course of history.[10]

This messianic time is one that operates not as a smooth progression, the predictable and empty accumulation of instants, but of shocks, of "standstill" moments or "constellations" that replicate or refer to one another, just as the French Revolution reproduced and doubled the Roman republic (395). The messianic implies less a human-like figure who comes to make everything better than a kind of opening, a shock administered to what otherwise would have been "homogeneous time" (397). The messianic is the "small gateway" that opens out of this time, through the repeated instant, and that leads to another time, one that at least holds out the hope of liberation. It is less a static Marxist end of history than it is the aperture that Benjamin refuses to call utopian (familiar as he is with the negative connotations of utopianism as condemned by Marx). A utopia is a closed space of perfect social harmony, perpetual, frozen in time; the messianic is the flash of another possibility, another life, which resides on the horizon, or erupts in the now *(der jetzzeit)*.

Benjamin still runs the risk of a Jüngerian fascist subjectivity when he affirms the destruction of individual reaction to art: Is art, if not auratic, then mere propaganda? If this were the case, the "critical" masses would be mere political pulp, subject to the manipulation of propaganda ministers who use as their primary tool kitsch, debased art in the service of the collective enthusiasm. Benjamin's task, then, is to prevent the aestheticization of politics, the hallmark of fascism. Jünger, with his cult of the machine gun, eliminates critical subjectivity, reduces art to mere agitprop in favor of ritual violence, and condemns aesthetics to a ditto-head repetition of a repressive political message (the masses want war). Benjamin must find a way to particularize the masses, render them critical intelligences, if not bourgeois individuals, and must reconceive the future as open to both hope and the possibility of contestation. What will the future preserve and pass on to future generations? War as endless and repetitive inner experience? Or repetition not as simple preservation, but as violent rupture, the opening to another time, that at least bears the hope of liberation?

As in the mechanical reproduction epitomized by film, messianic history is the shocking repetition that breaks the complacent and passive acceptance of what seems traditionally mandated and inevitable. (One can imagine the "messianic arrest of happening" as the arrest of the camera, breaking time apart in discrete instants.) Benjamin wrote "On the Concept of History" at a dark moment, just after the signing of the Hitler–Stalin Pact, a time when the easy assumptions of the Communist Left—that revolution was inevitable, that fascism was doomed by its own contradictions—were very much in question. No, history was not an easy ("dialectical") agglomeration of instants necessarily leading to a predictable end. And no, that end was not enshrined in some infallible doctrine, to be revered in hushed silence, gazed at in the auratic distance as it hovers there, patiently waiting for us to (finally) arrive. The future, liberation, was something that was not certain, was something that was not necessarily even a progression, but rather a repetition; it was wrested out of the past, seen first at a distance and then up close, a violent force of change that nevertheless was (unlike the "homogeneous" time of conventional Marxist history) known *critically*. The messianic was a product of astute independent analysis, not acceptance of a ritualized truth handed down from Moscow. Revolutionary action was inseparable from, yes, individual initiative and thought. That was at least the implicit force of Benjamin's critique, and the point at which it touched his analysis of aesthetics, and of culture as a whole, in his earlier reading of mechanical reproducibility.

The violent revolt against a complacent and passive historicism necessarily links that historicism to kitsch. Aesthetics and cultural production (and reproduction) are never far off—that is the danger. Kitsch is not just tackiness, or poor taste: it is unquestioning acceptance, aesthetic pleasure without effort or historical insight. The inevitable march of history to its happy end is kitsch. The auratic art object, untouchable in its art museum but reproduced on T-shirts and bags, is kitsch. Bourgeois culture and comfort is kitsch. Fascist sloganeering and simpleminded belief is kitsch. Benjamin's refusal of kitsch is also an affirmation of a revolutionary object—revolutionary both aesthetically and politically—that might have been taken for kitsch but for its explosive return. It is this distinction that separates Benjamin from Jünger, definitively. The kitsch object returns from the past as socially and politically destructive power, just as does the seemingly obsolete historical constellation.

Thus there is a linkage between kitsch and revolutionary art, and, one would assume, revolutionary historical practice. In a note in *The Arcades Project*, Benjamin writes:

Kitsch . . . is nothing more than art with a 100 percent, absolute and instantaneous availability for consumption. Precisely within the consecrated forms of expression, therefore, kitsch and art stand irreconcilably opposed. But for developing, living forms, what matters is that they have within them something stirring, useful, ultimately heartening—that they take "kitsch" dialectically up into themselves, and hence bring themselves near to the masses while yet surmounting the kitsch. Today, perhaps, film alone is equal to this task.[11]

Unlike auratic art, then, kitsch is "close" to the viewer, and one could say one of its prime features is uncritical acceptance (and enjoyment). Film brings the art object close as well, but its analytic aspect leads to a critical and political practicality on the part of the "masses" that encounter it.[12] This is an element of Benjamin's approach that comes from surrealism, and it is a way of linking the *flâneur*—that wandering observer of the strange, the unforeseen, questionable things and people—to revolutionary change. The surrealists were great walkers and observers, and Breton in *Nadja,* Aragon in *Paris Peasant,* among others, attributed a revolutionary and indeed explosive force to the visions and coincidences they met with on their urban rounds. Benjamin writes:

> [Breton] can boast an extraordinary discovery: he was the first to perceive the revolutionary energies in the first iron constructions, the first factory buildings, the earliest photos, the objects that have begun to be extinct, grand pianos, the dresses of five years ago, fashionable restaurants when the vogue has begun to ebb from them. . . . No one before these visionaries and augurs perceived how destitution—not only social but architectonic, the poverty of interiors, enslaved and enslaving objects—can be suddenly transformed into revolutionary nihilism. . . . [Breton and Nadja] bring the immense forces of "atmosphere" concealed in these things to the point of explosion.[13]

The fact is that these outmoded objects *were* kitsch, in their day. The musty old theatre interiors described by Breton, the accumulated junk Aragon's narrator sees and mystifies in the Passage de l'Opera, and all of his statues, were once kitschy but stylish locales and accoutrements. What then makes them revolutionary? Benjamin does not stress the dream state, or the miraculous nature of coincidences, so beloved by Breton. Nor does he seem to be enchanted by the supposed mystical power of the female "seer" *(voyante),* epitomized by poor Nadja, who ends up confined in an asylum. Rather, for Benjamin it is the return of the object, which once upon a time was an example of kitsch, a commodity fetish, as an uncanny thing that brings "to the point of explosion" the commodified and reified world of industrial capitalism, and that serves, we might say, as the narrow entry point of the messianic.[14]

The revolutionary object, that bit of heterogeneous junk, covered with dust, laying forlorn in a chest of drawers or in an equally forlorn shop window,[15] the one that confronts the flâneur as he or she wanders in arcades that are about to be pulled down—this junk is inseparable from the historical moment that repeats itself as the explosion of the messianic in the stalled progression of history. The repetition of the Roman Republic and the French Revolution are one and the same with the reassertion of "objects that have begun to be extinct" in the modernity of capitalism in crisis.

Benjamin makes clear the connection between the return of objects and the return of explicitly revolutionary moments in another fragment from *The Arcades Project*. His inspiration is now Proust: he transposes the return of things in memory as the historical and revolutionary memory:

> Indeed, awakening is the great exemplar of memory: the occasion on which it is given us to remember what is closer, tritest, most obvious. What Proust intends with the experimental rearrangement of furniture in matinal half-slumber, what Bloch recognizes as the darkness of the lived moment, is nothing other than what here is to be secured on the level of the historical, and collectively.[16]

The object, historical return and memory, and revolution are now brought together through the figure of sleeping—and awakening. The messianic, one might say, partakes not only of surrealist sleep, but of the Proustian "neuter,"[17] that moment between sleep and wakefulness where objects spin around and rearrange themselves, evoking different moments of personal, and now collective, history.[18] They reconfigure themselves, in shifting constellations that undermine the capitalist commodification and fetishization of "consumables." They return as "extinct" things with the revolutionary and analytic power of cinematic images, close to the viewer and more powerful for all that.

But what is the energy profile of these objects and images? It seems that the question of energy, so prominent in various models of technocracy—the Technocrats, Le Corbusier—is absent, both from Jünger and from the radical critique of Jünger's protofascism in Benjamin.[19] For Jünger, the explosive and elemental objects are always ready to hand, ready to serve as weapons or machines for the production of other machines in a posthistorical moment of technical completion. We never hear about coal or oil, though, or about the potential scarcity of energy inputs, how they would need to be managed, and so on. Similarly, in Benjamin, with the return of old junk as a critical force—the critical force of volatilized kitsch that blasts apart the complacency of Jünger's technocratic mastery—we never discover how these objects were produced, conserved, rediscovered, and revalorized. Each step of this process requires energy inputs, and Benjamin tells us nothing of this. Like the surrealist objects Breton presents in the *First Surrealist Manifesto,* or *Nadja,* the fragments from the past affirmed by Benjamin, while exploding the fetishes of capitalism, somehow manifest an energy expenditure (the "spark" in Breton, the "explosion" in Benjamin) that is never really accounted for.[20] Recycling, after all—of kitschy trash, of decisive historical moments—itself has an energy profile, an EROEI (Energy Return on Energy Investment) no matter how revolutionary that investment might be.

What would such an accounting amount to? This is perhaps the moment in which we must pass from an affirmative reading of Benjamin to a critical one, in which we rewrite a specific element of his analysis. For Benjamin, the bits of junk he (along with the surrealists) revels in have revolutionary potential because they are survivors from the past. They are emissaries of a bygone era, charged with the power of elusive memories, returning in and as moments of revolutionary (and messianic) change, on the personal level, as Proust or Baudelaire or Freud might have it, but even more so on a collective one. But as soon as we ask about the energy profile of heterogeneous objects, the energy embodied in statues or bric-a-brac from the *passages,* we pass from the past to the future—that is, asking about energy is asking about not just the past of the thing, its energy footprint and its explosive arrival in the present, but its future. If an object is fundamentally incomplete and unknowable, as Graham Harman and others would argue,[21] it is so because its future can never be fully grasped, and its future is a configuration of its future energy profile. How much energy will it consume as an explosive remnant of the past?

In section 12 of "On the Concept of History" (1940), Benjamin writes:

There is a picture by Klee called *Angelus Novus.* It shows an angel who seems about to move away from something he stares at. His eyes are wide, his mouth is open, his wings are spread. This is how the angel of history must look. His face is turned toward the past. Where a chain of events appears before us, *he* sees one single catastrophe, which keeps piling wreckage upon wreckage and hurls it at his feet. The angel would like to stay, awaken the dead, and make whole what has been smashed. But a storm is blowing from Paradise and has got caught in his wings; it is so strong that the angel can no longer close them. This storm drives him irresistibly into the future, to which his back is turned, while the pile of debris before him grows toward the sky. What we call progress is *this* storm. (392)

Which way, then, should the angel of history face? Is the angel of history also the angel of energy? What is the revolutionary future of energy?

Like all allegories, many interpretations of this one are possible. I would like to focus on the angel (who could be the "historical materialist," and—why not?—maybe a stand-in for, or fictional persona of, Benjamin himself) focused on the wreckage of the past growing "toward the sky." It is not just culture, it's all of history, all of the broken junk, dangerous pollution, and hideous crime that results from and contributes to historical and cultural "progress," which is faced by the angel, known, but also unknown (the future is not seen; the angel's back is turned). If Jünger simply ignores the energy sources fueling his technocracy, or folds them in to a larger machine aesthetics, Benjamin is able to tap into the *emergy* of the debris of the past as the driving force of the (or his) future.[22] But there is also an ambiguity concerning the direction the angel faces: a "chain of events appears before us," presumably *in front of us,* but the angel faces backwards. Is what is in front of us ("before us") *behind* us when faced by the angel? If we are facing forward, then is what will come for us already past for the angel? A version of the eternal return, in effect; the messianic is all the wreckage of history, and the violence of that wreckage blowing into the future, being repeated, with the angel looking back because the future is unknowable (what Nietzsche loved about it). But what is important is *how* the crucial events of the past repeat and reconfigure themselves as revolutionary moments of the future. This the angel can anticipate by not-knowing, not-seeing.

But who is "us" here, anyway? The reader/narrator combine? What do "we" have in common? The subjects of a degraded history? Or are "we" every reading-function that is not, precisely, facing backward? Are "we" the witness of a futurity as a double of the ruins coming from behind, from the past—and repeating itself into the future? Staring, projecting our voice onto its (already dead, ruined) face? To what extent is the angel itself part of this "us," to the extent that it is Benjamin's autobiographical double (how else does he know what the angel "sees"?), and Benjamin is speaking in the collective voice, with and for us?

So while the angel faces backward, *we* may very well face forward as well by looking back. We can't help looking at the future of and as recyclable ruins. As it was for Proust, the fragments of the past are spinning around us, coming from behind and forcing us to think about, to foresee the unforeseeable. But the wind from Paradise also means that, while we look forward, we cannot see forward. (The essay is entitled "On the Concept of History," not "On the Concept of the Future.") We can only see the past clearly, and the crimes that generate our culture grow ever greater, more monumental. The angel of history is (unlike Marx) not a scientist.[23] It refuses all prognostication. It is only an angel.

The repetition of the past, and all those junk (wrecked) objects as well, implies facing the future. The angel then may be bicephalous, with (another possible reading) the second head being our own, looking forward.[24] (If "we" are doubles of the narrator, and the narrator is personified by the angel . . . a metaphoric series.) Unlike the angel, "we" cannot help looking forward. Perhaps that is all that defines us.

The future in its unknowability is anticipated by looking both forward and backward. The future is infinitely distant but we gaze into its eyes. The object of history—the wreckage—is, like the surrealist object, scrounged and/or recycled as revolutionary through its very decay. Its explosive charge is its dustiness, its outmodedness, its uncanniness (both knowable and inalterably foreign), the bits of fluff sticking through its seams. Like Aragon's statue, it denounces the heroic plans it itself once celebrated. It is the bearer of the paradisiacal wind through its very depletion and entropic expenditure. And we look at it, its past, its future.

It is here that Benjamin's allegory of the future starts to take on implications for sustainability. The future is unknowable as is, but also in its depletion or depletability. The revolutionary fetish, Paradise, that blows the angel forward spends its force not just in the political and cultural upheaval it embodies, not just in the unknowability toward the future it confronts us with (allegorized in the delirious circulation of the neutral state between dream and waking), but in the unknowability of future energetic depletion as both salvation and fall. The ruins are recycled, providing energy, cultural and material, through their combustion, their donation of revolutionary remains. The ruins are the future; they are all that is left of capitalism (we can more easily imagine . . .), but recycled as the unfigurable messianic—

infinitely distant, but that which is nevertheless inevitably and incessantly re-represented, stared in the face, on the point of realization. Benjamin's counter-messianism (if not dystopia) of the paradisiacal wind blowing us forward reaches a point when it encounters the energy footprint of its forward movement. The object embodies not just the force of history, but the energy of history, and the potential of the repetitious depletion of that energy. "The forces of the redemption come not only from a transcendent intercession but from the very depths of catastrophe itself."[25] This is certainly an ambiguous redemption, one that stares directly into the face of the unredeemable.

What happens when the revolution runs out of gas? Not in terms of human effort or will, but quite literally when the EROEI of its fuel sources (up to now powering it) do not provide the needed energetic surplus to even enable us to think about Paradise, that of the workers, or of anyone else? Or when the true cost of fuel consumption is an unlivable, ruined world? Suddenly we (commentators, readers of Benjamin), if not the angel, face *forward,* and the wrecked, or outmoded, object is before us, staring back. It's all that is left, all that is on the left: wreckage as future fuel. Looking forward is perhaps what the angel does not want to do, because it reveals a vision of ever more depletion, the asymptote toward total and infinitely remote entropy. (The most high entropy.) Before us there is the object in its lack of plenitude as lack of forward motion and vision, lack of heat, lack of explosiveness, lack of maintainability, in a tortured landscape of heat and desert. The sun as never quite enough, but also too much. "We" are the smear of subjectivity, the remainder as pathology that cannot be seamlessly inserted in the eternal return of the same as happy ethical imperative. It takes a lot of energy to fuel a revolution, a war, even a backlash against revolution. It takes energy to pile up wreckage, to even maintain wreckage as wreckage and then tap into its energy stores in forward movement. Wreckage is embodied energy, but it is also what's left over when the energy stores start to peter out. Even maintaining a ruin (or a statue) is costly and controversial. It's the revolutionary object of the future, not the past, that is revolutionary precisely because it is what remains, and because, like Milton's Satan, it will not serve. It is the ghost of the commodity as fetish, in its format as a new and even more virulent fetish, elaborated in catastrophe-redemption against the commodity. It is the point of the future as non-knowledge: to really look forward is to gaze into the blinding dark sun of the depleted object and its tortured history. Our future as citizens of the planet.

But the wreckage always retains, no matter how minimally, some energy that can be utilized; it always fuels or drives us toward the future. It can always be recycled, following careful formulae. The wreckage provides the energy behind the "storm blowing from Paradise." And its future is always one of resistance as well, of hostility, of the remnant as what is repulsive, of what we would most like to throw "away" but cannot—when we think most constructively of future generations. It is always again the fetish in its most reprehensible (but also most desirable) self-assertion, our pathological glory as well as our fury to repress. Indeed throwing "away" itself has an energy profile, one that is often insufficient to overcome the residual energetic content of the excess that always remains, always more ruined, more tapped out, more obtrusive, in its energetic calling forth of sadistic repression.

This kind of object-based heterogeneity is thus always the blind spot of technocracy, and perhaps even, as in the case of Benjamin, of the most sophisticated technocratic antitechnocracy (after all, his is a theory that confronts both Marxist and Jüngerian technocracy from the standpoint of technical reproducibility). That debris thrown into the future is revolutionary because it serves as a point of unknowability, the unseeable, the rupture of the smooth, perfectly closed circle of the closed economy, Marxist (the materialist dialectic) or even Nietzschean (the seamless eternal return), of the future. The return is that of the ruin, of the high-entropy dirt of civilization, of all that is left after the fall from the peak. It remains after the demise of the Marxist claim to know the future perfectly in a scientific and technocratic manner. If the angel faces backward it may be to avoid facing this unknowability, as well as to embrace it while refusing it (one cannot stare into the face of, or represent, G-d). But facing does not mean knowing; facing means the confrontation with the face of the future, the infinitely and disproportionately distant, as it is situated in the interstices of historical repetition.

There is a danger in any model of historical recycling that it will turn into an eternal return of the sort analyzed by Benjamin at the end of Convolute D of the *Arcades* project. For Benjamin, the Nietzschean eternal return is mythic, because nothing happens or can happen: citing Karl Löwith, Benjamin notes "an attempt to eternalize all our doings and failings, an atheistic surrogate for religion" (117). But, interestingly enough, such a mythical atemporality has as its "complementary" double the kind of perfectibility one finds in technocratic sustainability. Benjamin states:

The belief in progress—in an infinite perfectibility understood as an infinite ethical task—and the representation of eternal return are complementary. They are the indissoluble antimonies in the face of which the dialectical conception of historical time must be developed. (119)

But therein lies the problem: a "dialectical" conception of time is somehow linked to a model of historical return (via Proust, the surrealists, etc.)—but how? Clearly Benjamin's idiosyncratic conception of "dialectics," incorporating the repetitive "constellations," entails a moment of "base" heterogeneity, a point in which the disruptive future resists easy vision or closure. What Benjamin neglects in this passage is the fact that there is always a resistant and ruptured subjectivity in relation to Nietzsche's eternal return of the same. The same, but with the add-on of a heterogeneous or pathological smear that observes, writes about, celebrates, and inevitably forgets (in madness) the return. The return impossibly opens to incorporate this metasubjectivity, and metacommentary. From the "perspective" of this deviant subjectivity (the aftereffect of devious tropes), the fall (as Bataille writes) is "final"; it is a one-time only deal, and opens the return to "deleteriously absurd" time. Yet this time is *in* the return, and that is its absurdity; the perfect return is opened out to what is most resistant to it, it contains the toxic, resistant element in and outside its closure.

This problem of the eternal return is exactly what Douglas Hofstadter has identified as a "strange loop." The Möbius strip about which Lacan and Žižek write (see chapter 5) is this kind of feedback loop, in which autoreference takes place on different levels, and on which no level can be privileged. A similar figure is the Klein bottle. This, as Hofstadter shows, is an aspect of self-reference in language, but also in logical systems (Kurt Gödel) and even the visual arts (M. C. Escher). Hofstadter writes:

Where language does create strange loops is when it talks about itself, whether directly or indirectly. Here, something *in* the system jumps out and acts upon the system, as if it were *outside* the system. What bothers us is perhaps an ill-defined sense of topological wrongness: the inside-outside distinction is being blurred, as in the famous shape called a "Klein bottle."[26]

Language "talking about itself" spins off a subjectivity ("surprise" at the "topological wrongness") that is itself part of the loop: it is the recognition that the loop closes only with a violation of its integrity, the rupture of the easy "inside-outside distinction." This opening, this surprise, is the point at which there is a subjective reaction, a subject, in other words, but a riven subject as only a spin-off of the faulty and impossible closure of the return. It is a rupture, an anamorphosis point outside the outside of the incessant circulation of the inside/outside, form/content distinction. Personifying this stain, as is inevitable (the loops are symbolic, linguistic) but also aberrant, means an autobiographical devil (Bataille's *Acéphale or ipse,* the "accursed share") or angel (Benjamin's messianic).

This angel faces backward, or (in our supplement to Benjamin) forward, but in hallucinatory blindness. The point of the focus of the angel's gaze, and/or blindness, the point of identification, is the moment of depletion of energy, the snag in the perpetual motion machine, awareness, but awareness of the "catastrophic" fall into time. The future in this version is dialectical in its recycling of that which most resists recycling: the very junkness of junk bringing the subject down. Highest-entropy junk, in other words, staring back from an infinite remove. Hence another eternal return, such as Bataille's, not the return as atheistic surrogate of God, seamless in its perfection, but as fallen temporality, the dirty return of heterogeneous decay. We might even say that the eternal return critiqued by Benjamin is that of a restricted (second-order) sustainability, a universe of mechanical reversibility and repetition, where what is lost always comes back in exactly the same form. Bataille's return (as in "the Obelisk"; see chapter 5), and Benjamin's (so-called) dialectical repetition, is a return as loss, the irruption of temporality that opens to both catastrophe and the possibility of a radical and perhaps unknowable innovation, entropy as faulty recycling (downcycling: something is always lost), as the proliferation of life in erotic frenzy. Bataille's return, like Benjamin's, is a moment of ecstatic (or messianic) deliverance not through a promise of eternity, aesthetic pleasure, or acceptance, but via a descent into an unmasterable and uncountable—and unaccountable—futurity.

Depletion asserts itself in the context of the historical drive to a pre-formatted progression, which is also the sheer circularity of a closed economy. Circularity now is generated in and through the monstrosity of decay. Benjamin's recurring, messianic history can never be anything but the failed representation of sheer circularity, the loop with the smear of meaning (semiotic drift), the lapse of the heterogeneous element in and against the return. This is not so much a split as a radical separation (in Frédéric Neyrat's formulation),[27]—that is, it is the point at which the perception, the grasping of the future, under the aegis of natural constraints, is blocked, but also enabled, by the opacity of "nature." The latter is neither radically "out there," simply foreign and opposed to us (yet exploitable), nor simply indistinguishable from our techno-sphere, our consciousness as technologically implemented. "Nature" is always again profoundly resistant, before us, demanding to be recycled, but also resisting that recycling in and through its infinite distance. That distance is inherently rhetorical. The only way we grasp "nature" is through representation: consciousness—our "human" consciousness, but also animal consciousness in general, there's no difference—works by comparing things, seeing similarities, and then acting on them. Consciousness is nothing but metaphor and metonymy (tropological systems) in the service of survival, with the recognition that tropes like metaphor are inseparable from catachresis, the trope of the originary loss of the primordial referent, the recurrently wrong signified.

Indeed it was the philosopher Thomas Nagel, in his influential article "What Is It Like to Be a Bat?," who noted that the only way to affirm the consciousness of other persons or organisms is to note that "an organism is conscious if there is *something that it is like* to be that organism." This is, Nagel argues, the way we can conceive of, or know, that other beings are conscious. But one can argue that this definition cuts both ways: while it indicates the awareness on my part of your awareness of yourself ("I know what it's like to be in your shoes"), it also indicates that our knowledge of others', and of necessity our own, consciousness is fundamentally rhetorical: it is based on the trope of simile. To be aware of ourselves, and of the world through our consciousness, is to be engaged from the first in the act of comparison. Consciousness is rhetorical, a deceptive play of figures, and knowing myself is only knowing what I am like (I, to be [self-] recognized, will always have to be "like" something else, if only "me" in the recurrent memories of "myself" in the past.)[28]

Science is metaphor-making writ large; before we and all other living things can use comparison and projection into the future to make sense of the world, of "nature," it is incomprehensible, or comprehensible, solely on the mythic level (which may very well contain its own truth). When memory works, as Benjamin would remind us, history and the world come into focus. The past returns for a second go round, but with a difference, a stain. The latter is internal to the process, both as forgetting, as the finitude of comparison and comprehension, and as the depletion of the energetic totality of the system, the totality of reason containing its own inevitable loss: the ignorance of the future into which we gaze.

Depletion is both a human-oriented term—depletion for us, for the human—but at the same time a signaling of the ultimate resistance or withdrawal of stuff to utilization, commercialization, and comprehension. "Nature" is the resistance put up by depletion in the very system of historical sense. In the seamless repetition of the closed economy there is the point of anamorphosis, of unreadability and surprise, that is integral to the establishment of that feedback circularity. Blindness is the energetic and exegetic exhaustion at the peak of signification, of cultural meaning.

Depletion returns, resistant in its monstrosity; like the heterogeneous object in Bataille, virulent in its challenge to a world that would ground itself in transcendent meaning (such as the hope of the eternally perfect eternal return). "Something like a spider or spit."[29] Anamorphosis, the specter at the depletion point of peak energy, thus is the moment in which the risk of the fragility of the object in its scarcity and exhaustion meets the virulence of the object as challenge to seamless aesthetics, economy, and sense. That is the "force or the shock" of the sacred object.

For this reason, it all depends on how one is situated "in" the anamorphosis; it is not a question of perspective—in or out of the circularity—but of the very possibility of signification. Anamorphosis and its profound duality are functions of rhetoric, not (perhaps *pace* Benjamin) merely contradictory aspects of a dialectical pairing in the act of seeing.

There are, no doubt, different ways of reading anamorphosis. As we've seen in the preceding chapter, Žižek approaches it through Lacan: as an offshoot or by-blow of the empty (sadistic) Kantian imperative, the subject is a residue of the process of perfect but empty (self-)reflection. Žižek notes:

> The spot of the mirror picture is thus strictly constitutive of the subject; the subject qua subject of the look "is" only in so far as the mirror-picture he is looking at is inherently "incomplete"—in so far, that is, as it contains a "pathological" stain—the subject is correlative to the stain.
>
> Therein ultimately consists the point of Lacan's constant reference to anamorphosis: Holbein's *Ambassadors* exemplifies literally the Hegelian speculative proposition on phrenology "spirit (= subject) is a bone (= skull)": the blind spot of the picture. In the reversal proper to the process of reflection, the subject experiences itself as correlative to the point in his Other in which

he comes across an absolutely strange power, a power with which no mirror-exchange is possible.[30]

One could just as easily reverse this, as Paul de Man does, and displace the subject; that is, the subject would not be constituted by an identification with sheer materiality (the skull, death), but rather act as a kind of reference to the play of tropes (prosopopoeia), which in their interaction engage with each other through anamorphosis.[31] The point in de Man is that one can never isolate irony, or definitively state that one text is ironic or not. Irony and its absence should, in principle, be controlled by knowledge: I *know* that such and such a text is ironic. I control the trope. But what if, as de Man states, "irony is always the irony of understanding, if what is at stake in irony is always the question of whether it is possible to understand or not to understand?" (166). In other words, understanding itself is subject to the vagaries of irony, of the play of tropes.

The anamorphosis of the trope is situated exactly at this point of non-certitude, the possibility of understanding or not that the text is ironic. Irony itself is ironized, and it comes to be situated in the very certainty that would necessarily control irony. Knowledge is, after all, just another trope—again, it relies on metaphor, the coordination of apparent similarities—and irony as a trope cannot be easily distinguished from metaphor (two things are similar in their opposition, etc.).

This entails an inevitable double reading, a moment in which the trope shifts from ironic to non-ironic, literal to figural, the instant of non-congruence when the *rhétoriqueur* (as Jean Paulhan would say) shifts from the recognition and awareness of the rhetoricity of the text (Terror) to his/her/its awareness of the meaning (Maintenance).[32] This "awareness" itself would be not so much a function of consciousness, but a certain tropicality—that is, the moment that, say, irony obtrudes, the mechanisms of rhetoric overwhelm, and the corresponding moment in which irony disappears and the contrary salience of indubitable and salutary meaning proceeds. Anamorphosis is the pivot between these two.

Sustainability is itself a figure (ironic or not), a metaphor of a certain life, or continuity of non-life, as plotted out in some way in relation to time. Technocratic sustainability, with its model of homogeneous, progressive (but repetitive) time, abstract and quantifiable energy and wealth, equivalency between abstract subjectivities, and so on, seems to generate its other with alacrity. It's hard to imagine Technocracy Inc. without contemporary

sustainability theorists (such as Callenbach in *Ecotopia*) who explicitly under-
score issues of inherent scarcity, violence, and coercion; it's impossible to
consider Le Corbusier's city of instantaneous solar elevation without that
of Bataille's labyrinthine abyssal time, or Jünger's model of technical perfection melded with aestheticized, incessantly recurring warfare without
Benjamin's version of reproducibility as historical return and angelic wreckage. All these doubles are conjoined by anamorphoses, the bicephalous
instant in which the literal moment reverses as the figural, and the figural
reflects back on the impossibility of stabilizing this relation of doubles. The
stain of their non-reflection is that of prosopopoeia, the trope through
which, as we saw in chapter 3, the recycled future is generated as infinitely
other. The subject's speech at the instant of the death of the subject.

The articulation point between dyads—inside / outside, form / content,
figure / ground, consciousness / matter, sheer repetition and decay—is itself
outside. It is the unthinkable chora that unites in division and rupture.

The movement of anamorphosis is one in which the blind spot, and the
stain, the point of textual, energetic, and economic depletion, both generate the double—and, why not, triple?—relation and forbid (suppress) its
easy coordination. This is why first-, second-, and third-order sustainability repeat each other as uneasy figures. As in Benjamin's model of historical return, each moment generates the next, but as trope, as irony that
cannot be sustained or isolated. Their relation is one of imperfect repetition, but it is also marked by the very peak that calls in death, absence, the
resistance of "the pathological self" and "the thing" that can never be fully
known: the unreadable stain in the phantasmic Möbius strip of circulating
dyads.

There is, then, no easy dialectical relation between levels of sustainability, since the process is not that of a linear progression, nor is it one of
repetition "on a higher level." As Werner Hamacher notes, paraphrasing
Benjamin, "History is not history as long as it does not happen. It cannot
happen if it merely follows a predestined form and goal."[33] If anything, it is
only a model of the return of a self-differing degradation. Benjamin, in his
theses on history, carefully avoids the promise of a posthistorical workers'
paradise, the triumph of the proletariat, or whatever.[34] Nor is it a question of
overcoming alienation. Yet Benjamin, unlike (for example) de Man, is careful
to note that there is still a revolutionary potential (or redemption) in historical return, and in the return of the object. Here he is going well beyond
the surrealists, for whom the object is somehow explosive and liberating in

itself, in its perturbation of waking consciousness, in its irruption of the dream. For Breton, surrealist revolution is revolution of consciousness, presumably to be enacted in anticipation of, after, or as a supplement to, economic and political revolution. Benjamin doesn't see this supplementarity. For him, the revolution of the object is part of the critical activity of the masses; this is why he's careful to consider film—a "popular" art form that has been embraced by the population as a whole—in a way that the surrealist object never could be. It does not accompany the revolution, it is the revolution. The explosion of the object, the moments of critical dismantling in which it returns, dismembered, fragmentary, reedited, its aura blasted, and blasting all other auras, serves as the narrow crack of the messianic gate.

Although the parameters of revolution have changed, one could argue the same thing in the passage from one mode of sustainability to the next. Passing from first- to second-level sustainability may be nothing more than a rhetorical shift, in which the meaning of the object is radically altered in and through its unavoidable, albeit minor, appropriation (figuration) by the human (as autobiographical figure). The unassimilable articulation points between orders are, in other words, the anamorphic distortions between opposing terms, the stains of each within the others. Moving from first level to second, the object is now no longer radically partial, unknown and unknowable, infinitely distant in a sustainability that both logically precedes, and succeeds, the human (and that can generate the human while *outside* it, outside the outside). Now it is grasped, counted, parceled out, maintained, conserved, surveilled for any signs of scarcity or insufficiency. It is the "solid object" Bataille refers to it in connection with what he calls homogeneity. What differs between the two sustainabilities is only the possibility of metaphor; in first-order sustainability, what sustains itself is the world (logically, if not temporally) blindly generating figuration (in and as, but not necessarily, the various animal/human species) but eluding its capture. Hence the machine as sheer rhetorical and mechanical performance in which the human is mere component: Paulhan's Maintenance, the Heideggerian ready-to-hand. The human (self-)signified entails a second-order world where energy is recycled without loss, where material is conceived, measured, doled out, conserved, and used. Where, in other words, the literal level and its sense are maintained, in the radical forgetting of anamorphosis: Paulhan's Terror, the Heideggerian present-at-hand. And third-order sustainability is the anamorphosis point at which the first two intersect.

The third-order object, shot through with the stain of not-knowing, is recalcitrant, depleted and depletable, outside, charged with social and erotic power and shadowed by the pathological loss of sense (a pathology that can never be remedied with sadism). It generates the promise of the future, no matter how suspect that performative might seem.

The second order nevertheless abides: it appeals, it calls out, and we respond, interpellated as humans. *We* (as humans) will continue to think of the world and its indefinite preservation not only out of selfish motives, but because we would know the world, establish it as an object of our concern and control. We are the aftereffect of this rhetorical strategy. The survival of our particularity, our stain, demands it, and out of that we generate the absolute, and the absolute necessity of constraint. We cannot refrain from being concerned with the carbon footprint of things, and restraint before it. We might not be able to defeat the specter of depletion, but we certainly hope to limit its effects, tame it, work around it. A certain number of signifying creatures will necessarily resist the ever-expanding ruins of the future. We are all, in other words, second-order technocrats. We want to live in a world of closed feedback loops, of successful and thorough recycling. And why not? We will, but maybe only as the self-pleasuring subjectivity that will be surveilled, remedied, and corrected as it traverses the transparent walls of the Klein bottle.

But on an impractical level—on, as Bataille would say, the scale of the universe—that's a different question . . . The ultimate unknowability of the universe, the devil's share, is not merely a factor in the practice of the scientific description of the world. The share returns.

There is *(il y a)* second-order sustainability, generated out of the mud and dirt of the old city, the horror of materiality without the human . . . And it is supplemented, but not supplanted, by *resilience,* the temporal elaboration of sustainability. That is the subject of the next chapter.

General Sustainability

7 Sustainability's Return

The search for sustainability in conjunction with one, single, and universal figure of the human can seem like a fool's errand. Sustainability is, however, more than just the ideal of a congruence between the human and a perfectly tailored series of feedback and autopoietic loops. If one imagines sustainability as, for example, the effort to effect "sustainable yield source management," the problem appears clearly. As Billy Fleming notes in an important article (which will serve as a springboard for my argument), if ecologists and designers have attempted to, for example, regulate and assure stocks of cod in northeastern fisheries, or Douglas fir in the Pacific Northwest, they necessarily are compelled to "control or hold constant in [their] models" other biota in the ecosystem, "in order to simplify the specified management regime."[1] But the general "collapse of fisheries and forests across the globe" (30) has shown the limitation of this approach. One cannot assure the sustainability of certain key stocks without paying attention to the larger ecosystem, and this means "embracing the complexity of ecological systems," and recognizing, in effect, that humans are not in a position to arrest change once and for all for their own benefit. A human-managed sustaining of biota and ecosystems proves elusive. Instead, "ecosystem-based management practices" (EBMPs) "redefine the goals of a system's performance away from a stable end state and toward one of managed change" (30).

The model of "managed complexity" would replace, "supplant," a sustainability model too mired in the notion of the static preservation of stocks, populations, and natural resources. The word commonly used for this new model of ecological governance is *resilience*; the latter is a way of managing in a way that downplays the strategic authorship of the human-technological subject. "Sustainability can be made, but resilience happens. . . . The concept is more dynamic, it is non linear, and it embraces uncertainty" (Stumpp, cited in Fleming, 30).

Fleming's criticism of the practice of sustainability could be applied to that formulated by the Technocrats and Le Corbusier as well. Ecological sustainability in the urban context would entail a vast strategic effort, well beyond the possibility of management.

> The flows of energy, materials, and waste that are consumed and produced by cities are . . . beyond the purview of existing urban policy frameworks. . . . Resilience, on the other hand, implies a more tactical approach to urban design and management in which small interventions are deployed in order to manage and minimize the impacts of a regime change. (30)

We recall Michel de Certeau's valorization of the "tactical" over the "strategic" in his influential essay "Walking in the City." The master plan, the godlike overview beloved by tyrants and planning experts, is to be replaced by a situational practice, one that does not claim overarching knowledge or authority.

But we should note as well in this celebration of resilience the return of the notion of management. Resilience may supplant sustainability, but the ideal of human control is not done away with entirely. Resilience, instead, is a more effective way of managing; when humans step out of the way, resilience in ecology, engineering, and society proceeds apace, and is in fact more effective. Sustainability in engineering is "utopian" (29) with top-down "control" exercised over systems: there is a lack of redundancy, a high degree of interconnectedness (preventing isolation of problems), and a slavish focus on efficiency, all of which can lead to rapid systemic failures (one thinks of the meltdown at Chernobyl, or the failure of levees in New Orleans during Hurricane Katrina). Resilient systems, on the other hand, are "highly distributed and horizontally configured," like green infrastructure, entailing, for example, "nature based strategies for flood prevention" (30). While sustainability entails "steady-state" models, resilience implies "dynamic" ones (29).

Social resilience as well entails a more horizontal ordering, in which problems are addressed through "the strength and extent of relationships, support networks, and institutional capacities within a neighborhood" (32). Rather than unitary direction in city planning, for example, a resilient social structure entails cooperation, and more effective recovery plans (in the case of natural disaster).

Resilience, then, would seem to offer a way out to the stasis-inducing and coercive tendencies of what I have dubbed second-order sustainability. It is both more effective, and more respectful of ecological and social structures that, by their complexity and diversity, tend to elude the grasp of centralized planning. Should we then simply assume that sustainability is *passé*, replaced by resilience as an effective way of conceiving ecological and eco-social relations?

One should stress that resilience entails a relation to time that is fundamentally different from that of sustainability. As we have seen in other contexts, sustainability assumes the possibility of a definitive return to a previous or current but endangered state, and therefore a time tending toward the timeless—that is, the denial of time as degradation, fall off, decay. As Fleming puts it:

> The tools of mitigation can be considered the instruments of sustainability. Collectively, they aim to optimize or balance a process to some idealized condition. But as ecologists and other scientists began moving away from this steady-state view of the planet, engineering scholars followed suit. (31)

The "steady-state view" is linked here with "mitigation"—a key word, which characterizes sustainability through its principal orientation: using the "tools available to engineers aiming to offset or minimize the effects of an undesirable process or byproduct" (31). An example of this might be the high-tech effort (geoengineering) to reduce climate change through reductions in CO_2 emissions.

Now, admittedly, this sort of amelioration is dependent on a single authority, as Fleming stresses, and thus it tends to be "top down" (hence strategic), rather than "tactical," "interconnected," and so on. But my point would be that *mitigation*—by definition an activity aiming to "moderate (a quality or condition) in force or intensity; alleviate"[2]—*works to stop or turn back time.* It refuses to recognize the passage of time and its effects.

Whatever one thinks of sustainability's chances in this, the salient point here is that resilience seeks to do just the opposite: the relevant term here is *adaptation* (31). The latter indicates not a return to some semblance of a previous or endangered state, a removal or moderation of an undesirable condition or intensity, but rather a modification or alteration that allows oneself

or one's productions to "become suitable to a new or special use or situation"; thus it is an "adjustment to new or modified cultural surroundings."[3]

In adaptation, time is recognized and its passage is accepted; there is, in
effect, no going back. While mitigation seeks to get us back to where we
were, adaptation accepts the new state of affairs and tries to make the best
of it. Hence the emphasis on multiple systems that can "fail safely," rather
than a single, potentially fragile, one upon which everything relies (31).
But the important thing to note here is the recognition of the inevitability
of failure—that is, the recognition that no matter how we try, things are
not what they were, that crises (typified by Hurricane Katrina) will assert
themselves, and that rather than trying to do away with these crises, we
accept them and rely from now on on systems that are "highly distributed
and horizontally configured." We are not concerned with mitigating the
hurricane (for example)— that is, eradicating it and its effects, returning to
the old, less intense hurricanes—so much as we are concerned with adapting ourselves, and our approaches, to it. More intense hurricanes are here
to stay; from now on we will be concerned with ways to deal with them.

One could indeed argue against Fleming, and make the case that there
is something to be said for mitigation, and even see it as more fundamental
than adaptation.[4] After all, in the end, to devote oneself exclusively to adaptation means to accept things that should be resisted, and (somehow) driven
back, rather than simply accounted for. Accepting the inevitability of yet
another extremely destructive hurricane, rather than working to create conditions that will—here's that word again—mitigate the actual intensity of
hurricanes, indicates a certain fatalism.

Of course the advocates of adaptation can argue that their way of pre-
paring for hurricanes—"nature-based strategies for flood protection" (31)—
are more effective than some grand, single strategy to make hurricanes less
severe or even do away with them. Rather than waving a magic wand and
eliminating disasters and their causes, various on-the-ground adaptations—
"multi-functional waterfront parks, ecologically functional breakwaters, and
coastal wetland restorations" (31)—will make life more agreeable in an era
of climate change and ever nastier natural disasters.

I don't want to argue against Fleming's version of resilience, but rather
only note that the resilience–adaptation strategy, commonsensical as it
might be, recognizes the inevitability of the passage of time, and the degradation and depletion we can associate with that temporal movement.
Temporality, the movement tending toward degradation, is associated by

Fleming with "horizontal" planning, with the absence, in other words, of the overweening subjectivity of the solitary expert, as well as the attempt to halt time or return to earlier states. The human in resilience is capable of only partial intervention, partial acts, and must share the stage not only with inevitable change, but with decay, the unforeseen, loss, depletion. In other words, resilience recognizes the failure of the unitary (and as Bataille would say, mono-cephalous) state of the world. If anything, resilience is an effort on the part of the human, working horizontally with all the other agents and actants in the world (such as parks, wetlands, breakwaters) to adapt to the catastrophic failures inadvertently authored by the strategizing planner.

Nevertheless, there is a strange relationship between resilience and sustainability. What does it mean to say that resilience *supplants* sustainability? That it comes after? On one level, of course, the statement is just an empirical observation: among engineers, social planners, ecologists, and many others, devotion to sustainability has been replaced by an affirmation of resilience. But on another level, we can note that to affirm replacing sustainability with resilience is to affirm the passage of time. Resilience comes after, but resilience is *already* the doctrine of temporality, of coming after. To argue that resilience comes after means that one is already in resilience, since resilience is the state (mental, operational) of affirming the passage of time. We assume time and its passage (resilience), and then find it necessary (resilience comes after). From the first (in time) we assume the temporal directionality of physical systems, rather than a mechanical notion of reversibility and repetition. We can never get outside resilience to determine its necessity. We affirm the horizontality of time, and ourselves as situated in the temporal hermeneutic circle.

And yet for all that, resilience contains, in itself, sustainability. It's as if the belated child contains in its womb the parent, the predecessor. Resilience maintains the ideals of sustainability. Fleming states:

> Thus, part of the allure of resilience theory flows from its embrace of dynamic equilibrium—or *brief moments of stability* in an otherwise tumultuous world—and the power that comes from understanding and *managing* the structural shifts that it implies. (34; emphasis added)

The characteristics of second-order sustainability—management, stability, the godlike overview of the telephone company—are once again affirmed, but now contained in resilience in miniature. Sustainability's affirmation of sheer repetition and perpetuity (always-again mitigation, "minimizing the effects" of the passage of time [30]) is still there, but now reduced to "brief moments," and all under the control of the manager ("managing the structural shifts").

Fleming recognizes this interpenetration of sustainability and resilience when he notes that, in fact, resilience is not simple. It so happens that

> these modes of adaptation can be envisioned along a spectrum from the highly centralized and vertical at one pole to the highly distributed and horizontal at the other. The highly centralized and vertical modes of engineering resilience grew out of the nineteenth century approach to the problems of sanitation, energy production and distribution, and flood protection. (31)

This raises an interesting question. What exactly, then, is the status of sustainability when it is both "supplanted" by and at the same time contained within resilience (on "the spectrum")? When the atemporal is always-already temporal? Adaptation, which Fleming sees as congruent with resilience (30), nevertheless manages, at one end of the spectrum, to mimic mitigation, in that in engineering, at least, it has a version that is top-down, single-solution oriented ("gray infrastructure," "'hard' solutions"). It "diverts some form of risk." This sort of adaptation involves the "planning, design, and construction of fortified coastlines, channelized rivers, and dam-generated reservoirs during the twentieth century" (31).

"Hard" resilience, in fact, looks a lot like sustainability, in its efforts to stop time and mitigate through "vertical risk reduction." The articulation point between the two, in other words, is not outside but inside sustainability. The fact that sustainability is not once and for all "supplanted," or is so only while the repetitious time of sustainability is maintained, indicates that sustainability itself is not in the past, but is always again in the present, in a sense surrounding resilience on all sides. It is around, and comes around in its inescapability; resilience can only leave it behind while maintaining it. The gesture of willing time out of the atemporal (resilience) can only itself be on the basis of perfect repetition (sustainability). The chora that generates them both, and presides over their difference, is also inseparable from the incessant instantiation of sustainability. We are within the horizontal temporality of resilience, which is at the same time lodged in and against, and always again emerging from, the fundamentally atemporal recurrence of sustainability. Instead of a one-way sustainability–resilience spectrum, one imagines sustainability like a giant cell, or bacterium, which has engulfed and is ruptured by the heterogeneous body of resilience.[5]

It turns out that we have never left sustainability. We cannot leave it. But sustainability is also never simply timeless, a homogeneous present or a perfect recurrence. Like the programming of cells, it mutates, or it contains the mutation within its cell. If a posthistorical or "end of history" state implies a stasis in which nothing ever changes, repeatedly affirmed, we could argue that such a timelessness is also a repetition of a Nietzschean eternal return. This was the point that Benjamin, citing Karl Löwith, made (see chapter 6). A theological realm of "eternal perfectibility" in this view is simply the antinomy, and the double, of the eternal return. One can certainly condemn this (or any) vision of posthistory, which Benjamin obviously does, but one can also note that this vision of posthistory is not easily escapable either. If sustainability is a utopian present in which dynamic change has been replaced by a stress on a maintenance and/or resurrection of the way things were before, it is nonetheless also a model of the return, the loss, if only fantasized, of a current state, accompanied by the happy reestablishment of that state without loss.

We love the time of our lives, the succession of events, the narrative, the spending and recovering, the drama of the cliff-hanger, and we love it so much we willingly, even eagerly, long for its repetition ad infinitum. We say yes to it. In sustainability, we affirm the possibility of loss—it galvanizes us, it is the basis of our practice—but we also refuse its ultimate necessity.[6] Sustainability is ours, perpetually. But it is so only against the threat of irreversible time.

Lodged in and against sustainability-circularity is, however, another return, that of resilience. The very aberrant autobiographical subjectivity of Nietzsche affirming the pleasurable and perfect circularity of return assures that there will always be a supplement to, an opening out of, the return. Resilience means that the threat of the passage of time cannot simply be laughed off, as at the end of a comedy. The return is still circular, but it affirms loss, failure, ruin, depletion, blight. A dirty eternal return, or an idiosyncratic (Benjaminian, but also Kojèvian and Bataillean) dialectic in which the endpoint, the stasis of the end of history, is doubled and "followed" by the repetitions of "jobless" negativity.[7] Hence adaptation, the steady loss of what we might want to hold dear and celebrate when it comes around again. In resilience there is still return, but return to a state that is imperfect, the best we can do. "You can always come back, but you can't come back all the way," as Dylan sang.[8] Or you can come back different, or differently. In the domain of social resilience, Fleming cites a 1943 study that indicates that "cognitive[ly] process[ing] or cop[ing] with a loss or disruption was the critical factor in the recovery of [resilient] children" (32).[9] In resilience, the disaster is not completely averted; rather it is incorporated, lived with, but (perhaps) gone beyond, as in the case of children traumatized in war. Thus we have a model in which sustainability incorporates resilience, without ceasing to perform as sustainability. In that case, we have a kind of smear in which the utterly foreign—the unidirectional time of resilience—is a constituting (always-already) supplement *within and outside of* the circular time of eternal recurrence without difference.

There are, then, two eternal returns, one perfect, perfectly happy, but static and managed by monocephalous experts (the one criticized by Benjamin), the other deleteriously absurd, lost in time's fall, scattered, rupturing utopia and returning always in and as fatal degradation (the one affirmed by Bataille). Sustainability looms as a future that we would reenact, that would sustain what we fear to lose, but that we can never simply be conscious of reaching for or attaining. This is not (or not simply) a technocratic future. It is, however, a future that returns while shying from our necessary plans or schemes, perhaps even oblivious to them. An asymptotic future that, for all we know, might very well be simply dead, or the reanimation of the dead in necessary fiction. Sustainability is the incessant and definitive concentration, the elaboration of verticality against time (Le Corbusier's towers), the happy end always-again ending without loss; resilience is the murmur, the scattering, the escape, the mortal, the fall, happiness only in the qualifying spectrum of horror (Bataille's Obelisk). The statue and its toppling are inseparable. Their scales are out of proportion, a parody of a larger assemblage. A bicephalous sustainability, looking back and also looking ahead out of timeless time is all that remains (in time).

What of resilience and sustainability in the larger movement of energetic planetary flows? Does the resilience / sustainability dyad operate not just in relation to human wants, but in relation to larger living, and indeed inanimate, systems? Autopoiesis, a term coined by biologists Francisco Varela and Humberto Maturana, is a way of thinking second-order cybernetics in biological systems.[10] Resilience in this context can be formulated not as a project of eco-engineering or social governance, but as the working and melding of bodies, both microscopic and immense, in the world. It unites the tiniest bacteria and the entire biosphere of the earth (Gaia). Both are self-regulating, moving forward through time and adapting, as best as possible, to the vicissitudes of the environment and sometimes catastrophic change. As biologist Lynn Margulis puts it:

> Cells and Gaia display a general property of autopoietic entities: as their surroundings change unpredictably, they maintain their structural integrity and internal organization, at the expense of solar energy, by remaking and interchanging their parts.
>
> Metabolism is the name given to this incessant buildup and breakdown of subdivisible components—that is, to the chemical activities of living systems.[11]

If we are to model a society, or an economy, on autopoiesis, we will see how human systems double (mimic, reproduce) biological and planetary systems: "life."[12] My interest is not in critiquing a method of analysis that sees human systems as models of autopoiesis, but rather in seeing autopoiesis as it was originally worked out, and then elaborated by Margulis, as a system that implies the human, but does not mandate it. A closed system—a cell, a body, a biosphere—has "self-making and self-maintaining properties"; they "maintain their own boundaries," unlike "mechanistic systems" (348). Most interesting here is that this process, on all levels, entails *intelligence*. Every cell, every body, every species, works to regulate itself, and indirectly, its own position in a larger ecology, which itself is an autopoietic structure. Resilience, lodged within and against sheer sustainability, is a function of adaptation, which, Margulis would argue, is a universal trait of life, and perhaps even of energy systems outside of (before, after, beyond) life. Negative inputs are dealt with, energy is channeled, the borders are (self-)regulated. The chemical mix and temperature scale are maintained. In this approach, these are not blind mechanical impulses; there is a guiding intelligence, on the part of every biological being, every body, every organism. There is no grand design, but there is a near infinity of tiny designs, on the part of every cell, of every living organism. This is resilience to a T, but the human is, ultimately, strangely lacking. We can imagine a noosphere, a thinking sphere of the earth, but the noosphere has no need of the human, or specifically human intelligence. Humans certainly can appear in the noosphere, they too have their autopoiesis, their self-regulating resilience, but theirs is just one more intelligence, neither necessary nor inevitable. Human intelligence is not a fluke; it is one possible version of the evolution of species in a process that, in the long run, seems mandated by matter itself. We are not isolated in the cosmos; we are integral to its larger workings. The indifference of the vast, terrifying Pascalian silence of space is now supplemented by a universe in which intelligence could and probably will pop up anywhere—but not necessarily *our* (human) intelligence.

Samuel Butler (1835–1902), critic of Darwin, held that all living beings are motivated not by purely mechanical inputs and outputs, but by intelligence. Margulis and Dorion Sagan write:

> Each living being, as Samuel Butler argued, responds sentiently to a changing environment and tries during its life to alter itself. . . . Gradually, in tiny increments, living systems with nonnegotiable demands for food, water, and energy transformed themselves in wily and persistent ways.
>
> What theologians called design, and considered otherworldly, was for Butler the result, in part, of Earth-bound thinking matter.[13]

"Earth-bound thinking matter," but not necessarily *human* thinking matter. Yet willy-nilly the human as well has emerged as autopoietic; but what strikes us nowadays is the human's endlessly resilient desire to escape the autopoietic. This is another way of saying that human civilization at the moment is not sustainable. But in the long-term view of things, which might not be so long term after all, humans too will deal with fluctuations in available energy resources, for example, and their activity as a species will modify itself accordingly. This will happen either through human volition or not. A happy adaptation could occur, in which our human intelligence triumphs and we save ourselves from a sudden and devastating die-off. Or not.

The human does represent, however, another turn of the screw, so to speak, in the sense that it seems to be (for the moment, here on earth) the only species capable of consciously reflecting on, and attempting to modify (one could argue, not so successfully) its own behavior through cognitive motivations. It is second-order cybernetics brought to a higher level, adaptation with technological hubris. Other organisms self-regulate, but it is through their direct responses to environmental inputs. Humans, hopefully, will do it in part through conscious activity, a larger plan. Hence the dream, and the promise, of second-order sustainability.

But what are the limits, the contours of this higher consciousness? What is the status of the self-awareness of this knowing, on the way to perfecting resilience, on the scale of the biological self-regulation of the planet?

It is the increasing role of intelligence in evolution—the noosphere—that provides a role for the human that sets it apart. Without intelligence, some would argue, autopoiesis could function perfectly well, as long as we assume that survival does not entail, or favor, human-style intelligence. This is the perspective of a purely mechanistic evolution: what survives does so by chance, and nothing in evolutionary history ever mandated the development of intelligence. If—if—humans are intelligent, it is simply by chance; the human species represented an evolutionary quirk that turned out (sort of) well.

But if we stick with Samuel Butler, and Margulis and Sagan's reading of Butler, then we can conclude that anything that could be characterized as human is really simply a (or one) continuation of all the developments in intelligence that have taken place since the very earliest organisms, indeed perhaps even on the part of "inanimate" things. Intelligence will be inherent in living organisms as they develop in and through evolution, by way of autopoiesis, and maybe throughout a universe capable of being the environment in which this generalized intelligence appears. This could be seen as the precise opposite of the Pascalian universe I discussed in the context of first-order sustainability, one in which the human is lost in vast and infinitesimally small space.

Humans might be different not because of some special technical skills—tools, language, and so on—but rather because they are *aware* of the role of autopoiesis, and of its necessity for their own, and planetary, survival. Thus self-referential human consciousness is itself inseparable from all the autopoietic systems that constitute it and open it out. In fact, human intelligence and subjectivity can be represented as simply another self-reflexive system, functioning in and through other self-reflexive systems. In that sense, the very notion of individual subjectivity can be put in question.[14]

And yet there is the difference in the human, not so much because human subjectivity and intelligence is different in kind in its sophistication and self-reflection, but rather due to its recognition of, and confrontation with, the impossibility of knowing, the impossibility of grasping the larger comprehensibility of the system. There is knowledge . . . of disproportion. This is the moment at the summit in which technological mastery fails, the "dark night" of not-knowing, the headlessness of the *Acéphale*. And it has to do with the point in which autopoiesis is grasped on a higher level as a comprehensible system, which is also the moment of the general loss of this (and all) comprehension, of this and all coherent "worlds."

Self-consciousness, then, lost in an infinite and ungraspable dispersion of other animate and inanimate intelligences, other self-consciousnesses, risks appearing as consciousness of that which defeats the all-inclusiveness of consciousness. Pascal's "disproportion" in the face of the lack of intelligence of the universe is now reconfigured as the highest knowledge once (and always-again) lost in not-knowing. This view of intelligence risks turning into an instance of the sublime (an exclusively aesthetic category), however, unless it is linked to an economic analysis.

We might turn here to Bataille's essay "The Economy on the Scale of the Universe," where he notes the fact that humanity's role in the biosphere[15] is essentially to squander the energy surplus that builds up in the system, and that humanity's is certainly the most spectacular, if not the only, release valve enabling its continued operation. Autopoiesis cannot be separated from flamboyant destruction.[16] There are any number of animals that release stored-up energy, once it has reached, in living things, the limits of its expansion.

> Free energy [in humans] flowers and endlessly displays useless splendor. But the excess share of energy could not have been liberated if it had not first been seized [emparé]. Condensation was necessary for expenditure. Human activity exploits the wealth of the earth through new means. In that way it extends the domain of life. Humans do not limit themselves like trees or insects to the occupation of space that's still free. In any case there was no space not filled to the maximum when they arrived. But by making use of new means, they invest considerable quantities of energy in installations that increase their power. They assure, and increase, living nature through the development of dead matter which must be, in the end, seen as one of the modalities of the extension of life.[17]

Bataille here is no doubt thinking of fossil fuels, which extend humans' power beyond that of other animals, who can only tap into energy sources that are readily available: the sun, chemicals in the soil, other animals. Humans, using their knowledge, can tap into much larger energy stores.

Bataille's main point, writing in 1946, is that, even though humanity seems impoverished—in the ruins of postwar Europe, destitution is universal—humanity is inherently wealthy. Humans alone, Bataille argues, are able to concentrate wealth—energy and matter embodying energy—far beyond what other animals are capable of. And yet, because of social injustice and war, the concentration and squandering of wealth results only in horror and death. The response, the properly "conscious" way of facing the problem of postwar poverty, lay not in hoarding resources, but in spending them, *in the right way*. Energy, after all, cannot be hoarded; it is either used to extend dominion or, facing blockage, it is expended, either disastrously or gloriously. To avoid even more war and destitution, humans must choose glory.

> Due to the fact that you have at your disposal all the resources of the world, since they cannot be endlessly extended, you must *spend them actively, with no other reason than the desire you have to do it*. If not you will have to go, passively, from unemployment to war. You cannot deny it: the desire is in you, it is intense [*vif*]; you cannot separate it from humanity. In essence, a human being has the responsibility here to spend in glory what the earth accumulates, what the sun lavishes. In essence, he laughs, he's a dancer, a party animal [*donneur de fêtes*]. (16; emphasis in original)

The Nietzschean register is clear enough in passages like this, but what I think must be stressed is the fact that at this highest awareness, this recognition that the surplus cannot indefinitely be recycled or stockpiled, there is a kind of madness, of not-knowing. This is the point at which any and all clever strategies fail. This self-reflexivity, of autopoiesis, of sustainability—stockpiling forever is not sustainable, it has reached its limits—lies not in some technocratic mastery, but quite the opposite: in delirium, festivals, laughter. The highest level of intelligence—the recognition of the limits of intelligence itself—is also the downfall of intelligence. The technical sophistication necessary for humanity to extend its dominion is ultimately inseparable from a larger oblivion (lack of mastery, embrace of the "absurdity" of time).

Bataille, in writing this, acknowledges, knows, what cannot be known: the truth of autopoiesis in this view is a kind of higher not-knowing, the point at which in Dionysian dance, erotism, laughter, the affirmation of life to the point of death, the future is opened out. This is not a "conscious" survival strategy; it is a dance, which may have, as an aftereffect, survival. The ultimate mode of adaptation, the ultimate resilience strategy, is not a strategy at all; its unforeseen, unplanned aftereffect may be a sustainability not fully separable from the opening to an unredeemable time.

But Bataille's (implicit) mention of fossil fuels serves as the transition from his era, when their use seemed to most people problem-free, to today, when energy resources represent the overfill and clogging, so to speak, of our environment, as Hubbert and Le Corbusier, among many others, already recognized in the 1940s.[18] Humans have reached the point, in other words, in which the freeing and spending of heretofore untapped resources has led to another saturation, another moment in which the environment is filled, and in which there is no more room to expand. Only this time it is waste—pollution, refuse—that has filled the environment and extended the "domain of life" into the domain of death.

Indeed, the change in the status of fossil resources means that Bataille's model of the liberation of excess energy must be reconceived. In Bataille's day, wars and social inequality were the "bad" way of consuming the surplus; the good, so to speak, lay in festivals, pleasure, eroticism, even (gasp) the Marshall Plan. Today the threat of war, and even global war, certainly remains, as does, to be sure, social and economic inequality, but they are joined by the blowback of the energy resources Bataille cited affirmatively as (ironically, from a current perspective) increasing the human power to expend. Today expenditure is betrayed by the very exuberant production Bataille celebrated. This means that the nature of consumption must be rethought; consumption as a mode of capitalist growth and concentration clearly results not in a festive burn off, but in the disastrous concentration of toxic residue.

The spending "without reserve"—the *dépense*—put forward by Bataille can now be rethought as the expenditure of the very concentrated waste that is filling every nook of the planet, piling up behind us and rushing ever forward, into whose abyss we stare (along with Benjamin's angel). What can be called waste is the very residue or aftereffect of a no longer viable model of expenditure.[19] For this reason, another consumption can be imagined, that of the free and orgiastic spending of the concentrated effluvia of a dying economic system. Bataille's critique of the late 1940s is notably lacking in any critique of capitalism, but that is perhaps because he could not see at that point the close linkage between capitalist consumption (outside of war and social inequality) and toxic consumption-destruction. He notes the problem of social inequality (unemployment, wealth inequality), but he does not trace it back to its source.

Bataille, then, imagines a sustainability–resilience combine in which capitalist production and consumption still plays a part. Bataille's sustainability model, I would argue, is still valid; it is, after all, a model of headless autopoiesis in which a flamboyant and spectacular consumption on the part of humanity serves as a way of opening out the planet to a further expansion and "glory" (and the continuation of that glory), a temporal movement toward the unknown and the infinitely remote. But what, in the end, is this glory?

If resilience is a temporal movement of inevitable loss (in resilience time and loss are one), it entails the death-bound embrace of "adaptation." In a depleted world of trash, trash itself is the only resource that can be expended. Recycling and expenditure are one. The festival, the celebration, of excess in this light takes place in the ruins of a capitalist world of excess. It is as easy to think the end of the world as it is to think the end of the capitalism, if the end of the world is an unthinkable *(dé-pensé)* celebration of the end of capitalism's model of accumulation and consumption—its ruinous model, in other words, of expenditure as reinvestment. The celebration and expenditure, in other words, of the wreckage hurtling toward our backward-facing better angels.

Sustainability "contains" this monster of temporality (resilience) in the sense that (third-order) sustainability is the inevitable aftereffect of the flamboyant destruction of the excessive object.[20] That object is charged with the power of community, but that power is now inseparable from the junked object's recycling as sacred fetish (religious or sexual). By consuming *(consumant)* what has already been consumed *(consommé)*—the embodied energy of refuse clogging our world—sustainability supervenes. To change consumption is to change an economic model, a world; in depletion, a world of peak everything, junk is all that is left of raw materials, and all that we can do is change our relation to our own refuse. All available space has been filled by it, and we cannot escape its gaze. This stuff is no longer simply an "economic asset"; it is instead the powerful cursed matter of collective activity and delirium. The energy of the world is in recycling, but recycling that does not entail the production of more stuff to be bought, compared, and discarded. It is instead the affective production of *mana*, of the object charged with the power of time-destined and death-bound exuberance.[21]

At first the temptation might seem to be the valorization of the totem as the symbol for, but also the motivation of, the community. The community in its mass subjectivity is ratified and continuously reaffirmed through the experience (such as the eating) of the totemic, sacred object. This is the model associated with Émile Durkheim's anthropology, and Durkheim hoped to link the affirmation of the community through the celebration of the totem with a modern humanity that would find its highest totem in the human.[22] This version, which certainly influenced Bataille, stresses the mass enthusiasm of the community in and through the sacred object. For example, we read in Durkheim's *Elementary Forms of the Religious Life:*

> Since religious force is nothing other than the collective and anonymous force of the clan, and since this can be represented in the mind only in the form of the totem, the totemic emblem is like the visible body of the god. . . . So if religious force, in so far as it is conceived as incorporated in the totemic emblem, appears to be outside of the individuals and endowed with a sort of transcendence over them, it, like the clan of which it is the symbol, can be realized only in and through them; in this sense it is imminent in them and they necessarily represent it as such. They feel it present and active within them, for it is this which raises them to a superior life.[23]

The individual is charged with enthusiasm, the power, or *mana,* of the sacred object, the totem. Through this power, which is a real (social) physical power, the individual is elevated to a "superior" life through his or her contact with (or ingestion of) the totem and its power.

Bataille rewrites this story by stressing the "cursed" nature of the totemic object, its "base materialism." The individual is not elevated, but cast down (or is elevated only to be cast down); the object itself is not a unitary source reflecting a transcendence. And yet for all this, for Bataille, there is still a community. There is still a grouping that orients itself around a sacred object, because it is accursed. But would such a community be an exclusive and exclusionary one (the "force of the clan"), defined by an orientation around a head, a leader, or rather some other grouping that precisely refuses or is incapable of union in and through a superior force or principle?

For the philosopher Jean-Luc Nancy, Bataille's model indeed fails to the extent that it posits an exclusivist community. For Nancy, all totems, of whatever sort, all sacred objects charged with *mana,* will always be linked to a larger community, one that plays the role of a subjectivity, with all the occidental philosophical baggage that that implies (subject/object, us/them, culture/nature, etc.). In *The Inoperative Community,* a commentary on the possibilities of a Bataillean community, Nancy writes:

> Community understood as a work or through its works would presuppose that the common being, as such, be objectifiable and producible (in sites, persons, buildings, discourses, institutions, symbols: in short, in subjects).

0

Products derived from operations of this kind, however grandiose they might seek to be and sometimes manage to be, have no more communitarian existence than the plaster busts of Marianne.[24]

Thus for Nancy the very viability of an object as an "objectifiable" token established in relation to a community of whatever sort is, to say the least, problematic. This iconoclastic view of the sacred is, I think, questionable: Why should community, of whatever sort, be irrevocably separated from the materiality of the object which would serve, in any capacity whatsoever, as a repository and vehicle of energy, of a sacred and transmissible force? Eliminating the dreaded "plaster bust of Marianne" eliminates, it would seem, the danger of the community constituting itself as a closed, self-reflexive entity in and through a hollow and repressive thing. What passes for a kind of idolatry of the statue in Nancy, however, is exactly the question that is most crucial for a world in which the consumption of charged objects is tied to desire, pleasure, deliverance, oblivion. What if the object of consumption is essential to a world in which consumption is to be rethought, at the point of ruin?

Consider that bust of Marianne. It is embodied energy, and it is consumed as such by the community (i.e., its stability is assured by the materials and energy that have gone into its fabrication, distribution, and maintenance). It's a mass-produced statue or statuette. It is in the *Mairie* in France—in thousands of them, in fact, since it is mechanically reproduced—and it represents the French Republic. It represents feminine beauty, desire, maternity, a host of things, many of which are probably objectionable, but which nevertheless need to be considered when thinking about energy use, expenditure, and politics as embodied in things. First, it represents the republic in the absence of a picture of the head of state. True, it might be accompanied by a photo of the French president, but it alone represents the totality and continuity of the republic through time. But as the surrealists and situationists well knew, it is also susceptible to *détournement;* its meaning can always be revised, parodied, turned on its head. The image can be desecrated, or it can be read in ways that have little to do with the original intent behind its production (assuming that "original intent" can ever be isolated). It can be taken as a very strong object of desire; it can be read as the detritus of a lost civilization, as a charged point in a nexus of inexplicable coincidences. Its carbon footprint can be measured, and that can be analyzed in relation to its signifying power in the civic space. But its energy is, in the end, quite different from that of a (supposed) inert object. Like Aragon's statues, it can speak in the mode of prosopopoeia of the inability of statues or the dead to speak. And, not least, it can be viewed, as Jane Bennett puts it, as "a creative materiality with incipient tendencies and propensities, which are variably enacted depending on the other forces, affects or bodies with which [it] comes into close contact."[25] Such assemblages can be read, in turn, as communities, linkages of human and nonhuman actants united and divided in common mutual misreading.

My point is that *mana* and the sacred, "electrical" charge of the totemic object, such as the bust of Marianne, are not necessarily in a straightforward relation to the constitution and sealing of an exclusionary community. Indeed, the object itself can be read as a community, a grouping of heterogeneous elements that negotiate in one way or another with each other and that leads to no higher or stable identity. *Pace* Nancy, there are objects, and there are communities. And they are connected in ways that reaffirm them: communities are objects, and objects are communities, and they communicate, perhaps in a Bataillean sense, across differences and distances, in ruptures of closed subjectivity. Sexual relations entail objects, organs, fetishes; communities entail delirious and pleasurable relations, political images, and things; all entail relations between organisms (vegetal as well as animal and animal), junk, emitting and consuming energy, in production, transportation, transport, conservation, recycling, and destruction (in landfills, in outer space, in orgiastic celebration,[26] etc.).

Channeling Levinas, Alphonso Lingis writes: "Community forms in a movement by which one exposes oneself to the other, to forces and powers outside oneself, to death and to the others who die."[27] That other, as we've seen in chapter 2, can also entail the ecological Other, as well as mutant metal, or stone, human hybrids (chapter 3: statues).

What then of the totem, and of *mana*? The totemic object can be seen as a mutant agent of autopoiesis, a fragment in and through which the community does not so much constitute (and regulate) itself but rather *communicates* through itself, which (as Nancy argues) would mean that it both shares and separates itself. Nancy supplements Bataille's notion of "communication" (the opening of the self in erotism and death) with *partage,* a word that, in French, has the sense both of "sharing" and "division" or "separation." Thus Nancy can write that "at every instant singular beings share [*partagent*] their limits, separate themselves [*se partagent*] on their limits."[28] Community is both separation and sharing simultaneously; the subject is not "one," but is riven in its connection with and through an other. For this reason, one can envisage a totem not of the unified clan or larger society, but of the union/separation of two—lovers perhaps, or readers,[29] but also of human–object or human–animal combines, or an amalgamation or assemblage of multiple connections-separations. Objects, humans, ecosystems, share and separate through their wounds. The totem is then the impossible point of autopoiesis or self-regulation in an unstable (headless) assemblage, a point where the self is not the self but only a split connection of split connections (Bataille's *ipse*). This is a node of refraction that leads not to a higher certainty, union, or organism, inside and outside (and least of all to isolable human selves), but rather to a momentary stasis or ecology of organisms, organs, and things. Sharing, shared, and separated.

The totem, according to Durkheim, is a kind of "badge": an "emblem, a veritable coat-of-arms whose analogies with the arms of heraldry have often been remarked" (113). The "totemic principle" that this "badge" represents, however, is much more than a stable grouping. Or, put another way, the grouping itself as represented/constituted by the totem (since the totem is a kind of speech act)[30] is inseparable from an instance of energy that is not so much embodied as expended. This is the "totemic principle," or *mana;* Durkheim notes:

> Does an individual come in contact with them [the totemic principles] without having taken proper precautions? Some receive a shock which might be compared to the effect of an electric discharge. Sometimes they seem to conceive of these as a sort of fluid escaping by points. (190)

The principles, embodied by totemic objects, carry with them a literal force. The object is not solid, but pierced by "points" through which "fluid," electrical energy, is emitted, streams, and shocks the "individual." The badge or marker, then, is not the depiction of a stable object, but of an expenditure of energy. *Mana* is enthusiasm, effervescence, force, also a principle of the recurrence of dissolution and death. If the sacred ritual serves to reenergize and reconstitute the community, this is an indication that the community itself is always riven by dissolution, is always teetering on the edge of extinction. The "electricity" of the mana-charged and expending object is the shock of the community coming together, of its operative and incongruous metaphors interacting, but also the shock of the fragmentation of the community, of its risk as it hurtles in frenzy toward its end. In principle, of course, Durkheim would argue that the totemic principle works to bring the community together as a unified, closed entity through sacred rituals channeling this force. But it can just as easily go the other way: the "left-hand" sacred affirmed by Bataille is the centripetal force that risks the very coherence of the community.[31] (The community is unthinkable without the ever-present risk of dissolution; even Durkheim must presuppose this risk, since the totem for him is involved in the never-ending task of reunification.) Sharing in left-handed ecstasy is division, explosion, the danger of the uncontrollable forces shooting out through the "points" of the fetish. The "badge" is a representation and a totem-act of an entity that is not an entity, or an entity tending toward dissolution at and after its moment of "sharing": a dissolute community. The dead (riven) community speaks (prosopopoeia) through the incessantly expended energy of the totem.

Thus two objects: one has measurable *emergy* content, which we can classify, store, know. We can see it embodied in forests, either as so many board feet of lumber to be cut, or, put another way, as potential natural capital, the gift of nature that keeps on giving, the gift that we must respect if we are to survive. That is the object of concern to second-order sustainability, the standing reserve (natural capital) whose proper management is necessary to the stabilization of the economy, the source of its wealth; respect for it is essential to the overarching health of the planet. The other object, that of the third order, is filthy, redolent of the energy charge left over after the major objects have been put to use and conserved (or destroyed). That is the object that flares at and beyond the limits to growth (the limits to, and the end of, capitalism). The risk it affirms is necessary, but only in the sense that unrecognizable excess—that which cannot be taken into account—must somehow be recognized. That impossible recognition is the task of third-order sustainability.

Nancy's *Inoperative Community* attempts to imagine a future community, a necessary task, for sure. While Nancy might eschew the totem, and *mana*, one can simply look around and see that both are still in force, and are not likely ever to go away. Why imagine, then, a future in which they have been extirpated? (Or only in force as literature, writing, etc.: the ultimate fantasy of the *République des lettres*.) In fact—and I will develop this point further in chapter 9—a future world of depletion, in which "Man" has both filled the world and exhausted it, will find both its *mana* and its totems in what's left over: refuse, recyclable materials that can both be repurposed, upcycled in bizarre and troubling ways, re-fetishized, re-venerated. With a difference. Re-use will clearly mean not melting things down ("down-cycling," as McDonough would call it)—the eventual carbon footprint is too great, the EROEI too small—but rather tapping into junk flows, re-appropriating, retrofitting: bricolage, DIY in short, and *détournement* as well.[32] Upfetishizing, we might call it. But the fragment, the object as sheer materiality in its rejected or reject status (as Irving Goh would put it), is also, inevitably, a *mana*-charged object. In a (by necessity) postpro-duction world, where the end of the world and the end of capitalism are coterminous, the economy shifts to a gift economy: *potlatch,* the exchange of desire and the destruction of wretched toys.[33] This is the revelation of the messianic: the apocalypse. There is nothing more to conspicuously consume (or rather consumption [in the sense of *consumation*] is now the affirmation of the conspicuous to its dissolution). In this sense, we recall the critique of capitalism of the Technocrats—the object must in future be tied in value to the energetic inputs that make it up—while arguing that the overweening Technical subjectivity will instead entail a subjectiv-ity opened out (as in Nancy) to finitude, death, and (following Bataille) erotism, laughter. The energy-charged object here bears the energy not simply of calculable inputs and outputs but also and above all of the vio-lence of the "cursed" sacred, the fire of its falling embers. The energy that does "work" (second-order sustainability) is recycled as the energy of the meditative, death-bound festival (third order). As a totem, the object entails (represents, emboldens) not the elevated subjectivity of the political or intel-lectual leader, but the riven, ritual subjectivity of the victim dying without hope of salvation. *Partage*—sharing and splitting—will characterize both a communal and a personal subjectivity that both is "in common" with oth-ers and differing with itself. A riven consciousness, perhaps, and one tied to the stuff of rejection and return, "base materiality" in the temporality of resilience.[34]

This intelligence, perhaps even if posited as a cybernetic "self-regulating" assemblage—if at least one links self-regulation to the death drive—is what is left over after the immanence of the seemingly self-less "hyperobject" (Timothy Morton) or "vibrant matter" (Jane Bennett). This way of conceiv-ing the object—that of "object-oriented ontology"—dismisses the subject by arguing that, by deconstructing the inside–outside (or nature–culture, etc.) opposition, we have done away with the need for, or viability of, the subject, and of course of the nature–culture divide as well (and this makes perfect sense in the context of first-order sustainability). But the subject this approach would eschew is really that of "imperative" heterogeneity, the all-knowing, all-controlling, and all-calculating control system (glorified as the savior of humanity) of second-order (technocratic) sustainability. On the other hand, larger incongruous assemblages imply an inoperative community, in Nancy's sense, and an inoperative subjectivity. Subjectivity returns, if only as a reject, in the repurposing and expending of whatever energy—physical, social, symbolic—is left over (and is unassimilable) at and after the end of the growth economy.

Note that Bataille's limits to growth are not the same as those of Donella Meadows et al. *(The Limits to Growth).* For Bataille, growth is limited in the sense that the system (biological, industrial, intellectual, sexual) produces *too much;* that which is in excess must, however, still be somehow consumed (rather than reinvested), thus preventing a disastrous oversaturation (and destruction) of the system. This results in the "need" for expenditure, which can never be coerced or repressed in communities, and which is perverted in capitalism. But note also that, for Bataille, since those objects in excess are of necessity *not* useful or useable, and are not objects of triangular desire, they will carry an affective (energetic) charge completely different from the placid and manipulable ones of modern consumerism. Their power will be in social action,[35] not measurable quantity. They will be as senseless as their expenditure: dramatized objects of meditation, eroticism, scrounging. The Meadows version is apparently the opposite: the ecological input system cannot produce enough and its stocks are finite; we are overconsuming, and we must carefully rein in our consumption so that it tallies with what can be produced.[36] Otherwise, there will be systemic collapse. I do not see these two versions of limits as contradictory, but rather locked in recurrence. To "save" the world,[37] if indeed such a thing is possible, one must recognize the limits to growth both in Bataille's sense and Meadows's—but the two imply radically different modes of recognition. Stocks of usable material are indeed finite, and this risks the depletion of the world, as Meadows argues. Meadows's solution is to requantify the world on a different basis and legislate accordingly, carefully marshaling resource and energy inputs and conserving the remaining stocks. This results in a new historical juncture, necessary but in complicity with the logic of the world it would limit. The world is facing exhaustion, to be sure, but on the other hand the world is also overfull, as Bataille argues, and the excess, and the tendency to expend, do not just disappear, even in the midst of an overall depletion. Expenditure on the part of communities cannot be coerced out of existence; the tendency is too profound. At the complete saturation of the planet with human-generated detritus, another kind of expenditure is set off. Third-order objects defy measure, defy control and coercion, and enable "us" (the inoperative community) to affirm in turn a sustainability based not on accounting, but on an*other*. Other objects, *another energy* (that of the power of *mana*), other consuming practices, other economies will incessantly supplement what's left of the world of utility and sense. The standing reserve, like the statue (of sense, of human dominion), falls.

In 1938, Bataille, writing for his "secret society," *Acéphale,* states:

> We affirm . . . that man [*sic*] must not be valued according to the useful work he provides, but according to the infectious strength he can apply to drawing others into a free expenditure of their energy, their joy and their life: a human being is not simply a stomach to fill, but an excess of energy to be squandered.[38]

8 Marxism, Meditation, Consumption

Perhaps the most important question posed by the Anthropocene is this: Will doing away with capitalism be necessary for the introduction of a regime affirming not just economic and social justice, but ecological justice as well? What would such justice mean, and how could it be brought about?

Such questions assume that the degradation of the environment that has been going on certainly since the advent of advanced capitalism is indeed inseparable from capitalism. Reversing, or at least halting, global climate change, for example, would necessarily mean not just changing consumption patterns, but above all the global economic system. Capitalism is the cause; the eradication of capitalism is the necessary, if not sufficient, condition for the reestablishment of a livable climate and healthy worldwide ecology, stabilized for the foreseeable future.

The Marxist critic Ian Angus, in his book *Facing the Anthropocene: Fossil Capitalism and the Crisis of the Earth System* (2016), ties the fundamental destructiveness of capitalism to what he calls the "metabolic rift," the disproportion in speed between the metabolic processes of "nature" (Angus's word) and the relentless rhythms of capitalism. In order to accelerate productivity, capitalism requires that natural processes be accelerated, to the point of ecological collapse. The incessant demand for growth—more unregulated production, more money in the system, more profits, more toxic stuff—leads to the collapse not just of local ecological systems, but now of worldwide systems. Angus writes:

> Nature's cycles operate at speeds that have evolved over many millennia—forcing them in any way inevitably destabilizes the cycle and produces

> unpleasant results. Fertile land is destroyed, forests are clear-cut, and fish
> populations collapse, all because capitalism needs to operate at speeds much
> faster than the natural cycles of reproduction and growth. (122)

Speed and growth, it would seem, are inseparable: more must always be produced, and more quickly. Slowness is inefficiency, loss of profit, loss of time. But while time is always more limited, and acceleration of consumption and degradation always faster, the finitude of available earth resources means that collapse is inevitable.

This is the fundamental tie between the Anthropocene and the capitalist epoch. Clearly the Anthropocene is not reducible to capitalism; Angus is reluctant to use the recent catchphrase "Capitalocene" because, in his telling, capitalism has preceded the Anthropocene, and the Anthropocene will still be in force long after the passing of capitalism (232). In Angus's view, what has intensified the ecological crisis of the earth has been the ever-greater consumption, over the last sixty years, of fossil fuels. The term "fossil capital" (Andreas Malm) indicates, however, that capitalism has been greatly accelerated through the use of fossil fuels so that economic growth is accompanied by "a sustained growth in emissions of carbon dioxide" (135).[1] It is the burning of first coal and then oil on a massive scale that has intensified the inexorable growth of capitalism worldwide, and the consequent ever-faster disruption of the climate.

Angus's identification of capitalism and ecological catastrophe is indisputable. What is in question is the thesis that only the elimination of capitalism can somehow heal the metabolic rift, and reestablish a justly proportioned world in which natural processes and human-led ones can coincide. Angus himself recognizes that the prime culprit is more fossil capitalism than capitalism per se. But one could argue, as Malm himself tends to, that fossil capitalism is a kind of inevitable outgrowth of earlier capitalism—that the need for ever-increased profits, the mobility of productive facilities, the docility of labor, all depend on the ever-greater implementation of the fossil fuel regime. Fossil capitalism, then, has been there, in germ, from the start, from before the start. But does Marxism offer an effective alternative? Angus notes that "capital exploits labor and nature to produce goods that can be sold for more than the cost of production" (113), but the fact remains that Marxism is a labor theory of value—that the value of goods is determined primarily by the amount of labor that goes into their production. Nature certainly provides the raw materials, but Marx's position in *Capital* is far from a "natural capital" kind of argument, such as that proposed by Herman Daly.

My point would be that a Marxist economic regime as an alternative is somewhat wanting: it is not an automatic solution to the crisis of the Anthropocene. Consumption in Marxism is not all that different from capitalism. One could cite the obvious fact that the communist regimes of the world, such as the Soviet Union, East Germany, and so on, in their day polluted just as much as, or more than, their capitalist counterparts. They rewarded their elites with more opportunities and more stuff. People voted with their feet because they wanted basic freedoms (of speech, religion), and they wanted to be able to work hard, make more money, and buy more stuff. Communist countries where consumption is the most restrained offer examples only of involuntary restraint—that is, poverty (moderation of the scale and pace of consumption) as the result of the harsh imposition of a badly planned economy, as in Cuba (nevertheless, or perhaps for this reason, one of the very few countries in the world, if not the only one, that today have achieved the sustainability gold standard: the conjunction of a very low per capita carbon footprint with a generally high level of human development [education, literacy, health care]).[2] One has the impression that, if given the chance, the citizens of communist countries would consume just as much, and just as happily, as the citizens of the western centers of capitalism.

I don't want to bash current communist regimes, or other countries that are called "developing," just because they, in principle, will soon have, or at least would like to have, the luxury of consuming (and wasting) as much stuff per capita as do we, the consumers of the West. Angus would argue that, once we have transitioned away from capitalism, these countries can have prosperity without the injustice and ecological ills of the "developed" world. And the West, too, will do the same, but presumably only by doing an about-face in its current modes of production and consumption. But the problem, I think, lies not only with capitalism and the metabolic rift, but with consumption itself. We identify consumption with capitalism, and Angus, quite rightly I think, associates fossil capital especially with the rise of particularly intense capitalist consumerism.[3] But nowhere does Angus consider what it means to consume. The Anthropocene is not simply the result of capitalism; it is the result of consumerism, which makes possible the purchase, use, and disposal of the ever-increasing quantities of energy-intensive materials for which capitalism is responsible and through which capitalists derive profits. Can we do away with consumerism, though, by simply doing away with capitalism? How?

We've seen, in the introduction, Bill McKibben's model of a nonconsumerist society: rural Vermont, in effect. Such a world is one in which people find satisfaction not in accumulating things and comparing their economic status but rather in being socially engaged on a personal and community level. A minimum but adequate income, volunteering, maintaining friendships, hanging out with others rather than just looking at one's smart phone and/or driving around ("multitasking")—all are antidotes to consumerism. *Gemeinschaft* rather than *Gesellschaft*. Perhaps Angus would say the same thing. The problem, of course, is that everywhere in the world, including in rural Vermont, people want more stuff. They want to eat more meat. They want markers of success and they want what is sold as comfort. Who is to argue that they shouldn't have it? People move from the country, where there may be some *Gemeinschaft*, but there is grinding poverty, to the city, where they get their high dose of *Gesellschaft*, so that their children have better opportunities—to live a better and more fulfilling life. And no one today, on the Right or the Left, criticizes them for it. Everyone is in favor of the end of poverty on a planetary scale, and for the right of people to raise their standard of living. Nothing could be more hypocritical than the criticism, on the part of jaded and well-traveled first-worlders, of people who simply want what those first-worlders already have. As the standard of living rises worldwide, which most of us see as a good thing, the metabolic rift widens. The Brundtland ideal of development as opposed to growth seems distant indeed. To give McKibben credit, his ideal of low consuming small-town life is at least an attempt to imagine what "durable" development would look like outside the trap of consumerism.

For what then would or could one renounce consumerism? For Guy Debord, the situationist, and a good Hegelian, consumerism is both the product and the method of the enforcement of alienation. In essence, in capitalism one tries to buy one's way out of alienation, which ironically only casts one further into alienation.

> From the automobile to television, all the *goods selected* by the spectacular system are also its arms for the constant reinforcement for the isolation conditions of the "lonely crowd."[4]

> But consumable survival is also something that must always augment, it's something that contains privation. If there is nothing beyond augmented

survival, no point where its growth can cease, it's because it itself is not beyond privation, but rather that it's become a richer privation. (41–42)

This would seem to reverse the model proposed by Angus; here it's the spectacle, as commodified, that enforces and proliferates the alienation/privation that characterizes capitalism. Growth is a function of this privation; it's almost as if consumerism breeds itself, and capital as a factor becomes much less prominent. People consume more to overcome their existential alienation, and this only intensifies their alienation. Thus we have the ever-increasing speed of alienation and intensity of consumption, another type of metabolic rift. In any event, Debord does not write of the fossil fuel model that makes for intensified capitalism, or of the ecological devastation that is its consequence; here it seems that if consumerism is taken down, capitalism will fall with it—rather than, as in Angus, the other way around. Debord's analyses are nevertheless crucial in that he identifies the central problem in consumerism. His alternative, offered not so much in *Society of the Spectacle* as in his earlier situationist writings, poses a *détournement* that, as in surrealism and Walter Benjamin, imbues the found object with a kind of parodic countermeaning and subversive force. As I will argue in the next chapter, this may be the most important tactic for repurposing consumerism.[5]

Assuming, rightly or wrongly, that the end of consumerism will beget the end of capitalism still begs the question: How then to wean people from consumerism? People cannot seem to get out of their craving for an ever "richer privation"; call it privation or surfeit, it satisfies to the very extent that it doesn't. Call it the potato chip theory of capitalism. That, after all, is the point that we can all agree on: if acquiring things was that satisfying, there would be no need to continue with the demand for more new things. One and done would be the full story, and capitalism, along with eco-catastrophe, would sputter out in an automatically no-growth world (the dream of eco-technocracy). So a certain frustration is inherent to, and presupposed by, a model of consumerism that nevertheless is in demand, and admired, nearly everywhere (it might have been "made in USA," as Jean-Luc Godard would put it, but it has become global). Perhaps people *want* this frustration—just as the satisfaction of desire is endlessly frustrated by consumerism, so too the satisfaction of frustration must endlessly be intensified by desire in consumerism. People like the tease, they are defined by it. As in the death drive, consumers like the heightening of tension (and the attendant frustration) before the ultimate release of energy. But is frustration the only way to intensify the lack of gratification offered by consumerism? How to imagine this lack? And how to conceive of the object associated with it? Is there another object or kind of object that might offer an intensified lack of both frustration and satisfaction? What would a consumption of another kind of object lead to? An object that's constituted less by measurable, "embodied" energy than by the virulent burn off of energy? Might the basic problem lie not just in capitalism per se, as in the way, in the fossil fuel era, the foundation of capitalism, consumerist consumption, is enacted? And does the problem lie not so much with consumption itself as with consumerism—that is, with a certain limited "experience" of the object?

In any event it's clear that what's needed is a more thorough consideration of consumerism and the consumed object. The Marxism of Angus does not allow for such interrogation. Nor really does that of Debord. Both assume that once somehow weaned from consumerism, people will be happy, nonalienated, nontormented by ecological degradation, and will never look back. This can clearly be seen in a long citation that Angus takes from Ernest Mandel, a prominent Marxist theorist. Mandel writes:

> We are convinced that once that satisfaction [of "basic material needs"] is assured in a society where the incentives for personal enrichment, greed, and a competitive behavior are withering away, further "growth" will be centered around needs of "nonmaterial'" production (i.e., the development of richer social relations). Moral and psychological needs will supersede the tendency to acquire and accumulate more material goods. (199)[6]

This is not that different from the Technocracy Inc. line of the 1930s and its eco-progeny; there, too, a rationalization of society was dependent upon, and presupposed, a fundamental human refusal of consumerism as a mode of life and a strategy for the fulfillment of desire (musical, artistic, and charitable activity would come to the rescue). Debord's argument has the virtue of showing that consumerism is more powerful than a simple psychological or social aberration instilled by capitalism—that it is, in a sense, a product of a dialectic of desire for satisfaction that is attainable only through frustration. But since Marxist theory in recent times seems to set relatively little store by the labor theory of value—Angus himself shifts the crucial speedup of capitalist value to the intensified surplus value provided by fossil fuels—we get to the point where the Marxist alternative is little different from that offered by the Technocrats. Perhaps one could say that the

Marxists are less hierarchical, more prone to considerations of social justice without the heavy burden of centralized (strategic) decision-making—but that is precisely the area where historical Marxism, as embodied in communist strategy, grotesquely failed. In practice, Marxism has never been able to separate itself from an intense centralization. How the populace might come to reject consumerism without a centralized (and coercive) strategy has never been made clear, either by Marxists like Mandel, or, as I've argued in chapter 4, by the (seemingly Right-leaning) Technocrats before them, or by the more progressive eco-critics who follow them.

Another way of putting this is that the state of exception needed to impose the reign of ecological law risks being identified with what Bataille would call "imperative heterogeneity." Sovereignty in this sense is the lawless act of imposing law, the unconditional origin of the conditional.[7] Every system of law, even the most humane and democratic, would seem to need a moment of instantiation, of institution, a performative in and through which law comes into action; but the paradox, and problem, is that that act of instantiation itself will necessarily be outside the law. But what are the parameters of this lawlessness? Does the sovereignty of legal/political institution necessarily imply some violent act of exclusion in the moment of foundation? This would certainly be the case for the fascist leaders whose "elevated" sovereignty is analyzed in Bataille's "Psychological Structure of Fascism." Perhaps there is another version of sovereignty, one in which the founding of a regime—economic, political—is *not* violent or coercive. Where, in other words, sovereignty is linked to "base" or subversive drives (as in Bataille) rather than to imperative and sadistic ones: the unconditioned without repressive hierarchies emanating from it.

E. F. Schumacher, in his well-known essay from 1973, *Small Is Beautiful: Economics as If People Mattered,* makes precisely this point: that an economy not based on a "Gross National Product" irrespective of what is being produced (consumption for its own sake, in other words) will necessarily entail a religious founding—in Buddhism. For Schumacher, the use of fossil fuels, which do violence to the planet, first and foremost goes against the tenets of Buddhism. The infernal dyad consumerism/fossil fuel consumption, each furthering the other, is obviously not the basis for a long-term economy because of fuel's finitude. Schumacher writes:

> Simplicity and non-violence are obviously closely related. The optimal pattern of consumption, producing a high degree of human satisfaction by

means of a relatively low rate of consumption, allows people to live without great pressure and strain and to fulfill the primary injunction of Buddhist teaching: "Cease to do evil; try to do good." As physical resources are every-where limited, people satisfying their needs by means of a modest use of resources are obviously less likely to be at each other's throats . . .

From the point of view of Buddhist economics, therefore, production from local resources is the most rational way of economic life.[8]

While Schumacher's position might seem commonsensical enough, I think his position marks a significant advance over the Technocrats and the Marx-ists. Both Technocrats and Marxists identify capitalism as the source of the problem—growing social injustice, ecological crisis—and both would re-place it. Both approaches rely on sheer rationality, and the stability of the object as a manipulable tool and repository of some quantifiable produc-tive input. In both cases, the state of exception in which the laws of their economic/political regime are instituted remains unspecified, and for that very reason one is led to suspect that some element of coercion (at least the threat of violence) will necessarily be involved. Schumacher, on the other hand, in putting forward Buddhism, emphasizes the fact that recy-cling and nonviolence are one and the same. Embracing an ethic of non-violence means instituting a regime of economic and political fairness; it also means founding an economy in which ecological degradation is a thing of the past—one that is, in common parlance, "sustainable."

> The teaching of the Buddha . . . enjoins a reverent and non-violent attitude not only to all sentient beings but also, with great emphasis, to trees. . . . Much of the economic decay of southeast Asia (as of many other parts of the world) is undoubtedly due to a heedless and shameful neglect of trees.
>
> Modern economics does not distinguish between renewable and non-renewable materials, as its very method is to equalize and quantify every-thing by means of a money price. (60)

A Buddhist economy, then, can only be instituted through nonviolence because its primary value is, precisely, nonviolence. Good recycling (up-cycling) is perpetual peace. This founding principle in a sense precedes any modern economy because it is a traditional religious (Buddhist) value: "cease to do evil." The law of recycling is based not on an unconditioned exception but on an eternal law, grounded presumably in values that are premodern and even prehuman: the laws of peace are those of trees. Bud-dhist economics entails conformity to laws of ecology that precede the insti-tution of economic laws through human violence, and the respect for these ecological laws is necessary for humans to continue living well, indefinitely, in the world.

While this theory is nicely coherent, it tends to neglect, I think, a sim-ple problem: people like to consume, and seem oblivious to *how* they con-sume. Schumacher's essay calls for an end to wanton consumption, and offers nonviolence as a way to attain this. Sustainability is nonviolence; it is inseparable from the politics of Gandhi and Dr. King. But the invocation of Buddhism is not in and of itself sufficient. There is a danger that Buddhism as a faith will become just one more alternative to consumerism, like artis-tic or athletic self-cultivation, or the volunteerism put forward by McKibben, along with many others.[9] All noble values, to be sure; all in principle can replace consumerism, but generally they do not. Why not?

People *like to spend;* they like to buy stuff, revel in the dissatisfaction of consumerism, they trash stuff, buy more, and go from there. They like being frustrated and engaging in high-risk behavior (the riskiest: risking the planet). If they're poor, they aspire to being rich (which is defined in the context of their culture: it is not an absolute) so they can be consumers. Consuming is the pleasure-laden sign that they have mastered the economy of the world. There's something about the quantifiable object—in terms of money, status, *jouissance,* whatever—that gets people going and gets them off, in the poorest countries and in the richest. There is an erotics of con-sumption. The object is not solely one of use value, and exchange value doesn't quite capture it either.

Any theory that would ground value in labor and above all in energetic inputs must, I would argue, consider what Bataille calls the "tendency to expend," not just on the part of the universe, but on the part of the post-modern public. Rather than a rigorous recycling, as Schumacher would have it, Bataille proposes, as we've seen, a universe in which there's always too much (or too much is produced). Natural systems themselves accu-mulate and transform energy from the sun; they cannot store it indefi-nitely, so they have to do away with it. In that simple sense, Bataille's theory is one of sustainability; all biological earth systems can only continue to maintain themselves by either "expending" what they cannot reappropri-ate or reinvest, or stop producing (or growing) in the first place (and then die off). Against Schumacher's generalized nonviolence, Bataille proposes a generalized violence: not of mean people, or of extrajudicial sovereignty, or of Carl Schmitt's or Ernst Jünger's endless conflict, but of earth systems themselves. We, as animals, as apes operating on a (perhaps) slightly greater level of sophistication than other animals, inevitably will realize that the wealth we produce will have to somehow be expended. We cannot artificially restrain ourselves to the point where we refuse to produce wealth; rather we will have to envision the best ways to spend it—to, yes, consume it. Therefore no ethical, religious, or political critique of consumerism will be up to the task: we are born to spend, and critiquing spending in general from a position of moral superiority is senseless.

But Bataille's violence of expenditure is not one (in principle) of hierarchical violence or wanton consumerist destruction. His sovereignty does not entail instituting the state, or enforcing an economic system; it is, rather, the sovereignty of the being who has (following Kojève) *nothing more to do*. Rather than founding a regime—of laws and distribution of wealth—that would accomplish something, this sovereignty is too low, too base; it is the unconditioned action of a nonagent (what Bataille called the *ipse*) losing itself in "not-knowing," in the impossibility of mastery and quantitative control.[10] It's what happens in the "ambivalence of the sacred," when sovereignty is the loss of the excess, the burn off. It is beneath or outside of the law, without taking on the role of somehow forcefully undergirding it (it is in this sense "outside the outside").

In this model the object itself is radically different. It is no longer good for anything, no longer a calculable term within the gross national product. It is not the embodiment of fossil capital. It is, on the other hand, the blind spot, the smear, in which the self in its deviance is constituted through its loss. Accumulation, stockpiling, bare life, utility no longer (or never did) characterize the object's pileup, encrustation, explosiveness, wasting away. Bataille's model is socially economic, but in and through religious practice. And, specifically, meditation. In meditation, the *mana* of the object, its ritual charge, is brought to bear on a reconceptualization of the world, and a radical alteration of the world in which consumption switches from being a measure of seemingly necessary and "useful" reckless, destructive pleasure (the vexed pleasure of the society of the spectacle: *consommation*) to the very action that will "save the world" *(consumation)*.[11] For rethinking the object, and rethinking the subject's economic and (non)subjective relation to it, is key to rethinking not just the future of economics but the future of the transformation of economics. In this sense, Schumacher was right:

Buddhist economics is the only economics that matters. The question is how we arrive at a world in which Buddhist economics matters. To do so we have to think consumption in a positive sense rather than a negative one. We all consume / expend extravagantly, and what we consume is other consumers consuming. Our sustainability always entails the loss of others' sustainability, and in that way, potentially at least, our own as well. The face of the consumed other—plant, animal, weird object—stares back at us from an infinite remove. Our sustainability, in other words, is the incessant risk of sustainability.[12] But our consumption is also the affirmation of a larger autopoiesis. The question is: How can we rethink consumption, just as we rethink sustainability, situating it outside of the capitalist—but also technocratic—orbit, and, with that, how can we rethink the object, in order to move toward something like "Right Livelihood"? How can we rethink energy "use," which constitutes us as beings on earth, away from the dour constraint / restraint model, and enact it as something that energizes, motivates, burns (in the space supplementing the subject–object distinction)?

Bataille was no Buddhist, and he at any number of points criticizes Buddhism.[13] But for the moment, I would like to argue that elements of his approach, specifically those having to do with meditation, are at least operating on the same turf as Buddhism. Consider, for example, how he describes his meditative practices in *Inner Experience*:

> I come back to ecstasy before the object.
>
> The mind awakening to inner life is, however, in quest of an object. It rejects the object which action proposes for an object of a different nature, but cannot do without an object: its existence cannot close in on itself. . . .
>
> I will say this, be it obscure: the object in experience is first of all the projection of a dramatic loss of self. It is the image of the subject. The subject tries at first to go to move towards its fellow being. But once it has entered into the inner experience, it is in search of an object like itself—reduced to interiority. . . . The situation of the object which the mind seeks must be objectively dramatized. Starting from the felicity of movements, it is possible to stare at a vertiginous point which should contain, in an interior fashion, all that the world holds *[recèle]* that is torn apart *[déchiré]*, the incessant slide of all to Nothingness. In other words, time.[14]

This "point," this object, is a transformation of the self, or of a loved one, in a death agony.[15] This is the point before which one meditates: an object that is an image of oneself transformed in such a way that one completely leaves the productive rounds of "action." The "identification" with an other is an identification with another in its (her/his) absence, its loss; it is an identification with oneself *as* loss. Hence Bataille's meditation before the image of the execution of a young Chinese man:

> In any event, we can only project the point-object through drama. I've had recourse to overwhelming images. In particular, I stared at *[je fixais]* the photograph—or sometimes my memory of it—of a Chinese man who must have been tortured during my lifetime. (119; translation modified)

The well-known image of a man being literally cut to pieces hardly makes for the usual feel-good themes of meditation exercises. But the image, or its memory, is an object of the sort that reflects back to the subject the very nature of its subjecthood—as riven, dismembered, emitting a kind of negative light: "Thus I cease being anything more than a mirror of death, in the same way that the universe is the mirror of light" (122). This may very well be the sovereign "stain" of Lacanian subjectivity, but notably lacking the imperative (and enjoyable) sadism that would enforce it.

This subjectivity, at the same time, has the very power of the totemic object as analyzed by Durkheim: with its power to shock, its emitting of fluid, electrical forces.[16] These are a sort of "vital principle" that can induce illness, but also can instill a shock "by which the reproduction of the species is assured."[17]

A totemic object, but, for Bataille, a cursed one, and an object not in a ritual that brings people together or aids in personal or social reproduction, but one in which the "self" "streams" out in the direction of its other—which is a *semblable,* a twin, death itself, a loved one, perhaps dead. The object of meditation, then, is an object whose importance is that it is from the past, represents or dramatizes, packs a physical punch, and delivers the subject not only to an "ecstasy," but to a "communication" outside of itself. (But why could it not be from the future, as well?)

Bataille specifically relates his meditation practice to that of St. Ignatius of Loyola, the founder of the Jesuit order, who recommended, in meditation exercises, that a postulant go into a "peaceful room" and "have the feelings he would have had on Calvary" (119). But St. Ignatius, of course, prescribes this meditation of agony and death along with a consideration of other, let's say, more life-affirming themes. For Bataille, it's death all the way down, but mediated, so to speak, via the totemic object (the photograph, what it represents)—a double of the subject—and a vision that puts the stable vision of practical objects itself in question.

Bataille's left-handed sacred strips, I would argue, the community-building power from the meditative process. At least at first. If anything, we could associate Bataille's practice in these passages with a Buddhist meditation on *tanha*, that is, on "thirst" or "craving." In the Buddha's Sermon at Deer Park, he indicates Four Noble Truths, and explains the cause of suffering *(dukkha)* and its cure. The cure for craving is not so much a furious effort to suppress it, but rather an affirmative meditation on it. As Robert Wright notes, following the Buddhist philosopher Miri Albahari:

> *Tanha* is inextricably tied to the sensation of self, and [the] overcoming [of] *tanha* is therefore tied to the experience of not-self. . . . *Tanha* is deeply involved in your sense that the self is bounded; *tanha* sustains and strengthens the sense of boundedness that, during the exterior not-self experience, weakens.
>
> After all . . . if you thirst for something—hot chocolate, say—then you are painfully aware of the gap between yourself and that chocolate, and that means you have a conception of the bounds of your self.[18]

Tanha, put another way, is a typical object of everyday consumption. It is, we could argue, the very motor of capitalist consumer society. When we want something, and we don't have it, that object is charged with a force, but not that of *mana*—rather it is the force that is absent. We could say it is a counter-*mana*. Rather than radiating some kind of social energy, the object only communicates to us, in its absence or in its disappointing or parodic presence, the limits of our own self, and the limits of discursivity (I do this to attain it, I avoid doing that to lose it) involved in its (momentary) attainment. Capitalism, to put it crudely, through the consumerism with which it is inseparable (and which is its motor), reinforces the bonds of the acquisitive and calculating self. Opening that self out to dread and loss—Bataille's unconditioned *ipse*—affirms the passage from capitalism to a gift economy, the point at which the energetic model of capitalism opens out to the end of the world, the unthinkable and blind future after capitalism.

Wright also makes the point, again via Albahari, that *tanha* involves not only the desire to attain, but the desire to be rid of (210). If something is undesired, it too indicates a "boundary," a hard border between self and not-self. One overcomes this *tanha* through a meditation that involves not a rejection of it, but rather a "feeling of aversion and anger [. . .] in a neutral way" (210–11). Rather than affirming by consciously rejecting, in other words (which only reaffirms the self as agent), one neutralizes through identification and affirmation. In Wright's case, he goes from feeling anger at a snoring fellow (non)meditator to simply "observing the aversion mindfully." The snoring ceases to be outside, and becomes simply a part of his nonself, a co-communication with the "exterior version of the not-self experience," which Wright expresses as "the feeling [of aversion] and his snoring as a kind of single system or organism, unified by communication" (210).

With this account in mind, we can reconsider Bataille's "Digression on Ecstasy before an Object." Here *tanha* for Bataille would be the fear of death, both his own and that of a lover, and of beings he doesn't even "know" (like the executed Chinese man, with whom he closely identifies). But there's much more to it than this; in Bataille's case death is both to be feared (hence it is the source of *angoisse*) and affirmed, desired. This entails the affirmation of life to the point of death, with both fear and affirmed (sacrificial) suicide, in a sense, neutralized through dramatization, representation. Meditation (like consciousness itself, but in a different way) is an aftereffect of the figural process of autobiographical self-nomination, the rhetorical machine working now to generate not the finite self so much as the loss of that self in the moment of death.[19] Hence the focus on a single point, with its power projected back onto the subject, which then loses itself in not-knowing, becoming the "mirror of death." Clearly, as in the Buddhist take on *tanha*, Bataille is neutralizing through accepting the very thing that he most dreads and (in an ascesis) desires:

> I fix a point before myself and I represent this point as the geometric space of all existence and of all unity, of all separation and of all anguish, of all unfulfilled desire and of all possible deaths.[20]

Here he is specifying the *tanha* that is outside him, projected outward. But immediately, the power of this object—imaginary, projected, and yet all too real—is internalized through what Bataille himself calls, in *Inner Experience,* "communication," the streaming movement of his self outward and back in which its limits (and his own) are overcome, in sovereignty:

> I adhere to this point, and a profound love of what is in this point burns me to the point of refusing to be in life [*être en vie*] for any thing other than what

is there, for this point which, being together the life and death of a loved one, has the explosiveness [éclat] of a cataract. (121; translation modified)

What's interesting now is that the affirmation of death in life, or vice versa, is also tied to the "life and death of a loved one." Bataille meditates on not only his own death, or finitude, or death in general, or the Chinese man's death, but on the death of another *who is loved*. We are not told who this person is—one could certainly speculate[21]—but what is most important is that the point, in meditation, allows the affirmation and accession to not-knowing through the representation of the infinite distance of the other in death. The meditating lover and the dying loved one form, as Wright would put it, a "single system."

The power of the object, then, is the rerouted power of the *tanha* not as consumable but in its state as affirmed point, as representation in a dyadic relation that opens out the isolation/boundaries of the self and its simple fear of death. It's not simply a question of neutralizing the object of fear or desire (or annoyance), and thus calming oneself, but of radically affirming it in anguish. The point is a fetish, we could say, but one that defeats the avid self that would cherish or attempt to maintain or restrict itself, and the object as well. Its power is linked to a "communication" with the other that overcomes both that other and the self that reflects and doubles it; both through meditation accede to a not-knowing. There is a social moment, in other words, but that moment is not of an exclusivist community; rather the *partage* is both a conjoining and a radical severance (death). Thus the movement toward the "cataract," the explosive "fluid escaping from points," is a linking of not-selves in a not-community. An inoperative community in the present, to be sure, but also in the past: the power of the point is tied to representations of lost ones, loved ones, personally known, or only imagined.[22] And why not others of the future, not yet born, or fated not to be born? The self is caught in an infinite Pascalian gap between two infinities: the infinitely small of the disappearing point, and the infinitely large of the space-time continuum in which lovers and others are "communicated with" and spent in the inconceivable spaces of past and (perhaps) future. Not the placid and feel-good meditation of Wright's Buddhism, perhaps, but a charged one in which all desires are energized, affirmed, and lost. In between, so to speak, the not-self, the *ipse,* is the opening out to a movement that denies its ideal proportions in limitation.[23] The fundamental disproportion of the meditating subject is one of streaming both outward and inward, in ecstasy. This ecstasy itself is the aftereffect of the rhetorical movement of representation and communication.

This post-Pascalian disproportion is that of time, but not one of a productive time, or of the happy eternal return as critiqued by Benjamin. Instead, the object-point is situated in a repetitive temporality of loss: a recurrence in which it incessantly, "at every moment of the experience," can represent an other, personified in a death agony: "it can flail its arms, scream, burst into flames" (118; translation modified). A dirty eternal return; the openness to time is the resilience of the economy of the not-self in ecstasy.

I would emphasize in all this the dual aspect of the object, both inner and outer. Inside, it is the point, relaying back to the rent subject its own lack of sharply defined identity, its own opening, in the *ipse,* to dissolution and "communication." But there is an outer one as well: time is not exclusively of the subject, but of the object (and its representation), in its incessant progress leading it into, and out of, death, its intimacy and infinite distance: the time of an eternal return of the fall. And between these two, linking but dividing them, stretches the line of anamorphosis, the outside of the outside, the sharing of separation and division *(partage).*

I mention this not only to recall my earlier discussions of time in Bataille and Benjamin's model of revolution and messianism, and of Nancy's community; what interests me here is the relation of time to the object in the world of consumption. The object charged with the totemic principle operates both in the practice of the meditating subject and in the larger messianic economy in society and history. Meditating on the eternal return of the dying or flaming object—personified or not—leads to *another* consumption, one tied not to simple satisfaction of imagined needs, but to the affirmation of an interiority in community with other lovers, in death or dissolution. The commodity fetish is consumed, set ablaze *(consumé),* in the "ecstasy before the object." The others are loved in their moment of dissolution, their absence from control or domination by the subject. They are the objects that resist fixed objecthood; they propose a kind of double identity for the subject at the moment they deny it. If capitalist consumerism *(la consommation)* entails a momentary jolt of competitive enthusiasm as marketing device, the objects of meditation are the explosion of the subject in joy ("before death") in a repetitious identification with an other whose moment opens out to an infinity (as Pascal would say) of fire *(la consumation).* Buddhist economics from this perspective cannot entail sober renunciation; such a thing is unimaginable, because historically speaking, at least, people have rarely been known to renounce, in a sober way, the consumption of objects (or their own consumption by objects).[24]

It's important to remember this other consumption when imagining a future economy, outside of the one we now know. Schumacher indicates the problem concisely:

> Modern economics . . . considers consumption to be the sole end and pur-
> pose of all economic activity, taking the factors of production—land, labor
> and capital—as the means. The former, in short, tries to maximize human
> satisfactions by the optimal pattern of consumption, while the latter tries to
> maximize consumption by the optimal pattern of productive effort. (58)

Productivism and consumerism go hand in hand; consumerism in this way has ties to the Marxist tradition, which stresses above all production and productivity and (albeit supposedly rationalized) consumption. As Jean Baudrillard puts it in *The Mirror of Production*:

> If there was one thing Marx did not think about, it was discharge, waste,
> sacrifice, prodigality, play, and symbolism. Marx thought about production
> (not a bad thing), and he thought of it in terms of value.[25]

Baudrillard in the same text (43) stresses the distance between Bataille's "symbolic" exchange—which entailed the charged destruction of both goods *and* values—and the quite literal exchange, based on use value, put forward by Marx.[26] Nevertheless, in *The Accursed Share* Bataille does invoke the ritual destruction of goods (potlatch) and, as I've already mentioned, links the burning off of surplus production that cannot be reintegrated into the economy—the Bataillean limits to growth—with religious practice. He does so precisely to demonstrate that ritual or sacrificial destruction as an economic strategy—planned or not—is profoundly linked to the repetitious moment of meditation in which the self focuses on, and loses itself, in the no-thing:

> It is a question of arriving at the moment when consciousness will cease
> to be consciousness of *something*; in other words, of becoming conscious
> of the decisive meaning of an instant in which growth (the acquisition of
> *something*) will resolve in expenditure [*dépense*]; and this will be precisely

self-consciousness, that is, a consciousness that henceforth no longer has *any thing as an object.*[27]

He adds in a footnote to the above passage: "If not pure interiority, which is not a thing." This not-knowing is what's left of intellectual practice in the absence of the thing that can be put to use, reinvested, and so on—and the opening-out of the self that would do that reinvesting. Or it's focusing on that absence, which is both self-consciousness lacking a thing (or self-consciousness of the self in "communication," its wounds bleeding) *and* an economic practice. The two cannot be separated. In this one brilliant move, Bataille ties together Vernadsky's notion of the burn off of material, economic and ecological surplus (the passage over the "limits to growth" as a tactic of the biosphere), *and* the mediative practices of religions of the past and future (including Bataille's home-brew ecstatic visions). He links, in other words, symbolic and material expenditure, and one can, in fact, argue that they can be situated on a continuum.[28]

As Timothy Morton has written, concerning Buddhism:

Meditation, Gödel's Incompleteness Theorem, and loopy self-reference all evoke nothingness. A meditating mind is thinking and not-thinking at the very same time. A coherent logical system must be able to talk nonsense in order to be true to its own terms.[29]

This paradox of meditation applies to economic analysis as well. The not-thinking of the not-self (the *ipse*) and the analysis of the economics of material excess can't be separated: when the limits of growth and sense have been reached, and even gone beyond, not-growth and not-sense become the objects of not-awareness. And they are objects not subjected to the logic of sense and (as Morton points out) non-contradiction.

Thus, I would argue that Bataille was wrong when he criticized Buddhism at one point for its supposedly inward-turning emphasis. The passage I've cited from the end of *The Accursed Share* indicates that, for Bataille, meditation and the analysis of the economic and social conditions of wealth are inseparable. Intellectual and symbolic expenditure are inextricable. But at other moments, he could lose sight of this. Marcus Boone, in an essay on Bataille and Buddhism, sees Bataille as critiquing Buddhism, and the Christian tradition as well, in that, as Boone puts it, "Bataille argues that . . . Buddhism underestimates action in the world, insofar as it thinks of it as not meriting a response."[30] Bataille, in Boone's estimation, would somehow link meditative practice to rituals of destruction *in the world*—a consumption not in its consumerist sense, but in the sacrificial sense. In a recorded discussion of his work, in 1948, Bataille states:

> The profane world must in its turn be destroyed as such, which is to say that everything in the capitalist world which is given as a thing which transcends and dominates man, must be reduced to the state of an immanent thing, by being subordinated to consumption by man.
>
>   This is profoundly opposed to all ascetic attitudes, such as are found in Buddhism . . . At a certain point, it is necessary to propose the consumption of the produced object outside of all utility, as the final end, because the final end of man is to destroy what has been made.[31]

In this view of things, one can imagine a postindustrial world where the destruction of goods in giant potlatches would supplement meditative practices. Piles of smoking junk surrounded by howling crowds would appear in every suburb. An interesting fantasy, to be sure, but a dystopia that, as Boone is right to suggest, could also simply veer back in the direction of high consumerism as we know it under capitalism; a California landscape with yoga and Zen studios interspersed among the Mercedes dealerships. Bataille himself famously suggests the Marshall Plan as a model of "immanent" expenditure, but the Marshall Plan, as is well known, had as its purpose the economic revival of Europe after World War II, with, no doubt, the reestablishment in Europe of an intensified consumer culture (of benefit, through trade, to the American economy). So how then to think about a nonascetic, and also nonconsumerist, consumption?

If one considers Schumacher for a moment, one realizes, though, that the model for an "immanent" consumption is there already. Schumacher's world would have some elements in common, no doubt, with the world of precommunist Tibet analyzed (critically) by Bataille in one of the chapters of *The Accursed Share*.[32] Surplus wealth would be spent not on consumer items but on monasteries that support meditative practices. It would, in other words, support the "destruction of what has been made." Or what could be made. More important, destruction in Schumacher's Buddhism would entail not the lavish expenditure on vast communities of do-nothings, but rather the simple act of meditating instead of producing or consuming (transcendentally). Meditation as expenditure of time and of stuff that has never been made—the gaze turning from the wreckage of the past to the messianic future—would complement and even found a life of "simplicity and non-violence."[33] The poverty of meditation is both its power and its extravagance.

Sustainability, in other words, would have to do not with a closed economy of planning and calculation, but with a practice that embraces the wasting of time instead of stuff—meditation from the perspective of a capitalist consumerist society is just a waste of time—and perhaps the destruction of objects on a small scale (one thinks of Tibetan butter art, or the elaborate sand mandalas that are created and then destroyed), small, degraded and imperfectly recycled objects being the only ones that remain. Time now entails not an anxiety-process fixated on the indefinite and featureless continuity-return of utilitarian life but rather the affirmation of the discontinuities of meditative practices. Practices that focus on the point that is the death of the world, of our world—in flames, in the pileup of destitute, charged and self-consuming artifacts.

This (nondialectical) resolution of the seeming contradiction between "death-bound" and ultimately "constructive" modes of expenditure is already present in Bataille—indeed it is the central concern of *The Accursed Share*. Bataille's main focus at the end of that work is, after all, the linkage between the "interiority" of his own harrowing meditative practices and the beneficial modes of mass-scale expenditure that will save the world from the nightmare of nuclear war. Replace (or supplement) imminent war with imminent (and indeed already upon us) cataclysmic climate change, and we see how timely Bataille's considerations really are. Just as, for Bataille (in 1949), the avoidance of nuclear war is ultimately inadvertent, an aftereffect of the embrace of expenditure without return ("self-consciousness" linked to international policies of giving), so today sustainability can only be the inadvertent aftereffect of a general economy of the fiery consumption in and of meditation. (And meditation-expenditure is an aftereffect of sustainability: resources—the limits of the self—are marshaled in order to be squandered [another version of the Marshall Plan].) To "detourn" Breton, sustainability will be meditative or it will not "be."

Few books published in recent years would seem to have less to do with questions of sustainability than Cormac McCarthy's *The Road*. The plot is simple to the point of absolute minimalism: A man and his son survive an unnamed, apocalyptic event. The earth has lost all life except the human: they, and small numbers of other survivors, are surrounded by dead towns, abandoned homes and shops, dead forests. The two set out on the road, pushing a shopping cart filled with food and their belongings, trying to reach the sea. Why? There is no reason; the man's wife has committed suicide precisely because she sees no reason to go on when all possibility of "success" has disappeared. But what does success in this context mean? What is survival? What is the future? What does the future mean when all one can do is stare at the accumulated ruins of the past? What is the future when there are no future generations? Yet the two face forward, and go on.

This is the starting point: How to meditate on what we fear the most, the ultimate *tanha*—not just global climate change, but the death of the world, total unliveability? The point at which sustainability becomes unthinkable . . .

The monstrosity depicted in the novel is our own: we too live with the suspicion that the world is already dead, that it is too late.[34] Bataille could meditate on his own death, or that of a loved one; he does not meditate on the death of his world, on the death of the world, both the social world, and the ecological world with humans in it. But there's something even more perverse here; it's not a question of the end of the world, but of its end *with us surviving*. Humans are the aftereffect of the destruction of their own world. People are still around, still certain, but all they can be certain of is their own death. Every other living thing, and all the other worlds, are gone. The "survivors" mourn themselves while still alive—and as they look forward. As Bataille well knew, death can never be "experienced." But it certainly can be meditated upon, which puts the limits of the self in question in ways more fundamental than does simple extinction.

So—extinction after the fact. The dream of surviving one's own death, all the while meditating on future death. This is the uncanny survival of extinction: the man and his son's journey, and its narration, after the death of everything. Meditation, as in Bataille, takes on an autobiographical cast. The dead world expresses itself: a prosopopoeia in which we visualize the world without us, but with us in it. Total extinction is also the complete lack of sustainability: "survival" in such a world means (according to the novel, at least) scavenging the few remaining cans of food from the shelves of abandoned houses and boats. Nothing in this world can be recycled (since recycling depends on cycles of life); there is no "ecology" in any sense.

This, then, is the ultimate meditation on what is most fearful: not just the end of the world, but the impossibility of death in the midst of generalized death. The ultimate autobiography written from beyond the grave. The certainty of death looms, but there is also separation from it, the inability to attain it. And not only that: the inevitable refusal to die, the inability to end it, the refusal of suicide. A meditation on death is not simply death. And indeed death is infinitely remote, because it can only be known, named, from the perspective of the still-alive. But it does not free one from death, either. No matter what we do, no matter how much stuff is scrounged, death awaits us. Why then keep scrounging?

The absurdity of the novel quickly reverses itself, and reveals personal survival as an absurdity. This is Camus territory *(The Myth of Sisyphus)*: Why not just commit suicide? For Camus, this was the central question in philosophy. Camus had his answer, but the question is still with us, perhaps even more acute now that the death of the world can be foreseen with such hallucinatory precision, if not with complete accuracy or certainty. The world has been fully built out: there is "nothing left to do."

Death would seem to be a necessity, but it is also an impossibility; infinitely remote, it teases with its promise and its refusal. Meditating on death, we are locked in our not-self, gazing on a death that is our double. Even if we embrace it, will it, it refuses us, and replaces itself with that which is closest to us: our will to die. Consider what the old man, Ely, says to the man (the unnamed protagonist) when they meet on the road. Ely is alone, abandoned, his survival a complete mystery.[35] Yet he makes clear that he has no need for the man or his son. Ely says:

> Things will be better when everybody's gone. . . . When we're all gone at last then there'll be nobody here but death and his days will be numbered too. He'll be out in the road there with nothing to do and nobody to do it to. He'll say: where did everybody go? And that's how it will be. What's wrong with that?[36]

This personification of death at first seems silly, until one considers it from the perspective of the one who wants to die. He wills his own death, in order to defeat death. It's a Christian strategy: I happily anticipate my own death, in the knowledge that eternal life will follow. But here eternal life only belongs to death. One has not escaped life, but only passed it on to a personification of death, which lingers indefinitely after life. Life remains in death after all life has passed from the scene, but only in the impersonal and in principle endless turnover of the rhetorical machine (is it solar powered?). Personification cannot be lost, or, put another way, rhetoric is the grounding of life that maintains life even in its absence, as its absence. As Blanchot noted in his famous essay "Literature and the Right to Death," language (a mechanism of tropes) signifies things in their absence; to exist as things (hence represented, representable) they must be mortal, already dead.

Just as life is tenaciously resistant in its absence, so too is sustainability. In the complete absence of sustainability, *there is* (*es gibt*: "*it gives*") sustainability. The man and his son, and indeed all the characters of the novel, live fully within their carbon footprints—if such a thing were still possible. They waste nothing, they conserve everything of use that they can find, they uphold the aftereffect (or deferred effect) of sustainability. The absence of sustainability returns as its own ghost, its own necessity, and its impossibility, in the retelling of the life / death story of the trip. Everything is picked over, saved, repurposed, evaluated from the perspective of survival. It is all carefully classified and organized in the shopping cart. Yet this is sustainability for nothing, since the man and his son will soon die, and there can be no future of humanity. But living in the absence of a future, the death of the earth, is also a call to be sustainable. It is as irrational as the drive to survive in the era of the seeming death of God. In fact, surviving is being sustainable—willing one's own self-sustaining in the face of certain and inevitable extinction, as a narration. It is an inescapable, even if derisive, imperative. There may be a drive to sustainability, as there is a drive to expenditure, each logically and practically following the other. Sustainability as *dé-penser*, spending in a compulsive rhetoric of not-thought.

Sustainability is retrospective, it is always too late: when its necessity is recognized, and enacted, there is the recognition that it can achieve nothing but its retelling. Poverty generates the awareness of the necessity of sustainability (as an aftereffect of a mode of adaptation); absolute poverty, the poverty of the future as void, generates absolute sustainability as a recounting of the future's demise. Sustainability always looks back; it remains in life after life has passed from the scene. Sustainability is the rhetoric of life, the representation of life as certainty, as a continuity, as a recognizable narrative with head and tail—but projected erroneously, as a wayward figure.

Just as there is a community in meditation—the community of Buddhist economics, of the *Acéphale*—so there is a community of sustainability after the death of sustainability. That's what unites and separates. Ely, the old man, refuses to believe in community. He tells the man:

> I think in times like these the less said the better. If something had happened and we were survivors and we met on the road then we'd have something to talk about. But we're not. So we don't. (171–72)

An absurd statement: of course they're survivors, so they should talk, have a community, no matter how minimal. But Ely's point is well taken: they have not survived. They are only the "dead on leave," as Céline would say. Talk, community, survival, narration are all over. So is godhood: the man suggests to Ely that his son might be god, and Ely quickly retorts:

> Where men can't live gods fare no better. You'll see. It's better to be alone. So I hope that's not true what you said because to be on the road with the last god would be a terrible thing. (172)

Silence, disbelief, are all that remain. But Ely himself cannot really believe it. At one point he lets slip: "There is no God and we are his prophets" (170). This post-Nietzschean gem nevertheless indicates a desire for, and even a recognition of, a community: he says this of himself and the man, even though the man has suggested that God would "know" of everyone's death, even if there were no one left on earth to know. It's Ely[37] who implicitly argues for this community, not the man. But community remains only in the story of its impossibility, the narrative of sharing and splitting.

If Ely denies community in bad faith, the boy affirms it, not in good faith, but out of sheer naivety. His father always wants to move on; the son wants to wait, and help the abandoned boy they meet on the road, as well as old Ely. The novel presents this help as both an impossibility and a necessity: they have practically no food,[38] but despite this absence the imperative to give becomes only stronger. The "good" for which the boy is constantly searching and arguing for is nothing more than the embrace of food as the gift that cements the community; the "bad," nothing more than the joining of people into a roving band through the enslavement and eventual consumption of others (cannibalism), the transformation of the other into bare life, murdered meat. (The ultimate moment of horror in the novel is the man's discovery of a group of ragged survivors held prisoner in a base-ment, and his realization that they are nothing more than the food reserve of a gang of monsters [110–11].)

The sacred object—*mana* charged—is on the other hand the food scav-enged in the ruins, the point of meditation where the future, the (illusory) promise of survival, is a point of social connection and death. Food is charged with the "glowing" energy of love, the love of the man who gives everything to his son—"everything" now reduced to a few cans of pre-served fruit—up to the moment of his own death, his own self-sacrifice. This is the ritual, preserved in the vanishing point of the holy of holies, the son as embodiment of the ethic of giving, the convulsive point of the con-junction of life and death, waste, degradation, and exaltation:

> The nights dead still and deader black. So cold. They talked hardly at all. He coughed all the time and the boy watched him spitting blood. Slumping along. Filthy, ragged, hopeless. He'd stop and lean on the cart and the boy would go on and then stop and look back and he would raise his weeping eyes and see him standing there in the road looking back at him from some unimaginable future, glowing in that waste like a tabernacle. (273)

It's unclear what the "waste" is here: Is it the wasteland that surrounds father and son, the universalized death of the planet? Or is the future itself waste, the unassimilable element that keeps the tabernacle from rising above the world, isolated in pure transcendence? Is the future itself, then, the con-junction of the waste of the past and the sacred glow, the downward pull of the "good" back to the subterranean realm of extinction?

Sustainability as a motivating narration absurdly survives the Gaia hypothesis; on a dead planet, where recycling no longer reigns supreme, the object still returns, is recycled, as a sacred food that joins the community as it faces its own remote yet imminent death. (The energy of the sacred object is never outside the social practice of the *ipse*.) One can read this as a Christian allegory, as does the woman in the community the boy joins after his father's death: "She said the breath of God was his breath yet though it pass from man to man through all of time" (286).[39] But the woman's view-point is only one among many, and is eminently questionable: How can "all time" be imagined in the case of a world facing its imminent demise? How can God authorize an eternity—and stand as its metonym—when survival seems likely only for another few weeks, if that? And yet Ely's pronouncement of the death of God seems equally limited, since the community continues to exist, if only in the community of prophets of God's death. The novel can instead be read as an allegory of a sustainability in which conservation, such as it is in its complete impossibility, is an aftereffect not of grim restraint but of the consumption of sacred objects whose *emergy* is supplanted by the bolt of love.

One can only think again here of Bataille's meditation-point, the union of death and life (God's death as life, God's life as death?). The endless narration of this story, this horror, returns as meditative practice: the deleteriously absurd time of the return, the projection of past into future, and the excavation of future in the past. Resilience is the boy's messianic time, a focus on the charged gift, the opening in which the hope of loss is conjoined to the loss of hope. The angel looks backward because sustainability is the unanticipated aftereffect of these practices (because they are not practices in the sense of subject–object operations): postconsumerist consumption.[40] Consumption after consumption, sustainability after sustainability. "The incessant movement of all into nothingness."

Bataille writes in a footnote at the end of *The Accursed Share,*

> And alone in fact the madman [the autobiographical and Nietzschean figure of Bataille himself] will arrive at the *self-consciousness* I speak of, for reason, being consciousness, is fully conscious only if it has for an object that which is not reducible to it.[41]

The object is both energetic and social, together, and to re-view its energy profile its social character must be fully understood and embraced, *jusqu'à la mort.* Self-consciousness, both "collective" and "individual" (as if they can be disentangled), through the incorporation of the socialized object, both mutates as self (it is now the not-self, the *ipse*), and as consciousness (it is now no longer simply human). Self-consciousness comes to inhabit the desert, passing over and recycling—meditating on—the ruins of the subject–object relation.

9 The Dead, the Future

Scrounging and Gifting the Ruins

The ruins of war and capitalist exploitation (of which Benjamin and Bataille were thinking) are now doubled by the ruins of "postconsumer" waste (plastic scrap, food waste, the remains of automobility and domestic display) that may or may not be recycled, may or may not be recyclable. The repetition of history as revolution, and revolutionary recycling, revolution as recycling, all start to fuse together. War, famine, exploitation, are now repeated, and recycled, in and through consumerism and its imminent exhaustion.

But the angel is moving forward, albeit backwards. Forward into what? Will future generations be established on the ruins of the past? The trash? How? What is futurity in a time when we are focused, more and more, on the precise results and consequences of past practices, and on the uncertainty of the future, of the very existence of future generations, of the future itself as a thinkable category? Must the future be seen as clearly as we see the past in order to enter into it and make it possible? Can we love, like Nietzsche, our ignorance toward the future, along with a commitment to it as a realization? Can there be an embrace of the uncertainty and forceful charge of the found object—all that may be left—along with the certainty of its practical modes of recycling?

First, a key strategy remains for incorporating the waste of the past into the present and its future: our relation with the dead. In Cormac McCarthy's *The Road* the dead were, quite simply, absent, or they remained only as nameless body parts, triggering horror and the flight instinct. Their absence was a shattering presence, but in anonymity: in their masses they were largely invisible, their bodies only occasionally seen, pop-up monsters quickly fled. In the same way, the world itself was already dead. But even in *The Road* there is a glimmer of messianic hope: the few survivors rummage around, find bits of food to eat and junk to use, thereby valorizing and incorporating the recycled, ever returning the past as a way toward the future. It's an absurd future, to be sure, and an unthinkable one.

Vinciane Despret, in *Au Bonheur des morts*,[1] is, for her part, concerned with the role of the dead in the current iteration of our society. Most often, she notes, in Western societies the dead are "present" only as "non-existent," or as "phantasms, beliefs, or hallucinations" (19). In other words, according to Despret, when we consider our relations with the dead, most typically we consider their influence on us in light of our own psychology, our own ability (or inability) to mourn, their influence on us as we have internalized it in our own personal psychologies. In Despret's view, the other way of seeing the dead (so to speak) involves understanding their *active* role in our lives; they entail things to do, a "being to do" *(un être à faire)*:

> [To] affirm that the dead have "manners of being" *[manières d'être]* which make of them quite real beings in the register that is their own, that they manifest modes of presence which count and whose effects one can feel, is to be aware of the fact that there has been, each time, a "being to do" and a living person who has welcomed this request. . . . [The] dead have things to do, but they themselves have to be the object of a fulfillment *[doivent faire l'objet d'un accomplissement]*. (19)

The dead, then, are not mere phantoms who haunt our memories and cause us, voluntarily or involuntarily, to do things, which may be in our interests, or not. Rather they are projects, strategies, plans, which are accomplished in conjunction with the living. They function in the mode of a speech act, in other words, causing things to be done, rather than as constatives, which indicate only their own terrifying or onerous nonexistence.

In a fascinating aside, Despret argues:

> These questions are close to those posed by ecology in relation to the objects it studies. This is why I can claim that my inquiry addresses ecology. Ecology, because it interrogates the conditions of existence of those it studies, sets itself off from the questions typically valued by scientists. For them, as Isabelle Stengers notes, the question of existence, when it is posed, most often is in the sense of "can one demonstrate that this (gravitational force, atoms,

molecules, neutrons, black holes . . .) 'really' exists?"[2] This is not the ecological question. It has to do with the needs that must be respected in the continuous creation of a putting-in-relation *[mise en rapport]*. (20)

One remembers here Hinchliffe's and Whatmore's discussion of the ecology of animals in urban ecologies, like the black redstart (chapter 2). What's of interest to the ecologist is not so much the simple determined "existence" or "presence" of an animal in a given space, but rather its relations, the conditions of its activities, the probabilities of its movements, its future, its absence, too.

Thus mourning, for Despret, should not be conceived of as a relation to an absent presence, of importance exclusively to the person who is upset over that nonpresence.

> Those who learn to maintain relations with their dead thus really do assume a labor, which has nothing to do with mourning. It's necessary to find a place, in multiple ways, and in the great diversity of meanings that "place" can take on. . . .
>
> The first question posed by those who have left us *[les disparus]* thus registers not in time but in space. . . . We have always, throughout our history—and the invention of Purgatory, as we'll see, is only one episode—tried to find a place to lodge them, to shelter them, from which the conversation can be continued. Everywhere where the dead are active, there is the designation of a place. (20–21)

Facing the past thus entails facing the future as well. In a specific place, the dead are engaged in a project, in conjunction with the living. The past is active as it is projected toward the future. The historical return of the dead is also their movement, in object relations, toward the accomplishment of future responsibilities. The spatiality of the actions of the dead imply engagement of objects, as well as bodies; just as the dead are accorded a role, so too, dead objects may have a role to play. Objects that have been written off, objects that are absent, "out of order," that are somehow incomplete or uncompletable, depleted or destitute, engage with the living in a future oriented task. The dead, those we have known, but also the dead of history, are never simply extinct; they return, and so too does their history, our history. Their recycling, I would argue, an ecological activity if there ever was one, also implies their position in the ecology of places—

both "natural" and "cultural." Giving a face to a name—prosopopoeia—is also the trope of the historical return of the dead, their action in the construction of a world which is also dead, or dying. The world peopled by the living can only claim its future by recognizing itself as the space of the dead, charged with their sacred power of putting-in-relation. Dead objects, evanescent junk, aroused and lost through prosopopoeia, "I see dead people," faces (of humans, of animals) ever more distant, all come together, repeated endlessly, in the future of a world trying to face away from extinction.

The dead, though I don't think Despret stresses it enough, nevertheless retain a sacred status in their active participation in the world. The sacred in this case is not a subjective phantasm but, as Durkheim argued, an objective energy that binds society together, no matter how tragically. Objective as "outside," but outside the inside / outside distinction. The dead, in their intervention, help forge a society quite different from one, based on oppositions, that is closed, exclusive, policed from above. Incorporated and embodied in dead objects, they return to power a society that is *partagé*, in Nancy's sense, both sharing and rent, impossible to unify in a conventional, exclusionary, or coercive sense. This base heterogeneity of the object, of the dead as imperatives and as objects, can be seen today, on the streets, in dumpsters. The dead are not imaginary, they are quite precisely defined, precisely viewed, identified with a locale though not "present," and their action works to repeat an ecological im-balance in which communities form and deform, repeating a revolution that itself is only a repetition, a return, of the past.

Jeff Ferrell, in *Empire of Scrounge,* recounts a number of facets of the year or so he lived out of dumpsters, by necessity. Unemployed—disgusted, he has quit his position as a tenured university professor—Ferrell realizes that he will have to reclaim material abandoned on the street (in Fort Worth, Texas) simply to survive. Food, usable furnishings, metal parts, construction debris, all can be reused, or sold; he furnishes his home, eats, gives away toys, clothes, and sells materials that can be recycled or reused. But scrounging quickly becomes more than simply an individual survival strategy. As a criminologist and sociologist, Ferrell establishes a reflective relationship, so to speak, both with the other scroungers he meets on his daily rounds, and with the people who have discarded what are, in many cases, objects of conspicuous consumption, or objects that have a deep connection with their (or others') past lives (or a combination of the two: both personal objects, and glamorous, pricey ones as well). Ferrell makes it clear that in going through trash bags full of other people's stuff, he is not interested in what would amount to spying on them; he never googles people to see who they are, what they have done, if they are dead.

> I decided not to utilize discarded keepsakes and mementos as entrees into broader investigations of people's lives . . . Mostly this resulted from a certain allegiance to the empire of scrounge and a commitment to my immersion in it—that is, from a desire to see if the empire could explain itself on its own terms, through its own ensembles of the lost and found.[3]

The empire of scrounge is another counterworld with its own rules, its own morality, its own fidelity to the absent ones and to charged objects, which nevertheless intersects with official reality at unforeseeable and ungraspable points. One can open other people's bags, look at their discards, without a sense of shame or guilt. Knowledge is an integral part of this empire, it powers this counterrealm on any number of levels, but a key level is indeed that of a deep understanding of other people's lives, on a sociological level, and on a dramatic, narrative one as well. Trash knowledge is a speculative one, almost novelistic in one sense, but in another hypothetical, necessarily incomplete, both frustrating and fundamental. We know others by their residue, what they leave behind, we form links with them not through what they think is essential but through what they consider inessential. We look into the face of the other only in that other's garbage, the dead skin on their countenance, the photographic gaze of their unknown eyes, the stuff they are sick of seeing piled up in their house. We accept their project as a *détournement*. The gaze of the face in its infinite distance, returned, is always the repetition of the absent life of the other; the "original" is not present but is in community with us, in the reject.

> With disconcerting regularity my scrounging uncovered high school and college diplomas, marriage certificates, achievement awards, family photos and photo albums, sports trophies, baby keepsakes, college annuals, and other detritus of human endeavor come loose from its place within personal and family history. . . . Did a discarded family photo album denote a death in the family, a sudden relocation, a family falling apart? Did a discarded high school diploma or college annual suggest an existential breaking point in someone's life, their death—or simply an overcrowded closet? (87)

At one point, Ferrell discovers a *Bear Cub Scout Book* from 1954, realizes he knows from his childhood the owner listed on the book's title page, and calls the man to see if he wants the book back. He is rebuffed; his friend had been cleaning out the home of his deceased mother, and "didn't want it returned" (89). Refuse, in other words, really is refused; but that is what gives it its power. Our scrounger goes on to reestablish, or fantasize life stories for, a number of individuals whose trash he studies: a young woman who grows up, goes away to college, receives hopeful letters from potential suitors (which Farrell reads), marries, moves away, and so on (93); a "prominent local physician" whose documents go all the way back to his bronzed baby shoes (94); a local yuppy, who dumps many expensive items still in their original boxes, unopened (92).[4]

What to make of all this? In the empire of scrounge, as in *The Road*, everyone is always-already dead. The narrative of all lives constitutes sign systems of the absent; all are open to interpretation, to reconstruction, based on traces that the subjects, or their surviving relatives, have deemed superfluous. But in their superfluity, their fundamentally fragmentary and incomplete natures, these objects alone allow one to enter into contact with the profound mortality of those who have, as the French would put it, "disappeared" *(disparu)*. What a society of acquisition calls waste is the truest thing, the most exciting, the most intimate: we *envisage* the absent others through their discards, we engage with them in their projects, of which they may very well be ignorant, to which they may be opposed.

Ferrell himself notes this linkage between scrounge and signs—after all, the book's title recalls Roland Barthes's *The Empire of Signs*—and he concludes his section on the recovery (if it could be called that) of people's personal discards with this observation:

> [All the refuse] accumulated for me into a deep deliberation on life's transience. . . . Digging amid the detritus of people's lives, I came away with a disturbing sense of existential rubbish—a sense that we'd best live our lives like they matter, because ultimately, we're all disposable heroes. (95)

This is no doubt true; one can even go a bit further, and imagine a profoundly Christian take on rubbish, in which the scrounger meditates on it as St. Jerome meditated on a skull. Without God, however, the meditation is a purely "existential" one, a melancholic reverie on our swift return to dust which, one can at least hope, will somehow be recycled, and not consigned to a Rock of Ages crypt. But, with Despret in mind, something else could be proposed; if indeed one can only know others through their cast-offs—starting with the appearance and perhaps touch of their skin (which after all is, on the surface, only dead cells, quickly cast off), and then moving to our memories of their words, their gestures, their gifts—then the dead are with us, physically, just as they were in life. The relation to the other is always through (their own) junk, and the continuing project of living with them, carrying out their wishes, their projects, in conjunction with our own, is part and parcel with reconstructing their lives, and our own, through the use of sacred (charged) objects.

With garbage, and with the violation of its sacrosanct limits (breaking open bags, for instance), the scrounger faces back, into a redemptive history.[5] The work of reclamation is always transgressive, a violation of the limits of privacy, of the official economy, of the integrity of a life as closed off from the wishes and plans of others. We work with them to carry out those projects, which inevitably are also our own, since the acts of the dead can only come forward when refracted through those of the living. They share with us, irrespective of their wishes. They are not phantasms, they are companions, helpers, agents, directors, but what they do they do through us, willingly or unwillingly. In that sense their residue carries a powerful, even sacred charge, linking us with them and with others who are (for the moment) living, in a shared but separated community. We act in the world with them, but in a strange way their anonymity is part of their reclamation from the past and projection (with us) into the future. The empire of scrounge is the key element in that anonymity: as Ferrell reminds us, trash in the empire is not to be used to look up or pester people in "real life," out there in the (other world); it is to contribute the elaboration of the "empire," which nevertheless is not closed. It is sheer resilience, openness to death-bound time. The dead, or the absent—the difference hardly matters—are reaffirmed, reestablished through scrounging, and their labor, if only through the discarding of things (which is not a simple destruction or elimination, but rather a construction and a deconstruction at the same time), points to the world to come.

Recycling and reclamation of the past, then, are one and the same. The dead are not only of the past, but for the future, as are any and all cast-offs. Theirs is the prosopopoeia of the absent, projected forward in time. The reject-subject eats trashed food, recycles reject-objects, discarded metals, puts to use the flotsam and jetsam of everyday life. Ferrell opens bags in which baby pictures and pizza boxes are jumbled together. The grid of cultural and semiotic oppositions has crumbled: nothing can be excluded or placed. The pileup of ruins is inevitably repurposed, one way or another. The returning, rejected consumer fetish blows apart the world of consumer fetishes. And yet all this repurposing is of the future. But which future? A future that is lovingly unknowable but at the same time acutely anticipated, a project shared and split between us, the scroungers, the dead, and refuse itself, all we have of the past—precise but decayed, disgusting, elusive, nourishing. It is a past constantly reconstructed, in the acts of reading, reinterpreting, dismantling, and violating. The bricolage, the recreation of tentative, interfering, and doomed classificatory grids, is the only work left, violating the limits between the undead historical past and the project of the unknowable future. Scrounged objects are sustainable in a different temporality, one just outside the parameters of human purposes and ends.

This is a world of third-order sustainability, making do with the historically charged past shuddering into the future, a community of sharing and rending. How indeed to pass from past to future, through the null point, the zero hour, the impossible presence/present of environmental horror? The dead help us into the future, but they too (like us) don't know where they're going. Sustainability would only seem to "work" if we know both where we are coming from and where we are going; we can account for what has been expended, and we can precisely calculate the who and what of the future, the resources and products that will be produced and the populations that will consume them. But there's another sustainability, a general one of base recycling and gifting, one that recognizes the past only as a project of and with the dead, the past generations, and the future as a transgression of the limits and objects of fossil capital. It puts "us" in question to the extent that "we" are not members of a closed community (living vs. dead, producers vs. consumers, etc.), but outsiders of the outside. Survival is of something that may not even be human in any conventional sense, monsters (the living dead) cast down into a chthonian repurposing that affirms the fetishism of the lowered carbon foot(print).[6]

But there is no bottom to it, no ground of proportion if there is no imperative elevation. The etymology of "to sustain" is "to hold up," the Latin *sustinere*.[7] But what is up when there is no stable position from which one can ascend? Sustainability's meaning mutates when there is no coherent scale of distance and direction, no basis for departure and no direction home. Sustaining in a *general* sense, then, would imply a moving or drifting across, through, or down (what Ferrell does) uncharted, deserted, or vague spaces *(terrains vagues),* rather than stability (holding) in elevation (up). Ferrell does hold up a bag of refuse, but only to speculate on its contents and how they can be recycled and reinterpreted.

Ferrell may write of scroungers who are "unwilling or unable to submit to corporate employment's increasingly demeaning constraints" (167), but I think there is more to it than this. This is a community not of planning, but of its suspension (Latin *suspendere,* to hang up,[8] but, again, without the "up"): the society of the future in which survival depends upon one's ability to exist outside any planned and administered framework.[9] Indeed, this utopia is a threat to any such framework, and that is perhaps its true messianic potential: the community of the recycling of the historical fragments of a society once certain that it had mastered its own history, that it could see the future with perfect clarity.

> Of all the discoveries I made, this understanding of the empire's diverse population was among the most important, and surprising. Minimum wage earners heading home in their work uniforms, immigrants lacking a green card, poor folks without a driver's license or steady home address, homeless men and women with their shopping carts, disabled folks supplementing a pension, old boys living rough by choice or change or necessity—all were there with me at the trash pile and the dumpster, all piecing together economic and physical survival one discard at a time. (166–67)

Under (and surreptitiously against) the radar of advanced capitalism and its ever-growing wealth gap, scroungers sketch out the future, collaborating with each other, co-operating, or simply swerving to keep from colliding. They can be considerate; Ferrell notes that they recognize each other's right to scrounge, respect the rights of the one who was there first, are happy to share things they have found. It is a sharing–gifting economy established under the aegis of necessity, but operating on the premise that wealth itself is only a discard, liable to endless repurposing and donation. Objects shine and call out on the street, waiting to be found, interpellating, then transferring their *mana* to the urban explorer.

> Riding on an old bike instead of a horse, serving as your own pack mule while pushing an abandoned shopping cart, you embrace the blessed uncertainty of prospecting: adventure, danger, disappointment, elation. (167)

Urban space is reconfigured as well: the scrounger has a kind of negative map of the city in his or her head, where all the spots (where discards accumulate), usually invisible, are most prominent, and the ceremonial sites and statues, embodiments of grandeur, are of interest only as spots where castoffs might accumulate. Scrounging and the gift economy are the aftereffect of marginality, ruination, and destitution, not planning.[10] Ferrell's community's methods "subvert and reinvent the city itself" (195). Ferrell compares the methods of the community he knows to the strategies of the nineteenth-century *flâneur,* celebrated by Baudelaire and Benjamin:[11]

> Lost to the flow of the city's streets, the *flâneur* is in reality not lost at all, manufacturing instead an emergent, microscopic map of city life—a map that, in its slow-paced human engagement, subverts the gridded certitude and hurried efficiency of city planners, law enforcers, and corporate developers. (195)

One could argue, I think, that there's something in scrap (or garbage) itself that directly results in this opening-out of the city. In this violation of the city's organization, its limits and limitations, in this overturning of the subordination of city life to purposeful and goal-oriented activity under the profit motive,[12] the object, incompletable and fragmented, transfers through a kind of sacred contact the power of its decomposition. By its very degradation, reject matter is the matter of the future: it defies technocratic measurement and control and, in so doing, it transforms the nature of urban density. It passes its rhythms, its densities, its temporalities, to the city. It draws people together on its own timescale, under its own initiative. The object is a synecdoche, a part for a whole, in which the whole is always just missing, and the part generates always another part, one in search of that elusive whole. The grid is replaced by the endless series. And the object uses the "person," the reject, in its everlasting, sustainable quest for another. The scrounger is an aftereffect of this desire on the part of the object.

> The empire of scrounge, I found, offered most everything I needed for surviving outside a cash-based consumer economy—but it almost never offered it quickly or predictably. As the weeks and months rolled by, needed items were found, little problems solved, to-do lists crossed off, if only I had the patience to let the solutions emerge. The ability of the empire to provide, in time, the particulars of my daily life I found remarkable. (188)

In classic sustainability theory, "we" must conserve, recycle, consume less, and so on to "save the earth." We, in other words, are already there, suffering from the guilt of the superfluity of our own existence, and necessarily practicing our calibrated parsimony—with ourselves, our community, our future. Our generosity to the future is in parsimony.

But perhaps it should be seen from the other way around—what's left of subjectivity (Bataille's *ipse?*) is only an aftereffect of this sacredness of scrounge, and, moreover, of our gift of scrounge to others, and to the future. In his book *Nowtopia*, Chris Carlsson studies a number of scrounger-like communities—"private programmers, outlaw bicyclists, and vacant-lot gardeners"—that are actively involved, in their separate communities, in reshaping politics, work, and the future of the economy (and ecology). In each case, the members of the community elude the nine-to-five of production, consumption, and alienation, with another mode of work, and of another consumption. Carlsson's workers engage in "freely given labor,"[13] establishing cooperatives and communities in which not only labor is contributed, but the fruits of that labor are given away. And it is given in the context of a sharing: of skills, practices, strategies. Carlsson's revision of utopia into nowtopia goes in the direction, then, not of precise and fanciful planning, but of improvisation and subterranean gestures that elude or even ignore the larger picture of the future. But in that way, in the "now," they are harbingers of the future, enactments of the future in which giving heedlessly goes some distance toward paying the debt incurred to the future, in the wanton destruction of resources and ecologies. The definitive critique of capitalism in this view is not a function of carefully elaborated theory or top-down socialist planning, but of the spontaneous gestures of many anonymous givers who work in the shadows, the crevices, the officially invisible spaces of a capitalism that is destroying itself.

Out of the end of the world of capitalism, then, there arises giving. Not so much people giving, though of course they do so, but giving that itself gives people who give. And act; as Carlsson puts it:

The "outlaw" biking subculture has no hierarchy flowing from wage differentials and ownership, because most of the culture takes place outside of monetary exchange or the logic of business. Instead, these bike hackers are all about doing, tinkering with the discarded detritus of urban life, inventing new forms of play, celebration and artistic expression. Theirs is a culture that is re-produced in action, not affirmed in acts of passive consumption. (116)

What is most striking is how both DIY bike mechanics and urban gardeners recognize the transformation—really the re-creation—of their own lives through their acting in, and giving through, their communities. And this giving is physical; not only knowledge and skills are passed on, but physical pleasures as well. As Carlsson notes, sharing the treasures of community gardens results in "the pleasure of human sociability and the pleasure of great-tasting, fresh food." One gives of oneself, but one also receives pleasure, both sensual and moral.

But what is giving? As in any potlatch, to not return a gift is considered antisocial; the gift instead is an important element in constituting and maintaining social relations, and for this reason it can seem hardly selfless. And one might certainly object that in both Ferrell's and Carlsson's social models generosity is inseparable from the desire for payback: I hope to be able to maintain my position as a scrounger, I hope to enjoy a more egalitarian society, and so on.

Certainly the ideal of recycling can be seen in this selfish-gifting mode. Why recycle? Out of pure generosity—to "save the earth"? But saving the earth also means preserving one's own position in it. One can even argue, on a grander scale, that interest in, and devotion to, the achievement of sustainability, in whatever from, is itself profoundly selfish: I don't want the world to change, so that I can look forward to my descendants, at the very least, enjoying the kind of life on earth that I have had. Not unreasonable, but hardly the kind of selflessness one sometimes imagines as fundamental to sustainability; after all, in principle, sustainability ostensibly would require some renunciation of pleasures, some deep self-sacrifice.

So much, perhaps, for any possibility of a "holier than thou" sustainability. Gaye Hawkins, in her thought-provoking book *The Ethics of Waste,* makes this point, following the arguments of the philosopher Rosalyn Diprose: that devotees of recycling engage in an exchange relation, with the payoff being self-satisfaction. What's more, this satisfaction is felt at the expense of others who give, and whose contribution is not recognized: all those who work for little pay, often in "developing" countries, or provide poorly remunerated services in first-world countries. To be a happy recycler, one must first consume, and on a grand scale.[14] Recycling is, in other words, an inherently yuppified activity. Without lavish consumption, there can be no recycling, and such consumption is made possible by the giving—of time, effort, and materials—by those who, precisely, are not adequately compensated. Some genuine element of giving must be forgotten, occluded, for it to seem, when it is overtly displayed, selfless; in modern capitalism, the truly forgotten giving is carried out not by the consumers, but by (what used to be called) the workers. Recycling, indeed the whole sustainability cult, is simply another form of postmodern hypocrisy.

But is this hypocrisy really an inherent aspect of all recycling, of all scrounging? Gaia, first of all, might not agree—after all, the biosphere does a good job of recycling: it's integral to its frolic, without any self-satisfaction. In the case of "modern" humans,[15] any thinking of sustainability assumes the long time-frame (long in a human sense, short in a biospheric one), and in that frame one cannot necessarily assume the stability of current relations of production and consumption. The decline of the fossil fuel fiesta might very well entail only heightened inequalities of production and consumption: the wealth gap will increase, and the small number of wealthy will be able, even more, to enjoy smugly their recycling. But a messianic (in Benjamin's sense) view of the future could also imagine the return of a radical depletion, one in which the future of consumption is the return of totemic scrap, and the kind of social relations one sees sketched out in Ferrell and Carlsson. In any case, a future of living off the ruins of consumerist culture is not even the future, but the present; in a number of American cities, the economy itself is based to a large extent on the scrapping of the industrial heritage of twentieth century capitalism, with an entire social stratum of non-smug recyclers.[16] Can one imagine Ferrell's scroungers as the remaining members of a community, living a hunter-gatherer life in the ruins not only of industrial consumerism but also of the hierarchies of "advanced capitalism"? What narrativized future could we shout out, à la Costanza—"Mad Max," "Ecotopia,"[17] or "The Road," or a melding of the three? What element of imperative heterogeneity, what "stable genius," could survive the mole-like "grubbing" of this inoperative community?

Hawkins is certainly right to signal the importance of Diprose's analysis; for the philosopher Diprose, in her book *Corporeal Generosity,* generosity does not come *after* the constitution of the "sovereign" self; rather it is the act of giving that generates the self. The self (so-called) is misunderstood, if it's understood to be primary, there from the first to do the giving, and to receive the benefits. If giving is seen as prior to the constitution of a (if not the) self, then the question of a self-interested giving is misplaced: there will be, in this model, no self there from the start, to be interested (in itself). As Diprose puts it:

> Generosity describes the operation that both constitutes identity and differ-
> ence and resists the full presence of meaning, identity and Being so that the
> self is dispersed into the other.[18]

How is the self dispersed in the other, in giving? If generosity truly is corporeal, what are the modes of the body's giving, in such a way that the
body itself, identified (momentarily, at least) with identity, will open out
to others, to other worlds? How will the body in its generosity be "dispersed into the other"? Diprose, referencing Nietzsche and Foucault, sees
self-identity as an "effect" of "body performance," and notes that there are
two aspects to this identity: first, that acts on the part of another body are
attributed to a stable identity; and second, that this is not an effect of a doer
but of "disciplinary productions of the law" (63). If, rather than reading the
other as a changeless identity that acts, one reads the other as an aftereffect
of his or her actions, there will then be a certain freedom. Not so much an
existentialist one, which depends on an already-constituted self with a history and a single personal "freedom," but rather one that is open to change
in action:

> It is because my body is always already given to the world and to the other
> that the relation between my body, the other, and the world is ambiguous
> and hence open to possibilities. (70)

This is a relation of invention, but one that through the body engages and
is engaged by others. But what kind of invention? And which possibilities?
Diprose imagines the body's relation to the world through an other in two
interesting examples: driving a car and wearing drag. In both cases there is
an adaptation of the body through the other, which is both incorporated
and, in a sense, controlled. Diprose writes:

> I structure the situation by the (prereflective) projection of my body onto
> the world. Through movement, I incorporate objects and others within the
> situation and resolve it according to the project at hand. I drive a car in this
> way; not by consciously calculating the distance between my body, the car,
> and the gateway but by the prereflective projection of my body (the gestures
> of which have been built up through mimesis and repetition) onto the world,
> making it a part of my body spatiality. (70)

There's little to dispute here, but the example is notable in that the "other's" incorporation works in such a way that the subject is put in a position of bodily mastery; nothing characterizes a "good driver" better than the absolutely instinctive gestures needed to navigate the car successfully through tight situations. Car and driver form a single steel-shelled self, aware (in principle) of nothing other than the driving. The self is a function of the machine. That is the very definition of automobility. Diprose's example is highly telling; she makes no distinction in this example between corporeal generosity generated exclusively through bodily movements (food-fueled) and those that are inseparable from fossil-fueled mechanical movement. How is corporeal generosity an effect of energy expenditure? What is its carbon footprint? Could it be measured? Could the mastery of the automobile through a corporeal generosity be an effect of the fuel consumption of the automobile—the car's corporeality? How to distinguish the two?

Diprose's second example is similar, despite its *éclat* (compared to car driving, at least):

> I would also perform drag this way, not by simply donning the garb of a foreign body and playing on the difference between that performance and the sex of my body but by implicitly incorporating the foreign body, its gestures, movements, and habits, into my performance. (70)

In another example, the physician and her patient are united not as two opposed subjectivities, subject and object, but as a kind of spatio-corporeal amalgam: "a situation through which the instrument [the stethoscope] and the other's body become part of her [the physician's] body spatiality" (117).

What is striking in these examples is that, out of various body parts, machine components, and dress, one body still emerges as master, and re-affirms a subjectivity, no matter how open to possibilities. One could, however, suggest exactly the opposite scenario: if there is to be generosity, it will come not as a consolidation or assemblage of authority, but as a breaking apart or dissolution of the self's illusory limits—physical, cisgendered, subjective, authoritative. One can imagine this in social situations, such as that of the scrounger, and in interpersonal and transgressive erotic relations (which are also, like scrounging, political), and certainly in practices of meditation. Rather than a self "in control" coalescing around or inserted into a body generously asserting itself through the incorporation of the other (which is laudable), there may be bodies appropriating parts, roles, fragments, stuff, microbes, in a way that always mimes not only their own physical coherence and mastery, but that of the other as well. That is implied in Despret's model, where the living incorporate the dead in such a way that they construct the dead, all the while putting into question the very mastery they had seemed to have as "survivors," superior to the dead through their momentary corporeal presence (aliveness). Corporeal generosity to the dead, in other words, might very well mean that my autonomy as a body is questioned by the role of the dead that I must construct (along with the participation of the dead) in order to constitute myself as a body, with a role in the world. Incorporating the dead, in the end, may mean much less incorporation (with all the psychic baggage that that implies) than a process of negotiation, mutual construction and destruction, and transgression of the limits of life and death. The dead incorporate me as much as I incorporate them. My body is not one, and my performance is not one, with an inside into which things are incorporated, or an outside to which it farms itself out, but a series of fetishes, phantasms, bits of superannuated trash, colliding with other bodies, other assemblages of charged and/or eroticized fragments, living, dead, inert and/or exuding uncontrollable forces and shocks. All this would be operating in an "outside" outside the outside.

Another way of thinking about corporeal generosity might be to imagine a relation in which giving entails not two clearly defined entities, bodies for example, or bodies and machines, but rather collections, series, of organs in transgressive relations, selves as pathological stains of pleasure. Thus there might be no implied subordination of one body to another (the car to the driver's body, the drag costume to the wearer) but rather the giving of body parts (their giving themselves, in effect) without any *telos*—such as the goal of sexual reproduction, for example.

Jane Gallop, writing of Pierre Klossowski's reading of Sade's *Philosophy in the Bedroom,* puts it this way:

Once any exchange is possible, once the *telos* (the vagina) is equated or equatable, then the substitutions can proliferate. The absolute value of a *telos* means its value is not a function of anything, not subordinate to any function. The possibility of an equivalent relativizes the value. The very positing of a substitute for the vagina assumes a grammar explaining that equivalency. That grammar opens the door for a potentially unending series of paradigmatic equivalents. Although Mme de Saint-Ange [a teacher in Sade's novel] only names four ("her hand, her mouth, her tits, her asshole") a page later Dolmancé (Eugénie's other teacher) adds the thighs and armpits to the list. The list is limited only by the imaginative capacities of the compiler.[19]

What can be taken as the *telos*—the vagina and its central role in sexual reproduction (and indeed sexual reproduction itself)—is now depicted as only a member of an endless synecdochic series of displaced and displacing body parts. If the *telos* really is unconditioned, not subordinate or dominant (thus depending on other subordinations), then it is indefinitely replaceable by simulacra. The "absolute value"—the founding sovereignty, in other words—of the vagina turns out merely to place it as one element in a series, much like the sun in Derrida's *"White Mythology"* (see chapter 5).

Corporeal generosity in this light entails the giving of body part to body part, with none privileged, none capable of incorporating or definitively excluding, none in control. The example of getting into a car and driving it through "the gateway"—an interesting enough example—can be scrounged, repurposed, as any number of things giving themselves to each other, constituting themselves as a series of charged and forceful units, rolling just about anywhere, on the loose. Ferrell on his bicycle scrounging and giving whatever he can find, for example: corporeal potlatch.

Of course in a Bataillean mode, this can be seen as an example of a transgressive eroticism ("communication"), but I would like also to stress the connections that can be made here with a future, *mana*-charged gifting community. Sade certainly had his community of libertines, and Bataille no doubt his headless ones as well, but one can think of this orgy of giving in the light of recycling, a donation that involves not just sexualized pleasures but also other forms of joyful corporeal generosities, ones that unite/split communities in *partage*. From the perspective of a general sustainability, one can imagine a practice that incorporates series of body and object-like fragments, given and giving, in a kind of community of the dying and newly born.[20] The ecstatic and horrifying dramatizations in meditation are accompanied by the corporeal actions of those who spend without return, in the very fragmentation of bodies (the fault line, the anamorphosis of subject-object, breaking down in the stain of the pathological). A parodic Brundtland would reaffirm a concern for the past (the heritage of community that is worth preserving) and the future (all those future generations for whose lives we [which we?] are somehow responsible). But rather than seeing this process as one of simple maintenance—a *telos,* so to speak, of the perfect and guilt-free reproduction of that summit called enlightened civilization—one can posit instead a base recurrence, a repetition not of perfect moments of revolution as accomplishment, but of moments of community in which the dead, the dying, along with those struggling in birth, come together with the living and the ruins of the past/future in projects of postcapitalist sociability. While second-order sustainability presupposes a complete absence of particularity—all subjects in the Technate are the same, their gender(s), "race," "culture," disability invisible or irrelevant—the third order affirms the fragmentation of these terms, their heterogeneous super- (or sub-)position in and through the intersecting tactics and figmenting faces of scrounging. *Consommation* (second-order consumption) is doubled and supplemented by (and lost in) *consumation* (third), and the footprint of rigorous measure is opened out by another foot, maximal carbon intensity super- (sub-)seded by the intensity of the fiery subject–object combine—in meditation, ritual, ecstasy.[21]

Future generations, of people, of animals, of conjoined communities of fragmentary objects, with the wind of Paradise in their faces, are always with us, always interpellating us, calling out for recognition, affirmation. The unborn are playing with us, and playing a role similar to the dead in Despret. The future, like the subject–reject combine, is of disproportion. Nongenital sexual activity always risks being doubled by sexual activity that actually leads to reproduction; Sade's series of body parts will always include penis and vagina, or some prosthetic simulacra thereof, and will always include the threat, and promise, of the giving of new life, of new assemblages of body parts called babies[22]—who themselves are quite happy to throw themselves, their parts, into an endless play of substitutions and simulations.[23]

Are birth and death commensurate? Many think not; in the Heideggerian tradition, I die alone; my death can only be mine, and mourning for another cannot rank with my anguish before what amounts to my own death. And yet the two would seem to go together, while not necessarily being perfectly symmetrical. Sartre, in *Being and Nothingness,* notes that

> death is a pure fact as is birth; it comes to us from outside and it transforms us into the outside. At bottom, death is in no way distinguished from birth, and it is this identity of birth and death that we call facticity.[24]

But the philosopher Dennis Schmidt, in an essay on just this topic, begs to differ: for him, there is a radical difference between life and death.

> To say that death is mine is to say that we die alone. No one can help me, no one can die for me. No one can carry me through it. No matter how much we want to keep company with the dying, death marks the ultimate limit of any companionship, of any help one can give.[25]

If one dies alone, though, one is always born with someone, if only one's mother:

> Birth . . . is never only "mine." Indeed it is in no way mine at all. Unlike many animals who are born and able to walk, run, and perhaps even to survive by themselves only minutes after birth, for us being born means that we require the help of someone else for years. (114)

This problem would seem to be fundamental to any thinking about sustainability. Does the individualized person (or subject) die alone? Does the humanized planet die alone? Does Gaia? On the simplest level, one could object that one's death is solitary, or (like birth) with others, depending on various circumstances. If a person has prepared well, is in a hospice, surrounded by loved ones, she or he does indeed die with others. But if I die under torture, or as the victim of some senseless crime, I then do indeed die alone. Just as a good birth, and a good childhood, depends "on a village," so too a good death depends on help from many others. In the future of ruins—economic, ecological, intellectual—dying alone, on the part of humanity, on the part of the individual, is a real possibility. Perhaps it is this that third-order sustainability must recognize and try to avert: humanity's death in isolation, struggling in hostility, hating itself and hating the future. Death with understanding, with acceptance, no matter how improbable, might indeed be linked to another birth; if not of humanity itself, then at least that of the planet.

The death of humanity does depend on many others, billions of others, to help it along, in one way or another. But that death may be only the death of our own species. One planet dies, and another is born, out of the ruins. A really dead planet, as in Cormac McCarthy's *The Road,* is the unthinkable not-knowledge, the first-order sustainability at the heart of our practice of the other sustainabilities, the other rhetorical projections of "life" (our concept) onto the ball of the Earth. Our finitude is inseparable from our anguish before death, the circumstances of our lives that it delineates, our understanding of the limited temporality that allows us to give our lives meaning in incessant gifts of prosopopoeia. But a life project, too, depends on others in a scrounging, riven community. Our relation to death is not a purely negative one; it entails also personal learning, growth, which again requires the help of many, as an adjunct to birth.

Playing off the birth and death of the traumatically humanized planet against one's own personal birth and death puts things in a new light. Death in the contemporary philosophical context is always individual; it does not seem to involve the death of a species, let alone of the planet as a whole. There is, no doubt, a disproportion of scale between the two; a personal death and the death of the planet as it is known "now" are two very different things. But any thinking about sustainability would have to think about and in this disproportion, and the ways that humans, as members of a species, identifying with their species, are caught between the extremely small (each individual life) and the incomprehensibly large (Gaia, the planet as a living system with humans in, for the moment, a starring role).[26] The species itself is caught in this zone of disproportion, dependent in myriad ways both on the individual acts of each member of the species, and on the vast number of acts of all the living organisms of the planet—of the planetary community of corporeal generosities.

Despret has indicated how the dead are with us, that they are perhaps not "alive," but certainly they are integrated into our activities and continue to do things in the world. In that sense no one dies alone; I continue to live, dead, along with the others I have known, and many others I don't know. And already dead I use self-referential language, as Blanchot would remind us. This could be considered as another being toward death: not as a simple awareness of my own imminent extinction, but as yet another project, rhetorical and energetic, I engage in with others, some living, some, like myself, dead. And birth as well can involve a being toward birth: I am not born once, but multiple times, my already-dying generation cannot be separated from the finitudes, the various projects, of those scroungers around me.

Birth and death, then, are difficult to distinguish; I am born and die always with others, but others who themselves may be fragmentary, themselves amalgams of body parts, organisms, and past objects that exude both force and mortality. If death is a return to a definitive fragmentation, it is one that I have constructed, no matter how badly. I have collected the pieces, arranged them, appropriated them, and now I let them go, I have spent them, given them, with the assistance, encouragement, and defiance of others. If I am born, it is through a phantasmic collection of desires, inputs of parents, chance meetings of organs, the reconstruction of dead objects of the past orbiting as my future.

Birth is a project, and so too is parenting; but as a parent one has no idea what will result from one's efforts. It is a dice roll, an exhilarating one to be sure, but nothing more than a leap into the unknown. One can offer "guidance," but the ways in which it will be interpreted are always unknowable. Parenting is impossible, or bound for complete failure, if one wants only a "mini-me," or a reflection of one's own fantasies about status and success. Parenting, as Hegel well knew, is an affirmation of one's own mortality, the giving of life is a step toward one's own demise. *Giving* birth is already a dying, an affirmation of the end as one prepares one's supposed successor.

The production of all those "future generations," then, is only part of a recognition of the fragmentary and unknowable aspects of the birth–death continuum. Sustainability is the aftereffect of those projects, because the expenditure they entail has to do not with stockpiling objects of prestige, or the engineering of a life whose trajectory and movement toward death is only measured through the number of things owned or accomplished, but with the repurposing of a future cobbled together with the charged prostheses and personal bits of detritus that pile up and indeed are thrown off through the unforeseeable movement of what we call history.[27] Birth, for this reason, can only be put forward in the context of ruin, of the vision of imminent planetary death (perhaps the ultimate "object" of meditation) that the *ipse* sees/foresees but defies. The history of technology, of nature, of capital accumulation and yawning wealth disparity accompanies us into a future of devastation, but perhaps also of survival. The zone of disproportion between planet and individual human finitude is that zone where planning repetitively fails, and where the event of meditation and corporeal generosity returns. If the earth is to be saved, it will happen on the anamorphosis-edge of planning and scrounging, planning as the inadvertent aftereffect of scrounging, scrounging as the last resort of doomed planning.[28]

Acknowledgments

It's been a long strange trip, from the "Bitu-Men" of the tar sands of Alberta to the oil refineries of the port of Houston; from the Grande Chartreuse of the Savoie to the Tibetan Buddhist temple of Philadelphia, with stops in between at Denys Lasdun's Keeling House in London and the faux Chauvet Cave in the Cévennes. Along the way I've made many friends, and had many contentious discussions. I'd like to thank in particular, both for invitations to speak and for their wonderful friendship, Imre Szeman, who very kindly invited me to the very first Petro-Cultures conference in Edmonton; David Cunningham, discussing parking-space micro parks with me at the surrealism conference he organized at the Courtauld Institute; the indefatigable Cymene Howe and Dominic Boyer at Rice; Thangam Ravindranathan, with whom I thought about dogs (both feral and domestic) and the absurd at Brown; Karen Pinkus, who fueled my interest in climate change and the underground at Cornell; Cameron Tonkinwise at the New School, working on postsustainability and design; the Pedal People (a bicycle garbage-hauling collective) in Northampton, Massachusetts; Vincent Bruyère, who was a wonderful colleague at Penn State and whose work at Emory on perishability is essential for understanding sustainability; Amanda Boetzkes; Jonathan Strauss; Wilda Anderson; Wayne Cristaudo, discussing Bataille's eroticism with me at Victoria Peak overlooking Hong Kong; Jeff Diamanti and Brent Ryan Bellamy; Jeffrey Jerome Cohen; Rich Doyle, urging me, in a meditation session, to be thankful; Nadir Lahiji; Martine Reid, with whom I contemplated the effect of the mistral on trees in Uzès; Chris Carlsson, whose knowledge of San Francisco geography is legendary; and Jeff Ferrell, with whom I found some valuable brass in a dumpster. Alphonso Lingis has always been a great and inspiring friend: I will never forget the day his whole house shook with dancing. And my dear friend Mark Conroy, who taught at Ohio State and with whom I carried on a running forty-plus year nihilist-intellectual comedy routine. Here in Philadelphia, I have greatly enjoyed discussions with friends at the Architecture and Design School at the University of Pennsylvania: Daniel Barber, Annette Fierro, William Braham, Joan Ockman, and Franca Trubiano.

Finally, this book is dedicated to my dearest companion of many years, Nan Moschella, who may very well see me (or avoid seeing me) participate at some point in the annual Philly naked bike ride.

Notes

INTRODUCTION

1. Swyngedouw, "Impossible 'Sustainability.'" Medavoi ("Sustainability") also notes the complicity between the use of the word and the "valu[ation of] social and natural living relations primarily for their convertibility into the abstract life of the [capitalist] economy" (344). This is certainly the case, but one also needs to ask what other economies (eco-technocratic, postcapitalist, utopian, messianic, gifting, meditative) have been or can be linked to the use or uses of the word.

2. Alaimo, *Exposed*, 178.

3. FrontStream, "The Three Pillars of Sustainability."

4. The full quote: "Humanity has the ability to make development sustainable to ensure that it meets the needs of the present without compromising the ability of future generations to meet their own needs" (paragraph 27 of part 3 ["Sustainable Development"] in section 1 ["The Global Challenge"] of *Our Common Future*).

5. Sachs, *Age of Sustainable Development*.

6. The term comes from social psychology; in another register—philosophy—one would speak (in a Sartrean mode) of "bad faith." For George Orwell (in *1984*) it was "doublethink."

7. Jenkins, "Sustainability Theory," 383.

8. Wackernagel and Rees, *Our Ecological Footprint*.

9. Actually, one and only one author to my knowledge has ever suggested this: the Marquis de Sade, in his book *Philosophy in the Bedroom* (in the section "Frenchmen, Some More Effort If You Wish to Become Republicans"). De Sade sees murder as a way of furthering the goals of "Mother Nature" in her constant cycles of birth and death (recycling)—as, in other words, an aid to a (first-order) sustainability (which, we could add, needs no aid). He therefore suggests that Mother Nature would be quite content if the entire human race were wiped out—this would only open the way for the development of other, equally worthwhile, species.

10. McDonough and Braungart, *Cradle to Cradle*, 113.

11. Jenkins, "Sustainability Theory," 383.

12. McKibben, *Deep Economy*, 109.

13. Woods, "Scale Critique for the Anthropocene," 138.

14. As reported by Benjamin, in "Franz Kafka: On the Tenth Anniversary of His Death," in *Selected Writings* 2, part 2, 794–818; 798. My thanks to Richard Block (Department of German, University of Washington) for suggesting this connection. One could retort that there may indeed ultimately be sustainability for us, but not the "us" of a purely anthropocentric, closed sustainability-community. See my comments on Jean-Luc Nancy and community in chapter 7.

15. See Harris, *Conscious*, 65–70, where the philosophical arguments for panpsychism are discussed. The very fact that we are conscious is an indication that the possibility of consciousness everywhere exists (it seems unlikely that it can exist here and not anywhere else: everywhere must be somehow open to it). If that's the case, maybe it is already everywhere, or at least the propensity to it is (a propensity would somehow be connected to it, or be a part of it). We just don't know—we aren't conscious of the parameters of consciousness, and may never be. Other than as a rhetorical trope ("I know what it's like to be a bat"), it remains opaque to us, in the very daylight of our awareness. First-order sustainability, which exists perhaps outside the warp of consciousness, or is somehow suffused with it, has the same puzzling and ultimately unknowable status.

16. An early observer of urban ecology, whose rambling observations on the various kinds of life in the city tended to (at least) minimize the centrality of the human, was Leonard Dubkin. See, for example, his wonderful book *Enchanted Streets* (1947).

17. Dominic Boyer's concept of "energopolitics" is certainly useful as a "transhuman register adapted to questioning the political interrelationship of humanity, energy, ecology and infrastructure" ("Energopolitics," 130). In the second part of this book especially, my analysis of eco-technocracy is an instance of considering energopolitics not just in the past and present of energy in its various economic, political, and social instances, as played out primarily in capitalism, but in its future in more or less sympathetic energy-oriented futures.

18. There are, then, not just three sustainabilities in this book, but three cities: the first-order city of an urban ecology of assemblages in which the human is simply one of a series of actants, more or less localizable; the second-order city of energy efficiency and technology-based consciousness at its summit; and a third-order city of scrounging, meditating, and giving.

19. Another term for which may be *Perishability Fatigue* (as analyzed in the book of that title by Vincent Bruyère).

1. OBJECTS, ENERGY, THE CHORA

1. Sagan, "Beautiful Monsters," 169–74, 169.

2. Sagan, 171.

3. Heinberg, *The Party's Over*, 19.

4. Morton, *Hyperobjects*, 116.

5. Defining life (and clearly delineating its qualities from the "inanimate") either here on Earth or elsewhere is by no means an easy task. What counts as life on

another planet ("lyfe") might be quite different from what we understand by it. See Bharmal, "Is There Lyfe on Mars?"

6. Shaviro, *Universe of Things,* 66.

7. Shaviro, 67.

8. "Bare life," as Giorgio Agamben would call it. See Agamben, *Homo Sacer.*

9. Harman, *Heidegger Explained,* 129–30.

10. Harman, 138.

11. Meillassoux, *After Finitude,* 28, 116.

12. Shaviro, *Universe of Things,* 67. Thacker's remark echoes, ironically or not, the remarkable book by Alan Weisman, *The World Without Us,* which presents a model of earth ecology as it would develop if humans were suddenly to disappear.

13. See Shaviro's discussion of Brassier in *Universe of Things,* 74–75.

14. Shaviro, 74.

15. A world, for not just the earth is in question. This world, however, would have to be differentiated from "life world," with its various degrees of perfection, as implied in Heidegger.

16. As Shaviro puts it in *The Universe of Things,* "If we accept that thought (or feeling, or experience) need not be conscious, then we might well be led to abandon the demarcation between mind and matter altogether" (81).

17. Shaviro, 83.

18. Bennett, *Vibrant Matter,* 5 (emphasis in original).

19. See Odum, *Environmental Accounting.*

20. Feynman, cited in Daggett, *The Birth of Energy,* 40.

21. Mirowski, *More Heat Than Light,* 75.

22. See, for example, Layzer, "The Arrow of Time," 559–69. On classical mechanics and contemporary concepts of temporality, thermodynamics, and quantum mechanics, see the classic *Order out of Chaos: Man's New Dialogue with Nature,* by Prigogine and Stengers.

23. Daggett, *The Birth of Energy,* 44.

24. Clausius, cited in Daggett, *The Birth of Energy,* 45.

25. Of course, Hegelian dialectics and the laws of thermodynamics were formulated independently, but both arose from the same nineteenth century *Zeitgeist.*

26. Daggett, *The Birth of Energy,* 42.

27. Plato, *Timaeus,* sections 50–54.

28. Sheldon, "Form/Matter/Chora," 193–222.

29. And even if timelessness (in a perfect return) is the ultimate ideal of sustainability as an ecological/social practice.

30. Derrida, *Khôra,* 23–24 (my translation).

31. Derrida, 25.

32. See Fleck, "Anachronisme et anachronie."

33. Morris, *American Heritage Dictionary,* 1296.

34. The same is true, of course, of any interactions one might have with a human interlocutor.

2. ANIMALS, SCALE, DEATH

1. Originally published in 1967.

2. Singer, *Animal Liberation*.

3. Descartes, *Discourse on Method*.

4. Derrida, *The Animal That Therefore I Am*, 60.

5. Chadwick, "Keystone Species."

6. Hinchcliffe and Whatmore, "Living Cities," 111.

7. My point is that Hinchliffe and Whatmore's model is inherently progressive because, without the overweening subjectivity that assigns inhabitants (animal and human) to urban spaces, and also eradicates them, animals and humans are in principle more free to carve out their own niches, to their own benefit, in collusion but also no doubt competition. This is clearly a utopian (or as I will call it later, after Walter Benjamin, messianic) goal when one pushes it beyond mere recognition of nonhuman/ human appropriation of space, and toward affirming and making possible that appropriation. Although Hinchliffe and Whatmore do not develop this point, they could note that the demand for ecological justice on the part of humans is part and parcel of this (re)appropriation of space; the refusal to live in ecologically contaminated areas, even the formulation of a kind of different occupation of urban space in the face of relegation to areas that are harmful, are elements of a "politics of conviviality" that inevitably will be anticapitalist if not postcapitalist. I will return to this in chapter 9 with a consideration of communities of scroungers and nowtopians.

8. Certomà, *Postenvironmentalism*, 100.

9. Woods, "Scale Critique for the Anthropocene," 136.

10. Pascal, *Pensées*, section 72 (my translations).

11. One can happily affirm the fact that a democratically elected noncapitalist regime (by humans, in collaboration with other "assemblages") could formulate and implement a global Green New Deal that would end and even reverse global warming. This would mean, however, not only the affirmative vote of the majority of the world's population in a fair and clean referendum/election, but the collective will to end consumerism as it has flourished under capitalism. It is consumerism, inseparable from fossil capital, as much as governmental decision-making, that is driving global warming. The problem of consumerism and its (so to speak) rethinking/reenacting is the subject of the last two chapters of this book.

12. Yong, *I Contain Multitudes*, 81–82.

13. Consider, for example, the role of social media in our society: everyone depends on it, uses it, and yet recognizes it as a (very profitable) toxin that is coming close to destroying the democratic public sphere.

14. As long as we hope that the assemblage can efficaciously do the work that responsible human subjectivity cannot, we face a situation where the assemblage is, in effect, a substitute for the subject, and not different in kind.

15. Levinas, *Totality and Infinity*, 195.

16. Sartre, *What Is Literature?* In Sartre's case, literature entails the mutual recognition of the other's freedom, on the part of both author and reader.

17. Anna Lowenhaupt Tsing, in *The Mushroom at the End of the World,* makes a similar point about matsutake mushrooms, both in Japan and in Oregon. These organisms are caught (or catch humans) in a complex play of presence and absence, visibility and withdrawal of prominence; they found both a capitalist economy and an economy of gifting, pleasure, and (social) marginality. One ecology (that of the old growth forest) is followed, after the clear-cutting of the forest, by a mushroom ecology (and economy). The parameters of the cohabitation of a capitalist and a gift economy (a main topic of Tsing's analysis) are not evident in her book, however. Can the two economies coexist indefinitely, as Tsing seems to imply? Can, in the future, fossil capital's authority continue to interpenetrate with the charged and elusive movements of the mushroom?

18. I use the word "world" to indicate that which is inseparable from human perception and intervention, of whatever kind. One can also speak of the "world" of black redstarts, whales, and even perhaps rocks—and that would be their world, and not ours (yet they no doubt intersect, in ways knowable and unknowable). Whether these worlds are "poor" compared to ours is certainly open to debate; as I've argued, one can think of an ecology as an assemblage of worlds whose actants are not necessarily localizable as subjects or objects, or are situated at some outside point linking but also interfering between the two.

19. This connection between human self-segregation, planning subjectivity, and fossil capitalism as the mark of the Anthropocene will be further explored in chapter 8.

20. Critchley, *How to Stop Living and Start Worrying,* 121.

21. See, in this context, Alphonso Lingis's version of Levinas's project: "Just when we walk around, what we see are not just shapes and forms and colors. There are distinct and independent things, that we see what they require. And if we get active, we sense the sorts of actions that could supply their needs. So, I always started from thinking about Levinas's idea that we see the other face as needy and putting demands on us and extending that across nature." "Interview with Alphonso Lingis," in George and Sparrow, eds., *Itinerant Philosophy,* 159.

3. STATUES, LANGUAGE, MACHINES

1. Zircon crystals from Australia have been dated to 4.4 billion years ago. See Oskin, "Confirmed," https://www.livescience.com/43584-earth-oldest-rock-jack-hills-zircon.html.

2. Statues are very hard to eliminate. Toppling one is bound to offend a lot of people; even once removed they tend to linger, resisting simple crushing and recycling (symbolic charge, if not permanence, trumps sheer sustainability of materials, at least in this case), popping up in other places, their meaning *détourné.* They are subject to constant reinterpretation, revalorization, and devalorization. Their significance lingers, refuses to die, even if their specific meaning is lost or even actively rejected. Their charged power remains, amplified by incoherence. The statues of Berlin's Siegesallee, erected in huge numbers by order of Kaiser Wilhelm II before World War I and celebrating all the Prussian emperors, were removed after World War II, but nevertheless stored; they're still around posing problems even today. See Oomkes,

"Berlin's Terracotta Army" (although the statues are not terra-cotta; they're marble), https://deademperorssociety.com/2014/04/27/berlins-terracotta-army-the-statues -of-the-kaisers-victory-boulevard/. The Confederate generals, soldiers, and politicians that are found everywhere in the American South are also notoriously hard to get rid of: "Silent Sam," a statue memorializing a confederate soldier at the University of North Carolina campus, was finally toppled by protesters in August 2018. The response of the state of North Carolina and the university was to condemn "mob rule" and require the re-erection of the statue at its former location. See https://en.wikipedia .org/wiki/Silent_Sam. In 2020, in the wake of the George Floyd killing, however, many Jim Crow–era statues really did come down, and yet the power of the acts of desecration and *détournement* aligned against them only demonstrated the resistance of their oppressive semiotic force.

3. See Du Camp, *Égypte, Nubie, Syrie,* a collection of photographic prints.

4. See the many references to Aragon in Benjamin's *Arcades Project.*

5. See Pessard, *La Statuomanie parisienne.*

6. See McWilliam, "Conflicting Manifestations." Aragon was not the only sur-realist fascinated by statues. André Breton's *Nadja* (1927) features a photo of the Dolet statue, and a contains a few cryptic remarks alluding to the statue's sinister nature and psychological implications.

7. The statues, as I've noted, were highly political, and many of the Left-republican ones (including Étienne Dolet; his empty plinth on the Place Maubert remained for almost fifty years) were melted down during the German occupation of Paris in World War II. See Freeman, *Bronzes to Bullets.* An excellent overview of Parisian statuary is Hargrove, *The Statues of Paris.*

8. Aragon, *Paris Peasant,* 153.

9. For more on the sacred charge of (cursed) objects, see my comments on Durk-heim and Bataille in chapter 7.

10. See Wernick, *Auguste Comte.*

11. De Man, *Allegories of Reading,* 180.

12. De Man, *Rhetoric of Romanticism,* 76.

13. De Man, *Allegories of Reading,* 298.

14. De Man, *Rhetoric of Romanticism,* 81.

15. See Nietzsche, *"On Truth and Lie."*

16. Deleuze and Guattari, *Anti-Oedipus,* 36 (emphasis in original).

17. On fuel in its various energetic avatars, see Pinkus, *Fuel.*

18. With this said, one can certainly note the importance of Deleuze and Guat-tari for thinking ecology. Guattari's *Three Ecologies* is essential, but other conclusions can also be drawn from their work; see, for example, Halsey, "Ecology and Machinic Thought."

19. Cited in Alvord, *Divorce Your Car!,* 54.

20. Illich, *Energy and Equity.*

21. See Cudworth and Hobden, *The Emancipatory Project of Posthumanism,* 66, for a perspective on Bruno Latour's model of the "parliament of things."

22. More on Holbein and anamorphosis, in the context of Lacan and Žižek, in chapter 6.

23. Paulhan, *Flowers of Tarbes,* 60 (emphasis in original).

24. De Man, *Rhetoric of Romanticism,* 285.

25. By "official America," I mean the current (2021) energy-intensive capitalist–consumerist society of the United States, characterized by ever-greater inequalities of wealth, the profound lack of social justice, and the self-sustaining of collective hallucination.

4. TECHNOCRACY, ENERGY ECONOMICS, UTOPIA

1. Jameson, "Politics of Utopia," 37.

2. On the difference between Marxist and energeticist modes of determining value, see my article *"Marxism, Materialism, and the Critique of Energy."* In this article I call, perhaps mistakenly, for a melding of the two modes of analysis.

3. In Marxism, the greed of the ruling class must somehow be eliminated, and acquisitiveness in general (even among members of the proletariat) must become a thing of the past, in order for the postrevolutionary epoch to come to pass. This moral transformation is the utopian component of both Marxism and theories of "natural capital."

4. The best overall history of Technocracy Inc. is Akin, *Technocracy and the American Dream.*

5. I will capitalize Price System throughout, following Hubbert. It is not entirely clear why he does so, other than to perhaps personify it as an evil. Neither Veblen *(The Engineers and the Price System)* nor Loeb *(Life in a Technocracy)* capitalize it.

6. Hubbert, *Technocracy Study Course,* 124. On Hubbert's authorship of the *Technocracy Study Course,* see the excellent recent biography of Hubbert: Inman, *Oracle of Oil,* which discusses the genesis of the Study Course (55–59).

7. Indeed, many economists of the 1930s and '40s struggled against the capitalist demand that private property and investment remain sacrosanct, as the bedrock of the capitalist system in which value was anchored in the price of gold. Both John Maynard Keynes *(The General Theory of Employment, Interest and Money)* and Georges Bataille *(The Accursed Share),* among many others, realized that real economic reform could be accomplished only by the lifting of debt (rather than its enforcement, even across generations) and by the redistribution of wealth through disbursement (i.e., gifting) as a larger policy. Keynes saw the crisis of the post–World War I peace as having to do with the refusal on the part of the allies to cancel German debt.

8. Today we don't even have gold—we have "legal tender," which is nothing more than the abstract token or measure freed from any specific scarcity, and thus reproduced, in debt (though lending), in ever greater quantities.

9. On the Continental Control, in effect the government of the Technate (the union of all North American populations), see the *Technocracy Study Course,* 228–230. Above the Continental Control is the Continental Director, "the chief executive of the entire social mechanism" (228).

10. Hubbert here anticipates McDonough and Braungart who, in *Cradle to Cradle*, argue for a total recycling model that also includes, as the most energy efficient practice, the leasing of things rather than their possession. (This is also an anticipation of the more recent idea of the "sharing economy.") See also the comments on ownership and consumer culture in Loeb, *Life in a Technocracy*, 52–53, for a consideration of the limits of private property in a Technocracy.

11. This was the thesis of James Burnham in his famous celebration of what one could call existing technocracy (in the USSR, Nazi Germany, and the United States), first published in 1941: *The Managerial Revolution*. George Orwell's *1984* is usually read as a critique of Stalinism, but in fact Orwell had Burnham's utopia in mind when he flipped it into a dystopia.

12. On the predictions of peaking oil production in the early 2000s, following Hubbert's curve, see Deffeyes, *Hubbert's Peak*, first published in 2001. A subsequent analysis of the cultural impact of the popularization of peak oil, especially as it resonated in the world of blogs and social media, and written after the threat of peak oil seemed to have passed, is Schneider-Mayerson, *Peak Oil*.

13. The House Un-American Activities Committee (HUAC) investigated Technocracy Inc.; its chairman, Martin Dies, regarded both Hubbert and Harold Loeb (author of *Life in a Technocracy*) with great suspicion. Hubbert was questioned as to his commitment to democracy in 1943 by Thomas P. Brockway, special assistant to the Board of Economic Warfare (BEW), and found wanting. Hubbert was eventually pressured out of government service. See Inman, *Oracle of Oil*, 87–94.

14. See Daly, *Steady State Economics*, and Helm, *Natural Capital*.

15. Costanza et al., "Value," 254.

16. Determining the carbon footprint (both internalized and externalized cost) of nuclear waste—buried for ten thousand years and demanding human vigilance for the same period—is a good example of how tricky the measurement of energy inputs can be. How would one set "boundaries" for this kind of analysis?

17. See, for example, Heinberg, *Powerdown*, 34–37, 45. Heinberg's central thesis in *The Party's Over* is that in the era of post-peak oil there will be little time or resource availability for the transition to renewables. Even though nowadays there is a recognition of voluntary, rather than geological/natural peak oil, the larger problem sketched out by Heinberg remains.

18. On the relation between the growth economy, money, and debt, see Heinberg, *The Party's Over*, 170–71. Heinberg's argument goes back at least to the Veblen–Hubbert critique of the Price System.

19. The recent Covid-19 pandemic has shown the fragility of the crust of civilization that has been taken for granted by the general public. The coordination of voluntary quarantining—self-restraint—has proven especially problematic.

20. See especially the brilliant chapter "Utopic Degeneration: Disneyland" in Marin's *Utopics* (239–57).

21. I will not linger over the contradiction of people "freely" choosing an alternative that they have been taught to see as inescapable.

22. This is, of course, a posthistorical variant of the situationist view that art is dead because art's revolutionary potential in the "society of the spectacle"—the postmodern world of consumer capitalism—is effectively zero. See Debord, *La Société du spectacle.*

23. For more on Kojève and his take on the end of history, see my *Bataille's Peak,* 73–88.

24. Thus we imagine the utopian space of ecotopia quickly flipping into a perverse and potentially repressive but sadistically pleasurable dystopia (Mad Max)—a flip already suggested by Callenbach. Ecotopia, in other words, is always-again opened out from within by Mad Max. See my discussion of Žižek's analysis of Lacan's "Kant with Sade" in the following chapter.

5. SOLAR ARCHITECTURE, SADISM, HETEROGENEITY

1. See, for example Flint, "Hazardous Business": "He became, in this widely shared view, a veritable force for evil, a destroyer of cities. He gave us blank walls, windswept plazas, and towers in the park; his wipe-the-slate-clean-and-start-over approach, seen in the 1925 Plan Voisin, a proposal for 60-story towers spaced well apart in the historic district of the Marais in Paris, helped inspire a dark era of urban renewal in this country." Le Corbusier thus becomes, in the attitude criticized by Flint, the embodiment of all the ills that destroyed the city in the postwar period. Prominent among these were all those high-rise, alienating constructions, and the prevalence of the car-centric urban grid. Hardly a model of what anyone would associate with sustainability . . .

2. My take on Le Corbusier's focus on solar energy and its use / control in this chapter may seem quite critical. Also worth noting, however, is the extreme (and laudable) technical sophistication of Le Corbusier's analyses of the role of the sun in an architectural program making use of a primary renewable resource. See, for example, Daniel Barber's presentation of Le Corbusier in *Modern Architecture and Climate,* including Le Corbusier's superb multipage analysis (reproduced in full in Barber's book) of solar architectural technology, with special focus on the *brise-soleil* (52–55).

3. Some critics do indeed link Le Corbusier to sustainability based on his concern for fostering and working with the solar. See, for example, Flueckiger, *How Much House?*; Kamal, "Le Corbusier's Solar Shading Strategy."

4. On Le Corbusier's connection with the 1920s technocratic and corporatist journal *Plans,* and his connections with Georges Bataille, see Stoekl, "Truman's Apotheosis."

5. Chandigarh is, admittedly, the furthest Le Corbusier got in designing a built and successful urban ensemble. See Lahiji, "'The Gift of Time.'" Note, however, that for Lahiji, Le Corbusier's Chandigarh plan is precisely a critique of the hierarchical structure of *La Ville Radieuse* (129), and thus consonant with Bataille's approach. Lahiji derives his inspiration here from the great architectural theorist Manfredo Tafuri.

6. De Pierrefeu and Le Corbusier, *La Maison des hommes,* 145 (my translations).

7. Le Corbusier, *City of To-Morrow,* 246–47.

8. As in Alexandre Kojève's *Introduction à la lecture de Hegel,* at the end of history, nothing new can happen. Humanity dies, in effect, since it is defined by its historical project (human liberation), and that has been completed. Le Corbusier goes a bit further, implying that not only is historical transformation (i.e., revolution) at an end, but urban change is as well.

9. Richards, *Le Corbusier,* 54–65.

10. De Pierrefeu, it seems, wrote the narrative text, Le Corbusier provided the sketches and commentary accompanying them. De Pierrefeu was serving mainly as Le Corbusier's mouthpiece: as Simon Richards puts it, "Even the most cursory reading reveals that he [de Pierrefeu] has been deeply inculcated into the Corbusian creed. . . . For this reason I will be treating de Pierrefeu's text as a reliable transcript of Le Corbusier's own ideals." Richards, *Le Corbusier,* 222n3. One should note, however, that de Pierrefeu emits a few openly fascistic and racist pronouncements along the way, which are not on display in Le Corbusier's other writings. Did Le Corbusier's use of de Pierrefeu allow him to both express his "real" political orientation while distancing himself from it (or obscuring his relation to it)?

11. De Pierrefeu and Le Corbusier, *La Maison des hommes,* 31–32 (emphasis in original).

12. This conjunction of the finitude of fuels theme and technocracy, in a French book published in 1942, is interesting: Were de Pierrefeu and Le Corbusier aware of Hubbert's work, and his *Technocracy Study Course?* Though they don't cite Hubbert, it certainly is possible.

13. Le Corbusier, *Destin de Paris,* 15 (emphasis in original, my translations). Winter was, it seems, like de Pierrefeu, another *planiste* who found Vichy-style corporatism appealing.

14. As a contributor to *planiste* (corporatist, technocratic) journals such as *Plans* and *Préludes,* along with Le Corbusier, Winter was very much associated with the technocratic "new right" tendencies that later attempted, without a lot of success, to gain traction at Vichy (Richards, *Le Corbusier,* 222n3). Winter's articles include topics such as the role of sports and labor, the psychological conditions of labor, the circulation of air (in homes), the importance of the peasantry, and the "laws of nature" that determine planning (these works are cited on the final page of the 1941 edition of *Destin de Paris*). Winter's interest in solar energy was paralleled by other French thinkers of the period, such as Georges Ambrosino, a physicist who, like Le Corbusier, had connections with Georges Bataille.

15. This argument is not exclusive to Le Corbusier: in a recent popular book, *Green Metropolis: What the City Can Teach the Country about True Sustainability,* David Owen argues that, indeed, big cities, due to their inherent energy efficiency (one can live without a car, etc.), and despite appearances, are the proper locus of sustainable living.

16. See Richards, *Le Corbusier,* 133–34.

17. This passage, which starts the famous "Divertissements" section in Pascal's *Pensées* (section 168 in the version edited by Philippe Sellier [Paris: Le Livre de Poche, 2000]), is cited in Richards, *Le Corbusier,* 133. In French: "J'ai dit souvent que tout le

malheur des hommes vient d'une seule chose, qui est de ne savoir pas demeurer en repos dans une chambre."

18. Pascal, cited in Richards, *Le Corbusier,* 133.

19. See Richards, "Antisocial Urbanism of Le Corbusier."

20. Le Corbusier, *The Four Routes,* 18.

21. See Leatherbarrow and Wesley, *Three Cultural Ecologies,* which contains a history of Le Corbusier's interest in monastic withdrawal. The authors trace much of Le Corbusier's project, and certainly his interest in a pairing of (monastic) social life and ecological harmony, to an initial visit to a Carthusian monastery at Galluzzo, Italy, in 1907. See especially chapter 6, "Alone-Together Naturally" (115–48). Another monastic project, which Le Corbusier designed for a community with which he had great sympathy, was the Dominican priory of Sainte Marie de la Tourette (1960). It contains one hundred monks' cells.

22. Pascal, *Pensées,* section 233, 116. The Dutton translation (1958) has this for the final words: "Even this will naturally make you believe, and deaden your acuteness." This is a nicer way of putting it, perhaps, but after all Pascal is quite straightforward: you will be mindless, like an animal *(cela vous abêtira).*

23. Kant, *Critique of Practical Reason,* 107–8.

24. Žižek, *For They Know Not,* 230 (emphasis in original).

25. This dilemma is also, of course, at the heart of Kafka's universe.

26. Žižek refers to the Lacan essay "Kant with Sade."

27. My point here is grounded in the fact that calculating carbon footprints and energy investments always comes up against the problem that such calculations can run on for infinity. Every agent and resource involved will have its own footprint, which entails yet more footprints, etc., all of which would have to be somehow calculated. Some "boundaries" must be set, and they are inevitably arbitrary, although no doubt useful. Thus, for example, Rauland and Newman, in *Decarbonising Cities,* make the point that "determining clear boundaries associated with the life cycle approach [of materials and services] is critical as boundaries are essentially infinite" (247). Without an arbitrary fixing of boundaries, the analyst risks floating into a zone of scalar disproportion (infinitely small or large carbon footprints; an infinite task of computation).

28. Sade was a Kantian as well in his version of the Kantian categorical imperative. "Act as you would want all other people to act towards all other people. Act according to the maxim that you would wish all other rational people to follow, as if it were a universal law." For Kant, duty is complete obedience to this dictum, without any admixture of ("pathological") personal will. For Sade this means republican, state-run bordellos in which every citizen prostitutes him or herself to every other, necessarily obeying the whims of any and all, but also dictating his or her whims to all others *(Philosophy in the Bedroom).*

29. Goh, in *The Reject,* posits his version of the reject as a kind of deconstructed figure of the subject in metaphysics.

30. The duality of heterogeneity is sketched out in Bataille, "The Psychological Structure of Fascism," in section 5, "The Fundamental Duality of the Heterogeneous World," in *Visions of Excess,* 144–45.

31. Bataille, "The Psychological Structure of Fascism," in *Visions of Excess,* 137–60; 138 (emphasis in original).

32. Bataille, "Rotten Sun," in *Visions of Excess,* 57–58; 57.

33. On the connections between the sun and the swastika (in Hinduism, etc.), see, for example, Wilson, *The Swastika.*

34. On Durkheim and *The Elementary Forms of the Religious Life,* see chapter 7 below.

35. Le Corbusier's urban ecology extends mainly to grass and trees.

36. These are the bizarre topics (such as "Eye," "The Big Toe," "Slaughterhouse," etc.) of a number of short essays by Bataille from the journal *Documents* (1929–1930), collected in Bataille, *Oeuvres complètes,* vol. 1, and in English in *Visions of Excess.*

37. Bataille, "Figure humaine," in *Oeuvres complètes,* vol. 1, 181–85; 182 (my translation).

38. Bataille, "Je ne crois pas pouvoir (2)," in *Oeuvres complètes,* vol. 2, 131–33; 132 (my translation). This fragment from the 1920s, unpublished in Bataille's lifetime, reads like a mashup of Pascal's two infinities with Nietzschean and surrealist takes on human insignificance and the clash of incongruous objects.

39. Bataille, "Je ne crois pas pouvoir (2)," 132 (my translation).

40. Hollier, *Against Architecture,* 60.

41. Gasché, "L'Avorton de la pensée," 25 (my translation).

42. Nietzsche, *The Gay Science,* 273 (section 341).

43. For more on Bataille's "Obelisk," see my *Bataille's Peak,* 98–104.

44. Bataille, "The Obelisk," in *Visions of Excess,* 213–22; 220.

6. ANAMORPHOSES OF THE FUTURE

1. Jünger, *On Pain,* 22.

2. Jünger, *The Worker,* 28.

3. See Blok, *Ernst Jünger's Philosophy of Technology:* "The elemental designates the earth as a fruitful domain of possibilities . . . on which the hope of a new determination of man and the world is placed. . . . Total mobilization describes the growing conversion of life into energy, in which man and the world appear *as* function, *as* work. The elemental refers to the force field that first appears with the total demise of the *animal rationale;* that which remains after this demise is elemental life and its motifs" (29).

4. The reactionary implications of this position are evident, and much writing on Jünger is devoted to a critique of his politics. See, for example, Neaman, *A Dubious Past.*

5. At the battle of Langemark (First Ypres, November 9, 1914); on the history and romanticizing myth of this battle, see Cowley, "Massacre of the Innocents."

6. On the type, and *Gestalt* (form) of the worker, see Blok, *Ernst Jünger's Philosophy of Technology,* 28–37.

7. One thinks of the role of war in Orwell's *1984;* the point is less "winning" than perpetuating a conflict that is the ultimate *raison d'être* of what one might call (parodying Louis Marin) a "degenerate technocracy."

8. Heidegger's critique of technology as a reading of Jünger's version of it is well known; no one, however, so far as I know, seems to have yet written extensively on the connections between Jünger's, Heidegger's, and Benjamin's versions of repetition, reproduction, and technology.

9. Benjamin, "Work of Art in the Age of Its Technical Reproducibility," in *Selected Writings,* vol. 3, 101–33; 104.

10. Benjamin, "On the Concept of History," in *Selected Writings,* vol. 4, 401–11; 396.

11. Benjamin, *Arcades Project,* 395.

12. This is the same action as that carried out by Atget, who, in his protosurrealist still photographs of urban Paris, strips the subjects of the kitschy aura that had been prevalent in later nineteenth century photography. See Benjamin, "Little History of Photography," *Selected Writings,* vol. 2, part 2, 507–30; 518.

13. Benjamin, "Surrealism," in *Selected Writings,* vol. 2, part 1, 207–21; 210.

14. Margaret Cohen, in *Profane Illumination,* her essential book on the relations between Benjamin and surrealism, rightly notes the connection between the world of questionably recycled cast-offs—both objects and people—and the larger "socially transformative potential of repressed libidinal forces" (110). In other words, for the surrealists, and Benjamin as well, the revolution is, on a collective as well as individual level, a matter of libidinal liberation as well as a conventionally economic political one, and this liberation is tied to a radical critique of the commodity fetish in capitalism. The world of the cast-off, such as the Parisian arcades in the 1920s or 1930s, is the privileged site / vehicle of this transformation.

15. Benjamin was of course deeply influenced by the presentation of forgotten, dusty and faintly fragrant objects not only in surrealism but in texts by Baudelaire, such as the poem "Spleen: J'ai plus de souvenirs que si j'avais mille ans."

16. Benjamin, *Arcades Project,* 389.

17. Roland Barthes cited the shadow area between sleep and wakefulness in Proust as a prime instance of what he called "the neutral." See his 1977–78 lecture series, *The Neutral.*

18. One thinks of the opening sequence in the first novel of *Remembrance of Things Past, Swann's Way,* and these famous lines (in the C. K. Scott Moncrieff translation): "Perhaps the immobility of the things that surround us is forced upon them by our conviction that they are themselves, and not anything else, and by the immobility of our conceptions of them. For it always happened that when I awoke like this, and my mind struggled in an unsuccessful attempt to discover where I was, everything would be moving round me through the darkness: things, places, years" (6).

19. Benjamin's only extended piece of writing on Jünger is his review essay "On the Collection of Essays *War and Warriors,* edited by Ernst Jünger," 312–21. In this piece, Benjamin rightly excoriates Jünger's fascistic take on mobilization and war. It is unfortunate, though, that Benjamin never engaged directly with Jünger's affirmation of mechanization and repetition / reproduction, which bears more than a few similarities with Benjamin's. While Benjamin never wrote on this aspect of Jünger, then, I think one can argue that he was at least responding to a cult of mechanization that was "in the air," which itself owed a lot, in Germany at least, to the influence of Jünger.

One can see a similar cult among the Technocrats in the United States: life will be modernized when it is fully mechanized, incarnating the predictable regularity of the machine. But in the German context this mechanization inevitably was directly assigned to the extremes of either fascism (Jünger) or Marxism (Benjamin).

20. As Breton writes in the *First Manifesto of Surrealism,* "The value of the image depends upon the beauty of the spark obtained; it is, consequently, a function of the difference of potential between the two conductors" (29). The two conductors are the two terms of the surrealist metaphor; the greater the aptness and incongruity of the metaphor, the greater the spark. I would argue that this image of metaphor is itself more than a simple metaphor; there is literally a spark, an expenditure of energy, in and through the coming together of tenor and vehicle in any metaphor, and especially in one particularly striking and incongruous. Metaphor, the process of being aware, of thinking and comparing, involves the usage of energy and results in the expenditure of energy, both in the brain itself and in the actions of a person or animal in the world. And that expenditure is rhetorical, an effect of the information and figurative structure of what has been called "consciousness"—which itself is not definable outside of rhetorical tropes, most notably metaphor and simile (see note 28).

21. See, for example, Harman, *Towards Speculative Realism:* "My perception of fire and cotton fails to use up the total realities of these beings, since they are describable at infinite length in a way that I can never approach. . . . Presence *means* relationality, nothing more. To consider an object in its being means to consider it in its withdrawal from all forms of presence, whether as something seen, used or just spatially present among other entities. All objects withdraw from each other, not just from humans" (124, 125). One could argue that "relationality" is figuration: all objects are comprehended as such through their similarity / difference with other objects. Harman's theory is one of rhetoric. And one can also compare Harman's relationality to the impossibility of establishing clear and finite boundaries to the carbon footprint of any given object.

22. And Benjamin's future is indeed a technocratic one (a fact often overlooked): it entails a technologization of art (if not a technocracy of art), first of all, that aids in the restructuring and reform of society (through the destruction of the religiously tinged aesthetic and societal "aura"), following the model of mechanical reproduction in photography and cinema.

23. It is fairly evident that Benjamin was no more an orthodox Marxist than was Bataille, though Benjamin was more than willing to play the Marxist while accusing Bataille of fascistic tendencies. Benjamin's "On the Concept of History" is a repudiation of Marxist and Hegelian dialectics—in fact the repetition of history in Benjamin is precisely *not* dialectical, there is no higher sublation, and that is the point of the essay (despite Benjamin's retention and repurposing of the term "dialectical"). Further, one looks in vain in Benjamin for any significant stress on the most important (and debatable) elements in Marx's economic theory, the labor theory of value and the tendency of the rate of profit to fall (what for Marx made his theory "scientific"). At most, Benjamin's Marxism consists of a remix of Marx's (via the Frankfurt School and Lukács) critique of alienation in commodity fetishism.

24. Benjamin's alter ego, the (questionably) bicephalous angel, has an evil twin: Bataille's fave, the *acéphale*.

25. Handelman, "Walter Benjamin," 348. Handelman, in her discussion of the angel, relates, as is clear enough in Benjamin's text, his political analysis to the Jewish traditions of the Talmud and its interpretations. In the passage from which I quote, she refers to the writings of Gershom Scholem and Geoffrey Harman.

26. Hofstadter, *Gödel, Escher, Bach,* 691 (emphasis in original).

27. That is, the radical separation of an earth from attempts at technological reconfiguration (in order to "save" it) as well as internalized appropriation (the earth as object or subject). See Neyrat, *The Unconstructable Earth.* He writes: "Nature is not simply natured nature (an object that is to be shaped or is manipulable), naturing nature (a producing subject), but also a *denaturing* nature—a movement of withdrawal, an anti-production preceding all production" (134).

28. Nagel tries, unconvincingly, to define his own "what it is like" as "'how it is for the subject himself'" rather than "'what (in our experience) it *resembles*'"—in other words he tries to define two ways of reading "what it is like" and set them in radical opposition (440n6). Nagel's version of "likeness" depends on an undefined subjectivity ("for the subject himself *[sic]*"). One would refer to some sort of authentic experience and understanding of consciousness (my own or others'), the other to a mere comparison (resemblance). But "how it is" also implies comparison: it is not just as it is (whatever that could mean), but *as* something else, since I am defining how it is necessarily in relation to something else ("how it is" implies definition, elaboration, explanation, etc.). There is no way to define "consciousness" or "subjectivity," or its workings, then, outside this play of catachresis, the trope of aberrant metaphor. To invoke subjectivity to make sense of the opposition only begs the question.

29. Bataille, "Formless," in *Visions of Excess,* 31.

30. Žižek, *For They Know Not,* 89–90.

31. De Man, "The Concept of Irony," in *Aesthetic Ideology,* 163–84; 177.

32. See Paulhan, *Flowers of Tarbes.*

33. Hamacher, "'Now,'" 63.

34. As Khatib points out in "Barbaric Salvage," Benjamin's future figure is not so much a proletarian as it is a barbarian: "The barbarian is a radical simplifier of life who can meet humanity's basic needs rather than endlessly complicating them from the standpoint of bourgeois reason and its fictitious causalities. Benjamin's 'new, positive concept of barbarism' also announces a new life-form, neither derived from a nostalgic past nor a prophetic future but from the poor now and the 'dirty diapers of the present'" (141). This new barbarian, it should be pointed out, is a tweaking of Jünger's, also conceived as an antibourgeois life-form, though Jünger, like so many men's men, does not concern himself with dirty diapers.

7. SUSTAINABILITY'S RETURN

1. Fleming, "Lost in Translation," 29.

2. Morris, *American Heritage Dictionary,* s.v. "mitigation."

3. Morris, *American Heritage Dictionary,* s.v. "adaptation."

4. As does Prof. Richard Weller of the University of Pennsylvania landscape architecture program (in conversation with the author).

5. See the landmark study by Lynn Margulis (Sagan), "On the Origin of Mitosing Cells."

6. As Karen Pinkus and others have pointed out, this "loving the world as it is"— preserving it as it is—depends on a perfectly arbitrary anthropomorphic choice of the present. "Sustainability, in other words, carves out a time that is workable around the human time of the now and the near future" ("The Risks of Sustainability," 72). I would argue, on the other hand, that a future elaboration of sustainability can nevertheless affirm the profound disproportion of timescales, anthropomorphic or not, in which it is always-again situated.

7. On jobless negativity, see Bataille, "Letter to Blank," in *Guilty*, 123–25. "Blank" was Kojève, whose famous seminar on Hegel Bataille had attended in the early 1930s.

8. "Mississippi," on the Bob Dylan album *Love and Theft*.

9. The work alluded to is Freud and Burlingham, *Young Children in War-Time*.

10. Varela and Maturano, *Autopoiesis and Cognition*.

11. Margulis and Sagan, *Slanted Truths*, 267.

12. See Luhmann, *Social Systems*.

13. Margulis and Sagan, *What Is Life?*, 185.

14. For example, Bruce Clarke and Mark B. N. Hansen write, in the context of Luhmann's work on systems and autopoiesis: "One of the capital advantages of the concept of the self-referential system (as against the notion of the subject) is its delineation of such a system's capacity to manage environmental complexity and indeed to derive its identity and its autopoiesis from its continual need to reduce the complexity of the environment by processing it through systemic constraints." *Emergence and Embodiment*, 11.

15. Although Bataille doesn't use this term, it's certainly implied.

16. See Margulis and Sagan's affirmative comments on Bataille's *Accursed Share*, in *What Is Life?*, 164–66.

17. Bataille, "L'Economie à la mesure de l'univers," in *Oeuvres complètes*, vol. 7, 7–16; 14–15 (my translation).

18. All of this recalls European technocrats' discussions of solar and fossil fuel energy in the 1930s and 1940s, of which Bataille was surely aware. See my remarks on Dr. Winter, in the context of Le Corbusier, in chapter 5. Bataille's friend, the physicist Georges Ambrosino, was also certainly aware by the late 1940s (if not quite a bit earlier) of the potential of solar energy as an alternative to fossil fuels: Bataille at one point cites him approvingly. See my *Bataille's Peak*, 39.

19. Waste is only expenditure *(dépense)* as provided by, and characterized under, capitalism.

20. Bataille's larger goal in the *Accursed Share* (in 1949) was to "save" the world from nuclear catastrophe through the affirmation of *dépense*, both as an international economic strategy and as a method of meditation. Today the larger threat is not only nuclear war, but environmental collapse. See my comments about this larger purpose of *The Accursed Share* in chapter 8.

21. Mana certainly is a time-worn anthropological category. But the word still retains its validity and usefulness. On the history of the use of the word *mana* and its potential meanings (and value) in current debates, see Mazzarella, *Mana of Mass Society.*

22. Thus Durkheim hoped to show that modern, republican society, affirming a Kantian humanism through civic festivals and identification with revolutionary symbols (the human being the ultimate sacred element), would embody a contemporary, and finally rational, sacred. This new social practice would replace Christianity as the cohesive backbone of French society—respecting the heritage and practice of religion while grounding it in rationality (and verifiable anthropological findings).

23. Durkheim, *Elementary Forms,* 221.

24. Nancy, *Inoperative Community,* 31.

25. Bennett, *Vibrant Matter,* 56.

26. Demolition derbies, *gilets jaunes* riots, and guitar smashing, for example. All are associated with certain social classes (or class revolt), and they are all frenzied potlatch rituals. They are located at the point where symbolic expenditure (a "potlatch of signs") and physical expenditure converge. They are scary precisely to the extent that one can never rest assured that they are merely minor forms of vandalism, but rather that in some sense they threaten the very premises of a seemingly stable, consumerist society. They, and many other instances, are the "safety valve" of violence that threatens to do away with safety. Such expenditure, it goes without saying, can also turn once again into a terrible affirmation of an exclusionary community (the occupation and sacking of state or national capitals, for example). The difference between the two lies in the fact that the heterogeneity of the rioting fascist mob has behind it, or rising above it and dominating it, a figure of imperative (sadistic) sovereignty—a Leader.

27. Lingis, *The Community of Those Who Have Nothing in Common,* 12.

28. This is my translation. Peter Connor's translation reads, for the second *partagent* "share each other on their limits," which is also good. See *The Inoperative Community,* 41. For the original French, see Nancy, *La Communauté désœuvrée,* 102.

29. See, for example, Maurice Blanchot's *The Unavowable Community,* which depicts the really radical community as one not so much of (lumpen) anarchists, mad saints, or lovers, as in Bataille, but readers. Literature, the text, in Blanchot's very specialized sense, is the last uncompromised thing tying a community together, after the disastrous horrors of the communist (Stalinist) and fascist communities. Nancy also elaborates his version of community against, or after, totalitarian politics, and he no doubt derives his iconoclasm, his profound suspicion of overt sacrificial engagement, from Blanchot as well. See, in this context, Nancy's critique of the sacrificial logic of philosophy in essays such as "The Unsacrificeable."

30. See my chapter on Durkheim in *Agonies of the Intellectual.*

31. And, of course, individual subjectivity. Bataille famously sees potlatch not as a calculated and calculating game of individual prestige, but rather at its most fundamental, as the fundamental and inescapable tendency to expend. See "The Notion of Expenditure": "The consequences [of potlatch] in the realm of acquisition are only

the unwanted result . . . of a process oriented in the opposite direction" (in *Visions of Excess,* 122).

32. From this perspective, DIY and scrounging/expending is the unplanned and unplannable aftereffect of the end of capitalism (consumerism, commodity fetishism), not the post-productivist phase of a planned eco-economy.

33. The end of the world (of productivism, infinite growth, the subject–object opposition) and the end of capitalism do not, however, "automatically" result in a gift economy; there is a *practice* (but not a constructive, subjective exercise of the will) in the inoperative community, as there is in communities of meditation and scrounging (see chapters 8 and 9). Simple collective passivity before the end of the world risks the return of feudal despotism and slavery.

34. Consciousness, and intelligence, are thus not synonymous with a closed, self-referential subjectivity. Consciousness—awareness—is a rhetorical function, the play of comparison and contrast in time (grammar). As Margulis and Sagan would argue, it is a function of life, but life itself is very difficult if not impossible to define, and could involve different chemicals and processes on different planets.

35. And in some circumstances, social justice: the demand for the power *for all* to ecstatically expend.

36. Note that for both Bataille and Meadows the crisis of limits that humanity faces is, paradoxically, not particularly human. For Bataille, all living organisms, under certain "favorable" conditions, risk outrunning their environment and growing (expanding and reinvesting) too much (and thus they face ecological crisis [economic crisis being a human variant of this]); for Meadows, at least implicitly, any organism could use up the available nutrients or resources and thus face population collapse. In both cases, the "need" for sustainability would not be a response to a particularly anthropomorphic condition, but to one common to all species and living systems. This most fundamental aspect of sustainability, then, the limits to growth, can be identified most directly with what I have called first-order sustainability (sustaining primarily outside the context of the human), and not second (or third).

37. But which world? An ostensibly perfectible one, arbitrarily determined in utopian narrative?

38. Bataille, *Sacred Conspiracy,* 334.

8. MARXISM, MEDITATION, CONSUMPTION

1. Angus cites here Malm, *Fossil Capital,* 11.

2. See Global Footprint Network, "Only Eight Countries," https://www.foot printnetwork.org/2015/09/23/eight-countries-meet-two-key-conditions-sustainable -development-united-nations-adopts-sustainable-development-goals/. While Cuba is not alone here, it is singled out among the eight as having a "very high level" of human development (HDI)—as opposed to just "high"—and along with that a very low level of resource consumption, due, one could add, to the involuntary poverty of its inhabitants. Leaving that poverty behind would, of course, end the desirable small ecological footprint enjoyed per capita by the Cuban population, and probably take it off the list of countries meeting the two key conditions for sustainable development.

3. Angus, *Facing the Anthropocene*, 155–58 ("Cars and Suburbs").

4. Debord, *La Société du spectacle*, 30 (my translation).

5. Debord's, and others', essential writings on drifting in the city and the *détournement* of objects and texts can be found in McDonough, *Guy Debord and the Situationist International: Texts and Documents*.

6. Angus cites Mandel, *Long Waves of Capitalist Development*, 83.

7. As Yelle puts it in *Sovereignty and the Sacred*, "Sovereignty is just another term for not being subject to conditions" (124). See Yelle's excellent discussion of Bataille and sovereignty (98–125). Hence one can found a nation on sovereignty—the sovereign is unconditioned—but, in the "base heterogeneity" of Bataille, sovereignty would entail the unconditional foundation of subjectivity itself (the self not subject to the conditions of limitation). Hence Bataille's meditation, which I link to Buddhist meditation. For an interesting take on sovereignty (in the negative sense) in relation to ecology, see Smith, *Against Ecological Sovereignty*.

8. Schumacher, *Small Is Beautiful*, 58–59.

9. Not to mention the fact that Buddhists recently (in Myanmar, for example) have been just as violent and exclusionary as anyone else.

10. "Not knowing" *(le non-savoir)* is associated by Bataille with the "blind spot" of understanding *(la tache aveugle de l'entendement),* a total understanding that impossibly embraces that which it cannot absorb *(Inner Experience,* 110–11). This blind spot of not-knowing could be considered as isomorphic to the "smear" in Lacan's reading of Kant and Sade (see chapter 5); the smearing both serves as the grounding of the distinct "pathological" self, but at the same time it is an opacity that establishes the self as deviant, necessarily rejected, unassimilable, its particularity a delusion. A sovereign self, in other words. "Not-knowing" at the summit of the philosophical system, at the most acute point of its vision, thus plays the same role in Bataille's meditative practice. Note that it is (logically) later that this smear-self is reintegrated as a kind of imperative heterogeneity, and hence associated with sadistic self-repression. We could argue that this later self is the self of fossil fuel consumerism, as well as of the effort to be free of this consumerism through constraint / restraint and object-manipulating technics.

11. See my comments on the difference between *consommation* and *consumation* in Bataille, in *Bataille's Peak*, 55. Bataille plays on the difference between the useful consumption of objects in capitalism *(consommer,* to wear out, use up), but also the sense of needless consumption in capitalism, as in *société de consommation; consumer* implies complete exhaustion of a resource, the fiery burn off of excess, in a positive (transgressive) sense.

12. My point here is that the total extinction of one species (say, deer) would inevitably mean the extinction of the other (wolves) that prey upon it. More deer means more wolves, which shrinks the deer population. The deer come back, after the wolves die off, and the cycle repeats itself. Ecology is always ecology in time; it consists of self-distorting feedback loops that are maintained over shorter or longer periods and then fade away or collapse. Any given ecology in this sense is inseparable from temporal finitude, both constituting it and limiting it; under any circumstances it must be seen as tragically finite (a function of, and victim of, entropy).

13. See Boon's discussion of Bataille's take on Buddhism in "To Live in a Glass House," 51–53.

14. Bataille, *Inner Experience,* 118 (translation modified).

15. On the psychological and interpersonal aspects of Bataille's meditative practice, see Hunt, "Secular Mysticism." Bataille's method may not have been as haphazard-seeming as it appears in *Inner Experience.* Jean Bruno, in "Les techniques d'illumination chez Georges Bataille," notes that there were, in fact, six stages of meditation, each logically following from the preceding, and that could have been transmitted (taught) to adepts. Bataille's *Acéphale* group may have had as its real "secret" (it was a so-called secret society), then, a method of meditation taught in group sessions on a regular basis to what would have amounted to Bataille's followers. See on this, for example, the clear outline of a practice of meditation addressed to one of the members of *Acéphale,* Isabelle Farner: *The Sacred Conspiracy,* 451.

16. This fetish-waste object can also be associated with the aesthetic object, to the extent that it is not exhaustible within systems of use and knowledge. See in this context Boetzkes, *Plastic Capitalism.*

17. Durkheim, *Elementary Forms,* 190.

18. Wright, *Why Buddhism Is True,* 209.

19. Bataille's meditation entails "dramatization"—representation, in other words. Like consciousness itself, it is a rhetorical structure, a function of the operations of comparison and contrast.

20. Bataille, *Inner Experience,* 121 (translation modified).

21. Bataille could very well have been thinking here of the death of his lover Laure (Collette Peignot); Maurice Blanchot also wrote of Laure's death, lightly fictionalized, in *Death Sentence.*

22. Hence, perhaps, the rather bizarre inclusion, in *Inner Experience,* of a shaggy-dog story having to do with a family in which the accidental death of one member triggers the death of another, until the whole family is wiped out (121).

23. The *ipse* is not absence of self, but (to simplify) the self opened out in meditation and death. It is the self of ecstasy rather than of servile labor. Harris, in *Conscious,* notes the contingent nature of the self, added on to consciousness as a kind of faux closure: "Though it may be impossible for someone who hasn't experienced something like this to imagine it, consciousness can still persist without an experience of being a self, and even in the absence of thought" (51). This consciousness could be associated with Bataille's *ipse.* Consciousness, that mysterious sauce that may be everywhere (panpsychism), in every rock and every animal, and is yet nowhere, indefinable beyond simile, is not identifiable with the self. In meditation, one passes away from a certain self, controlling, controlled, the subordinate of imperative heterogeneity, but nevertheless consciousness remains, an ineradicable smear. Consciousness, the rhetorical structure itself ("what it's like to be a bat" [or human]) is the residue that defies the perfect transparency of the moral law and the meaning of the closed economy of energy accounting. In the same way, Michael Pollan, in *How to Change Your Mind,* notes that in psychedelic experience activity in the brain's "Default Mode Network (DFM)," associated with "higher order 'metacognitive' activities" such as

"self-reflection, mental projection, time travel, and theory of mind—the ability to attribute mental states to others" "falls," leading to the "dissolution" of the "sense of self" (416). In psychedelic experience, then, the weakening of the DFM leads to the experience (in the Bataillean sense) not of a classic subjectivity but of one opened out (to death, the future), which we could associate with Bataille's *ipse.* See also, in this context, Piper, "Psychedelics, Transgression, and the End of History."

24. Of course one could mention the desert fathers, monastic orders that embraced extreme poverty, Carthusian hermit-monks who live alone and spend all their time studying holy texts, etc., but those are exactly the same orders that spend or spent enormous amounts of time engaging in hypnotic, repetitive prayer, chanting, and meditating on the wounds of Christ. In other words, they engage in an unproductive contemplative practice that wastefully embraces the *mana*-charged power of the object.

25. Baudrillard, *Mirror of Production,* 42.

26. Baudrillard in this text criticizes the emphasis on production and productivity among avant-garde critics of the period, such as Julia Kristeva, who also invoked Bataille (and wanted to assimilate "textual production" to a Bataillean expenditure). From Baudrillard's perspective, the Marxist cult of production was identifiable with a closed economy of utility and sense that could not have been further from Bataille's concerns.

27. Bataille, *Accursed Share,* 190.

28. See, for example, Braham, *Architecture and Systems Ecology,* 147–50. Writing of the concentration of energy resources in the maintenance of a domestic home, Braham makes it clear that simply using condensed energy resources (electricity, fuel oil, natural gas, food) is not enough to keep the system running; also necessary is *information,* from the education of engineers and architects to the regulation and amplification of the flow of resources "from more primary forms of production" (149). The larger point is that the concentration and dispersal of energy stores is as much a symbolic act as it is one of purely physical action. This is perfectly consistent with Bataille's pairing of the physical destruction of excessive elements as in potlatch rituals with the symbolic destruction of language, for example, in poetry. Bataille's meditative practices are both symbolic and physical, to the extent that the meditator is engaged on a physical level, but also a symbolic one (he or she meditates before a dramatic representation). In any event, an easy distinction between the physical and the intellectual is no longer operative; they are connected (if that's the word) through the anamorphoses of rhetoric. Braham also, interestingly, notes that "there is no simple boundary of analysis evaluating the cost of information" (148). Information is the element *par excellence* that eludes simple accounting when it comes to considering inputs.

29. Morton, "Buddhaphobia," 234.

30. Boon, "To Live in a Glass House," 52.

31. Cited in Boon, "To Live in a Glass House," 53. In Bataille, *Œuvres Complètes,* vol. 7, 437.

32. A current economy not based on production-consumption but on the ethics of Buddhism is that of Bhutan, which measures its success in "gross national happiness"

rather than "product." See Long, *Tantric State*. Such an economy, as Bataille noted, inevitably affirms economically useless activity rather than sheer production and perpetual (impossible) reinvestment.

33. See, for example, Derrida's *Given Time*, where the only thing that really can be a gift is time; everything else implies some economy of return, benefit, etc. In the same way, one can say that the only thing that can really be "wasted" is time, but wasted time also—inevitably—means wasted stuff, on many different levels: things not made, things allowed to decompose (and hence recycle themselves, at least in some cases), things as religious or aesthetic objects (charged with delight or ecstasy), things as sexual toys or fetishes (charged with sexual pleasure), things allowed to actively destroy themselves (the "self-consuming artifact").

34. Or that we must face with a very real fatalism at least the possibility of a general demise, however it might be defined. See, for example, Scranton, *We're Doomed, Now What?* and Thacker, *Infinite Resignation,* books that came out almost simultaneously in 2018.

35. Eli in the Old Testament (Book of Samuel) is the biblical patriarch who was incapable of reigning in the unacceptable behavior of his sons; God punishes him, resulting in his and his sons' deaths. This may or may not be relevant.

36. McCarthy, *The Road,* 173.

37. Or whatever his name is: he has even disavowed the name he gave earlier (167).

38. Indeed, the novel seems to revel in its lack of verisimilitude; the man and his son trudge on for what seems weeks, for hundreds of miles, yet eating only what almost always seems the last, or the next to last, can of preserved fruit or meat.

39. One can certainly obtain Death-of-God Christian readings in *The Road*, stressing, for example, the importance of grace, without higher values: "Only through belief in grace can man realize his [sic] *telos* in McCarthy without grounding his actions in Truth and Justice." Hawkins, *Cormac McCarthy's Philosophy,* 99.

40. From this perspective, the single gaze morphing into a two-way gaze would be the equivalent of the two incompatible / cohabiting gazes of anamorphic vision.

41. Bataille, *Accursed Share,* 197n22.

9. THE DEAD, THE FUTURE

1. This book was published by the University of Minnesota Press in 2021 under the title *Our Grateful Dead: Stories of Those Left Behind.* All translations of it here are my own.

2. Despret refers to Isabelle Stengers, "Penser à partir du ravage écologique," 154.

3. Ferrell, *Empire of Scrounge,* 89.

4. It should be noted that, in his book, Ferrell joyfully ignores the difference between "scrap" and "waste" (or "refuse"). This distinction has been defined by the Institute of Scrap Recycling Industries in this way: "Simply put, scrap is not waste. Waste—often called 'trash,' 'refuse' or 'garbage'—is a material that has no value and is not wanted. Wastes are disposed of because they are no longer useful. In contrast, scrap—often called 'recyclable material' or 'secondary material'—is a valuable

commodity sold in the global marketplace according to industrywide, globally recognized specifications as a raw material in lieu of virgin materials for manufacturing.
Worldwide, more than 800 million metric tons of scrap commodities are consumed
each year." https://www.recyclingtoday.com/article/isri-comments-china-revisions
-identification-standards-for-solid-wastes-general-rules/.

Ferrell's entire project could, however, be characterized as conflating the two: his
research indicates that everyday refuse (discarded photographs and mementos of all
sorts, worthless bits of stuff that reflect back on lost lives) can be of inestimable
value in understanding the past, reconfiguring the future, bringing the dead back to
life and carrying out (and defying) their wishes, instilling the sacred in everyday life,
and so on. In its own way, garbage is even more valuable than the scrap with which
it rubs shoulders, but outside the framework of the "useful" in capitalism. Indeed the
characterization of "waste" or "garbage" as such makes sense only within the logic
of capitalism.

5. Ferrell's task can therefore be seen as a kind of secular reenactment of the Mass.

6. As Bataille put it, "I defy any art lover to love a painting as much as a fetishist
loves a shoe." (In "L'Esprit moderne et le jeu des transpositions," in *Œuvres complètes*,
vol. 1, 271; 273.) Or, put another way, one could defy any sustainability advocate to
love a low carbon footprint as much as a fetishist loves a shoe.

7. Morris, *American Heritage Dictionary*, s.v. "to sustain."

8. Morris, *American Heritage Dictionary*, s.v. "to suspend."

9. Benjamin's "messianic" is of course (from his perspective) the only possible
alternative to the repressive and technocratic history-less future worked out by the
Marxists-Leninists-Stalinists of his era.

10. Here I must differ from Timofeeva, who, in her brilliant article "From the
Quarantine to the General Strike: On Bataille's Political Economy," valorizes Marxism as the primary model leading to a society of greater leisure, in which one can
engage in "employment" (163). As I have attempted to argue above (in chapters 4, 5,
and 6), planned (economically and ecologically) efficient societies are not in a position to affirm a sustainability model oriented primarily around an affirmation of
expenditure, free play, "the Sunday of life" (Queneau), etc. (Such affirmation is as
untenable as the support of meditation at the top of Le Corbusier's technically impec-
cable towers.) It is only when these—and scrounging, in Ferrell's sense—are disen-
gaged from eco-technocracy that a general sustainability can be evoked. That said,
the ground of eco-technocracy (second-order sustainability)—that is, the ground of
sense, quantification, and putatively stable, denotative representation—can never be
dispensed within an economy attempting to stem the ravages of capitalism, either
present or past.

11. And, of course, to the situationists as well, the practitioners of the *dérive*, the
passage through an inventive repurposing of urban space.

12. The famous French graffiti on this topic is that unholy trinity of working life,
"*Métro, Boulot, Dodo*" (subway, work, sleep, though sadly it doesn't rhyme in English),
usually scratched—where else?—on the walls in the Métro.

13. Carlsson, *Nowtopia*, 95.

14. Hawkins, *Ethics of Waste,* 113.

15. "Modern" as opposed to *Homo erectus, neanderthalensis,* etc. Those "primitive," "early" humans at least seemed to be pretty good at recycling and didn't get too puffed up about it (from what we can tell, at least, after having scrounged their trash piles, bone dumps, and burials).

16. See, for example, in the *New York Times,* "Scrappers," by Jake Halpern. Scrapping, a version of scrounging that targets only the most profitable elements recycled (such as copper and aluminum), is a process that nowadays involves reclaiming the discarded material of the leftover infrastructure that produced the city itself. As Halpern puts it, "In short, we have a glut of garbage from the objects that we have discarded, but we also have the derelict infrastructure that once made and sold the stuff" (52). The recyclers of Buffalo are heavily engaged in the actual recycling of what's left of the physical remains of industrial Buffalo. (This could be another way of thinking about corporeal generosity: the body, in effect, is that of the city.) Most of this scrap, of course, is sent to China.

17. Of course as I pointed out (in chapter 4), Callenbach's *Ecotopia* already contains some pretty savage Mad Maxian mythemes.

18. Diprose, *Corporeal Generosity,* 7.

19. Gallop, *Intersections,* 78–79.

20. This, I think, is what Clare Colebrook in *Sex after Life* is getting at when writing of "becoming-woman": "Once becoming-woman opens 'us' (we humans) to the notion that becoming is always singular, always the becoming of this or that singularity and always in responsive relation, then writing would be presented with the tireless and ongoing destruction of genders and proliferation of sexes; it is not that there are beings—women—who become. Rather, what something is is its rhythm of becoming" (165). One could argue that that "rhythm of becoming" is also a "rhythm of depletion." A regime of the "becoming-woman" might be seen as an alternative to both patriarchy and matriarchy, with matriarchy associable with hunter-gatherer societies, and patriarchy with agriculture-based ones. (See, on this topic, Scott, *Against the Grain.*) Of course a "becoming-woman" society would be a postcapital and postfossil fueled variant of a hunter-gatherer society, but the gathering now would be recycled as scrounging.

21. The Green New Deal will be erotic or it will not "be." See Pettman, *Peak Libido.*

22. Although Sade himself, it goes without saying, was fanatically opposed to the reproduction of the species, given his cult of human extinction . . .

23. Here one thinks of Julia Kristeva's argument (in her book *Revolution in Poetic Language*): she associates the semiotic chora with the pre-oedipal stage of development, a maternal/feminine period "before" the supremacy of the denotative function, and the body unification, enforced by the law of the father. The notion is a good one, I think, but I would associate it less with an actual temporal moment in human physical and psychic development than with the logically post-facto physical acts of scrounging and DIY improvisation, both "practical" and corporeal (and erotic).

24. Sartre, quoted in Schmidt, "Of Birth, Death," 114.

25. Schmidt, "Of Birth, Death," 114.

26. Lynn Margulis and Oona West write: "We reject the analogy that Gaia is a single organism, primarily because no single being feeds on its own waste nor, by itself, recycles its own food. Much more appropriate is the claim that Gaia is an interacting system, the components of which are organisms." "Gaia," 225.

27. One thinks of Franz Kafka's prescient short story "The Cares of a Family Man" (473), a highly suggestive parable, in which a peripatetic bit of rubbish (Odradek) scoots around in a correct bourgeois interior, too insignificant to capture but too disruptive to ignore, all the while reflecting ironically on the environment in which it "lives."

28. It can be objected that "individual" acts (meditation, scrounging) alone, like the individual choice to recycle analyzed by Gaye Hawkins, are finally not enough, at least in the current economic and political conjuncture, to make any real difference in the struggle against the ill effects of the Anthropocene. This may be true, but it should also be remembered that, in a democracy, people (individually responsible subjectivities) must independently choose, by voting, the correct path, the right version of the Green New Deal. Even in a coordinated and planned governmental response, individual choice is necessary, as Robert Costanza rightly noted in his article on "possible futures" that I discuss in chapter 4. One must also foresee (in the wake of Benjamin), as I have tried to do in the later chapters of this book, a historical moment (apocalyptic, messianic) in which "all bets are off" as to the continued viability of the mechanisms (late capitalism, representative democracy) that characterize the fossil fueled civilization that we know.

Bibliography

Adler, Mortimer J. *The Difference of Man and the Difference It Makes*. New York: Fordham University Press, 1993. (Orig. pub. 1960.)

Agamben, Giorgio. *Homo Sacer: Sovereign Power and Bare Life*. Translated by Daniel Heller-Roazen. Stanford, Calif.: Stanford University Press, 1998. (Orig. pub. 1995.)

Akin, William E. *Technocracy and the American Dream: The Technocrat Movement, 1900–1941*. Berkeley: University of California Press, 1977.

Alaimo, Stacy. *Exposed: Environmental Politics and Pleasures in Posthuman Times*. Minneapolis: University of Minnesota Press, 2016.

Alvord, Katie. *Divorce Your Car! Ending the Love Affair with the Automobile*. Gabriola Island, B.C.: New Society, 2000.

Angus, Ian. *Facing the Anthropocene: Fossil Capitalism and the Crisis of the Earth System*. New York: Monthly Review Press, 2016.

Aragon, Louis. *Paris Peasant*. Translated and introduction by Simon Watson Taylor. Boston: Exact Change, 1994. (Orig. pub. 1926.)

Barber, Daniel A. *Modern Architecture and Climate: Design before Air Conditioning*. Princeton, N.J.: Princeton University Press, 2020.

Barthes, Roland. *The Neutral: Lecture Course at the College de France (1977–1978). Translated by Rosalind Krauss and Denis Hollier*. New York: Columbia University Press, 2005.

Bataille, Georges. *The Accursed Share*. Vol. 1, *Consumption*. Translated by Robert Hurley. New York: Zone Books, 1988. (Orig. pub. 1949.)

Bataille, Georges. *Guilty*. Translated by Bruce Boone. Venice, Calif.: Lapis Press, 1988. (Orig. pub. 1945.)

Bataille, Georges. *Inner Experience*. Translated by Leslie Anne Boldt. Albany, N.Y.: State University of New York Press, 1988. (Orig. pub. 1943.)

Bataille, Georges. *Oeuvres complètes*. Vol. 1. Edited by Denis Hollier. Paris: Gallimard, 1970.

Bataille, Georges. *Oeuvres complètes*. Vol. 2. Edited by Denis Hollier. Paris: Gallimard, 1970.

Bataille, Georges. *Oeuvres complètes*. Vol. 7. Edited by Thadée Klossowski. Paris: Gallimard, 1976.

Bataille, Georges. *The Sacred Conspiracy: The Internal Papers of the Secret Society of Acéphale and Lectures to the College of Sociology*. Edited by Marina Galletti and Alastair Brotchie. Translated by Natasha Lehrer, John Harman, and Mayer Barash. London: Atlas Press, 2017.

Bataille, Georges. *Visions of Excess: Selected Essays, 1927–1939*. Edited and translated by Allan Stoekl with Carl Lovitt and Donald M. Leslie Jr. Minneapolis: University of Minnesota Press, 1985.

Baudrillard, Jean. *The Mirror of Production*. Translated by Mark Poster. St. Louis, Mo.: Telos Press, 1975.

Benjamin, Walter. *The Arcades Project*. Edited by Rolf Tiedemann. Translated by Howard Eiland and Kevin McLaughlin. Cambridge, Mass.: Harvard University Press, 1999.

Benjamin, Walter. *Selected Writings*. Vol. 2. Part 1, 1927–1930. Translated by Rodney Livingstone and others. Boston, Mass.: Belknap Press of Harvard University Press, 1999.

Benjamin, Walter. *Selected Writings*. Vol. 2. Part 2, 1931–1934. Translated by Rodney Livingstone and others. Boston, Mass.: Belknap Press of Harvard University Press, 1999.

Benjamin, Walter. *Selected Writings*. Vol. 3, 1935–1938. Translated by Edmund Jephcott, Howard Eilman, and others. Boston, Mass.: Belknap Press of Harvard University Press, 2002.

Benjamin, Walter. *Selected Writings*. Vol. 4, 1938–1940. Translated by Edmund Jephcott and others. Boston, Mass.: Belknap Press of Harvard University Press, 2003.

Bennett, Jane. *Vibrant Matter: A Political Ecology of Things*. Durham, N.C.: Duke University Press, 2010.

Bharmal, Zahaan. "Is There Lyfe on Mars? New Concept Broadens Search for Alien Organisms: Research Suggests Standard Definition of Life May Be Too Restrictive for Complexities of Space." *Guardian*, July 30, 2020. https://www.theguardian.com/science/2020/jul/30/is-there-lyfe-on-mars-new-concept-broadens-search-for-alien-organisms.

Bjornerud, Marcia. *Timefulness: How Thinking Like a Geologist Can Help Save the World*. Princeton, N.J.: Princeton University Press, 2018.

Blanchot, Maurice. *Death Sentence*. Translated by Lydia Davis. Barrytown, N.Y.: Station Hill, 1998. (Orig. pub. 1948.)

Blanchot, Maurice. "Literature and the Right to Death." In *The Work of Fire*. Translated by Lydia Davis, 300–44. Stanford, Calif.: Stanford University Press, 1995.

Blok, Vincent. *Ernst Jünger's Philosophy of Technology: Heidegger and the Poetics of the Anthropocene*. London: Routledge, 2017.

Boetzkes, Amanda. *Plastic Capitalism: Contemporary Art and the Drive to Waste*. Cambridge, Mass.: MIT Press, 2019.

Boon, Marcus. "To Live in a Glass House Is a Revolutionary Virtue Par Excellence: Marxism, Buddhism, and the Politics of Nonalignment." In *Nothing: Three Inquiries in Buddhism,* by Marcus Boon, Eric Cazdyn, and Timothy Morton, 23–104. Chicago: University of Chicago Press, 2015.

Boyer, Dominic. "Energopolitics." In *Fueling Culture: 101 Words for Energy and the Environment,* edited by Imre Szeman, Jennifer Wenzel, and Patricia Yaeger, 128–31. New York: Fordham University Press, 2017.

Boyer, Dominic. "Energopower: An Introduction." *Anthropological Quarterly* 87, no. 2 (Spring 2014): 309–33.

Braham, William W. *Architecture and Systems Ecology: Thermodynamic Principles of Environmental Building Design, in Three Parts.* London: Routledge, 2016.

Breton, André. *Manifestoes of Surrealism.* Translated by Richard Seaver and Helen R. Lane. Ann Arbor: University of Michigan Press, 1969. (Orig. pub. 1924, 1929.)

Breton, André. *Nadja.* Translated by Richard Howard. New York: Grove Press, 1960. (Orig. pub. 1927.)

Bruyère, Vincent. *Perishability Fatigue: Forays into Environmental Loss and Decay.* New York: Columbia University Press, 2018.

Bullock, Marcus. "Walter Benjamin and Ernst Jünger: Destructive Affinities." *German Studies Review* 21, no. 3 (1998): 563–81.

Burnham, James. *The Managerial Revolution: What Is Happening in the World.* Westport, Conn.: Greenwood, 1972. (Orig. pub. 1941.)

Callenbach, Ernest. *Ecotopia: The Notebooks and Reports of William Weston.* Berkeley, Calif.: Banyan Tree Books, 2004. (Orig. pub. 1975.)

Camus, Albert. *The Myth of Sisyphus and Other Essays.* Translated by Justin O'Brien. New York: Alfred A. Knopf, 1955. (Orig. pub. 1942.)

Carlsson, Chris. *Nowtopia: How Pirate Programmers, Outlaw Bicyclists, and Vacant-Lot Gardeners Are Inventing the Future Today!* Oakland, Calif.: AK Press, 2008.

Certomà, Chiara. *Postenvironmentalism: A Material Semiotic Perspective on Living Spaces.* New York: Palgrave Pivot, 2016.

Chadwick, Douglas H. "Keystone Species: How Predators Create Abundance and Stability." *Mother Earth News.* June / July 2011. https:// www.motherearthnews.com / nature-and-environment / wildlife / keystone-species-zmoz11zrog.

Clarke, Bruce, and Mark B. N. Hansen. *Emergence and Embodiment: New Essays on Second-Order Systems Theory.* Durham, N.C.: Duke University Press, 2009.

Cohen, Margaret. *Profane Illumination: Walter Benjamin and the Paris of Surrealist Revolution.* Berkeley: University of California Press, 1993.

Colebrook, Claire. *Sex after Life: Essays on Extinction. Vol. 2.* Ann Arbor, Mich.: Open Humanities Press, 2014.

Cooper, Barry. *The End of History: An Essay on Modern Hegelianism.* Toronto: University of Toronto Press, 1984.

Costanza, Robert. "Visions of Alternative (Unpredictable) Futures and Their Use in Policy Analysis." *Ecology and Society* 4, no. 11 (2000). https:// www.ecologyandsociety.org/ vol4/ iss1/ art5/.

Costanza, Robert, et al. "The Value of the World's Ecosystem Services and Natural Capital." *Nature* 387 (1997): 253–60.

Costea, Bodgan, and Kostas Amiridis. "Ernst Jünger, Total Mobilisation and the Work of War." *Organization* 24, no. 4 (2017): 475–90.

Cowley, Robert. "Massacre of the Innocents." Historynet. Spring 1998. https://www.historynet.com/massacre-of-the-innocents.htm.

Crist, Eileen, and H. Bruce Rinker, eds. *Gaia in Turmoil: Climate Change, Biodepletion, and Earth Ethics in an Age of Crisis*. Foreword by Bill McKibben. Cambridge, Mass.: MIT Press, 2010.

Critchley, Simon. *How to Stop Living and Start Worrying*. London: Polity Press, 2010.

Cudworth, Erika, and Stephen Hobden. *The Emancipatory Project of Posthumanism*. London: Routledge, 2018.

Daggett, Cara New. *The Birth of Energy: Fossil Fuels, Thermodynamics, and the Politics of Work*. Durham, N.C.: Duke University Press, 2019.

Daly, Herman E. *Steady State Economics*. 2nd ed. Washington, D.C.: Island Press, 1991.

Debord, Guy. *La société du spectacle*. Paris: Gallimard/Folio, 1992.

de Certeau, Michel. "Walking in the City." In *The Practice of Everyday Life*. Translated by Steven Rendall, 91–110. Berkeley: University of California Press, 1988.

Deffeyes, Kenneth S. *Hubbert's Peak: The Impending World Oil Shortage*. New ed. Princeton, N.J.: Princeton University Press, 2008.

Deleuze, Gilles, and Félix Guattari. *Anti-Oedipus: Capitalism and Schizophrenia*. Translated by Robert Hurley. Preface by Michel Foucault. Introduction by Mark Seem. New York: Penguin Classics, 2009. (Orig. pub. 1972.)

de Man, Paul. *Aesthetic Ideology*. Edited and with an introduction by Andrzej Warminski. Minneapolis: University of Minnesota Press, 1996.

de Man, Paul. *Allegories of Reading: Figural Language in Rousseau, Nietzsche, Rilke and Proust*. New Haven, Conn.: Yale University Press, 1979.

de Man, Paul. *The Rhetoric of Romanticism*. New York: Columbia University Press, 1984.

de Pierrefeu, François, and Le Corbusier. *La maison des hommes*. Paris: Plon, 1951.

Derrida, Jacques. *The Animal That Therefore I Am*. Edited by Marie-Louise Mallet. Translated by David Wills. New York: Fordham University Press, 2008. (Orig. pub. 2006.)

Derrida, Jacques. *Given Time: I. Counterfeit Money*. Translated by Peggy Kamuf. Chicago: University of Chicago Press, 1994. (Orig. pub. 1991.)

Derrida, Jacques. *Khôra*. Paris: Galilée, 1993.

Derrida, Jacques. "White Mythology: Metaphor in the Text of Philosophy." *New Literary History* 6, no. 2 (Autumn 1974): 5–74.

de Sade, D. A. F. *Justine, Philosophy in the Bedroom, & Other Writings*. Translated by Richard Seaver and Austryn Wainhouse. New York: Grove Press, 2007. (Orig. pub. 1795.)

Descartes, René. *Discourse on Method and Meditations on First Philosophy*. Translated by Donald A. Cress. New York: Hackett, 1999.

Despret, Vinciane. *Au Bonheur des morts: Récits de ceux qui restent*. Paris: La Découverte / Poche, 2017. Published in English as *Our Grateful Dead: Stories of Those Left Behind*, trans. Stephen Muecke (Minneapolis: University of Minnesota Press, 2021).

Diprose, Rosalyn. *Corporeal Generosity: On Giving with Nietzsche, Merleau-Ponty, and Levinas*. Albany: State University of New York Press, 2002.

Dubkin, Leonard. *Enchanted Streets: The Unlikely Adventures of an Urban Nature Lover.* Boston: Little, Brown, 1947.

du Camp, Maxime. *Égypte, Nubie, Syrie: Paysages et monuments.* Paris: Gide et J. Baudry, 1852.

Durkheim, Émile. *The Elementary Forms of the Religious Life.* Translated by Joseph Ward Swain. London: George Allen and Unwin, 1915. (Orig. pub. 1912.)

Dylan, Bob. *Love and Theft.* Columbia Records CK 85975, 2001, compact disc.

Fernandez-Galianto, Luis. *Fire and Memory: On Architecture and Energy.* Translated by Gina Cariño. Cambridge, Mass.: MIT Press, 2000.

Ferrell, Jeff. *Empire of Scrounge: Inside the Urban Underground of Dumpster Diving, Trash Picking and Street Scavenging.* New York: New York University Press, 2006.

Fleck, Frédérique. "Anachronisme et anachronie," *Fabula.* October 7, 2011. http://www.fabula.org/atelier.php?Anachronisme_et_anachronie.

Fleming, Billy. "Lost in Translation: The Authorship and Argumentation of Resilience Theory." *Landscape Journal* 35, no. 1 (2016): 23–36.

Flint, Anthony. "The Hazardous Business of Celebrating Le Corbusier." Bloomberg CityLab. November 11, 2014. https://www.citylab.com/design/2014/11/the-hazardous-business-of-celebrating-le-corbusier/382584/.

Flueckiger, Urs Peter. *How Much House? Thoreau, Le Corbusier, and the Sustainable Cabin.* Berlin: Birkhauser, 2016.

Freeman, Kirrily. *Bronzes to Bullets: Vichy and the Destruction of French Public Statuary.* Stanford, Calif.: Stanford University Press, 2009.

Freud, Anna, and Dorothy Burlingham. *Young Children in War-Time: A Year's Work in a Residential War Nursery.* London: George Allen and Unwin, 1943.

FrontStream. "The Three Pillars of Sustainability." September 25, 2013. https://www.frontstream.com/blog/the-three-pillars-of-sustainability.

Gallop, Jane. *Intersections: A Reading of Sade with Bataille, Blanchot, and Klossowski.* Lincoln: University of Nebraska Press, 1981.

Gasché, Rodolphe. "L'avorton de la pensée." *L'Arc* 41 (1971): 11–27.

Georges, Bobby, and Tom Sparrow, eds. *Itinerant Philosophy: On Alphonso Lingis.* Brooklyn, N.Y.: Punctum Books, 2014.

Gibson-Graham, J. K. *A Postcapitalist Politics.* Minneapolis: University of Minnesota Press, 2006.

Girard, René. *Deceit, Desire and the Novel: Self and Other in Literary Structure.* Translated by Yvonne Freccero. Baltimore, Md.: Johns Hopkins University Press, 1976.

Global Footprint Network. "Only Eight Countries Meet Two Key Conditions for Sustainable Development as United Nations Adopts Sustainable Development Goals." September 23, 2015. https://www.footprintnetwork.org/2015/09/23/eight-countries-meet-two-key-conditions-sustainable-development-united-nations-adopts-sustainable-development-goals/.

Goh, Irving. *The Reject: Community, Politics, and Religion after the Subject.* New York: Fordham University Press, 2015.

Guattari, Félix. *The Three Ecologies.* Translated by Ian Pinder and Paul Sutton. New York: Bloomsbury Academic, 2014.

Halpern, Jake. "Scrappers: The Big Business of Scrapping in Postindustrial America." *New York Times Magazine,* August 25, 2019, 50–59.

Halsey, Mark. "Ecology and Machinic Thought: Nietzsche, Deleuze, Guattari." *Angelaki* 10, no. 3 (2005): 33–55.

Hamacher, Werner. "'Now': Walter Benjamin and Historical Time." In *Walter Benjamin and History,* edited by Andrew Benjamin, 38–68. London: Continuum, 2005.

Handelman, Susan. "Walter Benjamin and the Angel of History." *Cross Currents: Religion and Intellectual Life* 41 (1991): 344–52.

Hargrove, June. *The Statues of Paris: An Open-Air Pantheon.* New York: Vendome, 1989.

Harman, Graham. *Heidegger Explained: From Phenomenon to Thing.* Chicago: Open Court, 2007.

Harman, Graham. *Towards Speculative Reason: Essays and Lectures.* London: Zero Books, 2010.

Harris, Annaka. *Conscious: A Brief Guide to the Fundamental Mystery of the Mind.* New York: HarperCollins, 2019.

Hawkins, Gay. *The Ethics of Waste: How We Relate to Rubbish.* London: Rowman and Littlefield, 2006.

Hawkins, Ty. *Cormac McCarthy's Philosophy.* London: Palgrave MacMillan, 2017.

Heinberg, Richard. *The Oil Depletion Protocol: A Plan to Avert Oil Wars, Terrorism and Economic Collapse.* Gabriola Island, B.C.: New Society, 2006.

Heinberg, Richard. *The Party's Over: Oil, War and the Fate of Industrial Societies.* Gabriola Island, B.C.: New Society, 2003.

Heinberg, Richard. *Peak Everything: Waking Up to a Century of Declines.* Gabriola Island, B.C.: New Society, 2007.

Heinberg, Richard. *Powerdown: Options and Actions for a Post-Carbon World.* Gabriola Island, B.C.: New Society, 2004.

Helm, Dieter. *Natural Capital: Valuing our Planet.* New Haven, Conn.: Yale University Press, 2015.

Hinchcliffe, Steve, and Sarah Whatmore. "Living Cities: Toward a Politics of Conviviality." In *Technonatures: Environments, Technologies, Spaces and Places in the Twenty-First Century,* edited by Damian F. White and Chris Wilbert, 105–24. Waterloo, Ont.: Wilfred Laurier University Press, 2009.

Hofstadter, Douglas R. *Gödel, Escher, Bach: An Eternal Golden Braid.* New York: Random House, 1989.

Hollier, Denis. *Against Architecture: The Writings of Georges Bataille.* Translated by Betsy Wing. Cambridge, Mass.: MIT Press, 1990. (Orig. pub. 1974.)

Hubbert, M. King. "Energy from Fossil Fuels." *Science* 109:2823 (February 4, 1949): 103–9.

Hubbert, M. King. *Technocracy Study Course.* New York: Technocracy Inc., 1940.

Hunt, Harry. "Implications and Consequences of Post-Modern Philosophy for Contemporary Transpersonal Studies: II. Georges Bataille's Post-Nietzschean Secular Mysticism, Phenomenology of Ecstatic States, and Original Transpersonal Sociology." *International Journal of Transpersonal Studies* 32, no. 2 (2013): 79–97.

Illich, Ivan. *Energy and Equity.* London: Marion Boyers, 1974.

Inman, Mason. *The Oracle of Oil: A Maverick Geologist's Quest for a Sustainable Future.* New York: Norton, 2016.

Jameson, Fredric. "The Politics of Utopia." *New Left Review* 25 (January–February 2004): 35–54.

Jenkins, Willis. "Sustainability Theory." In *The Berkshire Encyclopedia of Sustainability,* edited by Roy C. Anderson, 380–84. New York: Berkshire, 2010.

Jünger, Ernst. *On Pain.* Translated and with an introduction by David C. Durst. Candor, N.Y.: Telos Press, 2008. (Orig. pub. 1934.)

Jünger, Ernst. *Stürm.* Translated by Alexis P. Walker. Edited and with an introduction by David Pan. Candor, N.Y.: Telos Press, 2015. (Orig. pub. 1923.)

Jünger, Ernst. *The Worker: Dominion and Form.* Edited by Laurence Paul Hemming. Translated by Bogdan Costea and Laurence Paul Hemming. Evanston, Ill.: Northwestern University Press, 2017. (Orig. pub. 1932.)

Kafka, Franz. "The Cares of a Family Man." In *The Complete Stories.* Translated by Willa and Edwin Muir, 473. New York: Schocken Books, 1995. (Written in 1919.)

Kamal, Mohammed Arif. "Le Corbusier's Solar Shading Strategy for Tropical Environment: A Sustainable Approach." *Journal of Architectural Planning Research and Studies* 10, no. 1 (2013): 19–26.

Kant, Immanuel. *Critique of Practical Reason.* Translated by Werner S. Pluhar. Introduction by Stephen Engstrom. Indianapolis: Hackett, 2002. (Orig. pub. 1788.)

Keynes, John Maynard. *The General Theory of Employment, Interest and Money.* New York: Prometheus Books, 1997. (Orig. pub. 1936.)

Khatib, Sami. "Barbaric Salvage: Benjamin and the Dialectics of Destruction." *parallax* 24, no. 2 (2018): 135–58.

Kojève, Alexandre. *Introduction à la lecture de Hegel: Leçons sur la Phénoménologie de l'Esprit professées de 1933 à 1939 à l'École des Hautes Études.* Edited, from Notes, by Raymond Queneau. Paris: Gallimard, Collection Tel, 1980. (Orig. pub. 1947.)

Kristeva, Julia. *Revolution in Poetic Language.* Translated by Margaret Waller. New York: Columbia University Press, 1985. (Orig. pub. 1974.)

Lacan, Jacques. "Kant with Sade." *October* 51 (Winter 1989): 55–75.

Lahiji, Nadir. ". . . 'The Gift of Time': Le Corbusier Reading Bataille." *In Surrealism and Architecture,* edited by Thomas Mical, 119–35. London: Routledge, 2004.

Layzer, David. "The Arrow of Time." *Astrophysical Journal* 206 (June 1976): 559–69.

Leatherbarrow, David, and Richard Wesley. *Three Cultural Ecologies.* London: Routledge, 2017.

Le Corbusier. *The City of To-Morrow and Its Planning.* Translated by Frederic Etchells. New York: Dover, 1987. (Orig. pub. 1947.)

Le Corbusier. *Destin de Paris.* Paris: Sorlot, 1941.

Le Corbusier. *The Four Routes.* London: Dobson, 1947.

Levinas, Emmanuel. *Totality and Infinity.* Translated by Alphonso Lingis. Pittsburgh: Duquesne University Press, 1969. (Orig. pub. 1961.)

Lingis, Alphonso. *The Community of Those Who Have Nothing in Common.* Bloomington: Indiana University Press, 1994.

Loeb, Harold. *Life in a Technocracy: What It Might Be Like.* Syracuse, N.Y.: Syracuse University Press, 1996. (Orig. pub. 1933.)

Long, William J. *Tantric State: A Buddhist Approach to Democracy and Development in Bhutan.* New York: Oxford University Press, 2019.

Lovelock, James. *The Revenge of Gaia: Earth's Climate in Crisis and the Fate of Humanity.* Foreword by Sir Crispen Tickell. New York: Basic Books, 2006.

Luhmann, Niklas. *Social Systems.* Translated by John Bednarz Jr., with Dirk Baecker. Palo Alto, Calif.: Stanford University Press, 1996.

Malm, Andreas. *Fossil Capital: The Rise of Steam Power and the Roots of Global Warming.* London: Verso, 2016.

Mandel, Ernest. *Long Waves of Capitalist Development: A Marxist Interpretation.* London: Verso, 1995.

Margulis (Sagan), Lynn. "On the Origin of Mitosing Cells." *Journal of Theoretical Biology* 14, no. 3 (1967): 225–74.

Margulis (Sagan), Lynn, and Dorion Sagan, eds. *Slanted Truths: Essays on Gaia, Symbiosis, and Evolution.* New York: Copernicus, 1997.

Margulis (Sagan), Lynn, and Dorion Sagan. *What Is Life?* New York: Simon and Schuster, 1995.

Margulis (Sagan), Lynn, and Oona West. "Gaia and the Colonization of Mars." In Margulis and Sagan, *Slanted Truths,* 221–34.

Marin, Louis. *Utopics: The Semiological Play of Textual Spaces.* Translated by Robert A. Vollrath. New York: Humanities Press, 1984. (Orig. pub. 1973.)

Mazzarella, William. *The Mana of Mass Society.* Chicago: University of Chicago Press, 2017.

McCarthy, Cormac. *The Road.* New York: Vintage, 2006.

McDonough, Tom, ed. *Guy Debord and the Situationist International: Texts and Documents.* Cambridge, Mass.: MIT Press, 2002.

McDonough, William, and Michael Braungart. *Cradle to Cradle: Remaking the Way We Make Things.* Berkeley, Calif.: North Point Press, 2002.

McKibben, Bill. *Deep Economy: The Wealth of Communities and the Durable Future.* New York: St. Martin's Press, 2007.

McWilliam, Neil. "Conflicting Manifestations: Parisian Commemoration of Joan of Arc and Étienne Dolet in the Early Third Republic." *French Historical Studies* 27, no. 2 (Spring 2004): 381–418.

Meadows, Donella H. et al. *The Limits to Growth.* New York: Signet, 1972.

Medavoi, Leerom. "Sustainability." In *Fueling Culture: 101 Words for Energy and the Environment,* edited by Imre Szeman, Jennifer Wenzel, and Patricia Yaeger, 342–45. New York: Fordham University Press, 2017.

Meillassoux, Quentin. *After Finitude: An Essay on the Necessity of Contingency.* Translated by Ray Brassier. New York: Continuum, 2008. (Orig. pub. 2006.)

Mirowski, Philip. *More Heat Than Light: Economics as Social Physics, Physics as Nature's Economics.* Cambridge: Cambridge University Press, 1989.

Morris, William, ed. *The American Heritage Dictionary.* New York: Houghton Mifflin, 1973.

Morton, Timothy. *Hyperobjects: Philosophy and Ecology at the End of the World*. Minneapolis: University of Minnesota Press, 2013.

Morton, Timothy. "Buddhaphobia: Nothingness and the Fear of Things." In *Nothing: Three Inquiries in Buddhism*, by Marcus Boon, Eric Cazdyn, Timothy Morton, 185–266. Chicago: University of Chicago Press, 2015.

Nagel, Thomas. "What Is It Like to Be a Bat?" *Philosophical Review* 83, no. 4 (October 1974): 435–50.

Nancy, Jean-Luc. *La Communauté désœuvrée*. Paris: Christian Bourgois, 1991.

Nancy, Jean-Luc. *The Inoperative Community*. Translated by Peter Connor et al. Edited by Peter Connor. Minneapolis: University of Minnesota Press, 1991.

Nancy, Jean-Luc. "The Unsacrificeable." Translated by Richard Livingston. *Yale French Studies* 79 (1991): 20–38.

Neaman, Elliot Y. *A Dubious Past: Ernst Jünger and the Politics of Literature after Nazism*. Berkeley: University of California Press, 1999.

Neyrat, Frédéric. *The Unconstructable Earth: An Ecology of Separation*. Translated by Drew S. Burk. New York: Fordham University Press, 2019.

Nietzsche, Friedrich. *The Gay Science*. Translated with commentary by Walter Kaufmann. New York: Vintage Books, 1974. (Orig. pub. 1882.)

Nietzsche, Friedrich. "On Truth and Lie in an Extra-Moral Sense." In *Philosophy and Truth: Selections from Nietzsche's Notebooks of the Early 1870's*, edited and translated by Daniel Breazeale, 53–62. New York: Humanities Press, 1990.

Odum, Howard T. *Environmental Accounting, Emergy and Decision Making*. New York: Wiley, 1995.

Oomkes, Robin. "Berlin's Terracotta Army—the Statues of the Kaiser's Victory Boulevard." Dead Emperors' Society. April 27, 2014. https://deademperorssociety.com/2014/04/27/berlins-terracotta-army-the-statues-of-the-kaisers-victory-boulevard/.

Orwell, George. *Nineteen Eighty-Four*. New York: Harcourt Brace, 1949.

Oskin, Becky. "Confirmed: Oldest Fragment of Early Earth Is 4.4 Billion Years Old." Live Science. February 23, 2014. https://www.livescience.com/43584-earth-oldest-rock-jack-hills-zircon.html.

Owen, David. *Green Metropolis: What the City Can Teach the Country about True Sustainability*. New York: Riverhead, 2009.

Pascal, Blaise. *Pensées*. Introduction by T. S. Eliot. New York: E. P. Dutton, 1958.

Pascal, Blaise. *Pensées*. Edited by Léon Brunschvicg. Paris: Flammarion, 1993.

Paulhan, Jean. *The Flowers of Tarbes, or, Terror in Literature*. Translated and with an introduction by Michael Syrotinski. Urbana: University of Illinois Press, 2006. (Orig. pub. 1941.)

Pessard, Gustave. *La Statuomanie parisienne: Étude critique sur l'abus des statues*. Paris: H. Daragon, 1912.

Pettman, Dominic. *Peak Libido: Sex, Ecology, and the Collapse of Desire*. Cambridge, UK: Polity, 2020.

Pinkus, Karen. *Fuel: A Speculative Dictionary*. Minneapolis: University of Minnesota Press, 2016.

Pinkus, Karen. "The Risks of Sustainability." In *Criticism, Crisis, and Contemporary Narrative*, edited by Paul Crosthwaite, 62–77. London: Routledge, 2011.

Piper, Alan. "Psychedelics, Transgression, and the End of History." In *Breaking Convention: Psychedelic Pharmacology for the 21st Century*, edited by Ben Sassa et al., 237–52. London: Strange Attractor Press, 2017.

Plans. Paris. 1931–1932. (Review edited by Philippe Lamour; contributions by Le Corbusier, among others.)

Plato. *Timaeus*. Translated by Benjamin Jowett. Project Gutenberg. January 15, 2013. http://www.gutenberg.org/files/1572/1572-h/1572-h.htm.

Pollan, Michael. *How to Change Your Mind*. New York: Penguin Press, 2018.

Potts, Matthew L. *Cormac McCarthy and the Signs of Sacrament*. New York: Bloomsbury, 2015.

Prigogine, Ilya, and Isabelle Stengers. *Order Out of Chaos: Man's Dialog with Nature*. London: Verso, 2018.

Proust, Marcel. *Remembrance of Things Past*. Vol. 1, *Swann's Way*. Translated by C. K. Scott Moncrieff. New York: Henry Holt, 1922. (Orig. pub. 1913.)

Rauland, Vanessa, and Peter Newman. *Decarbonising Cities: Mainstreaming Low Carbon Urban Development*. New York: Springer International, 2015.

Recycling Today Staff. "ISRI Asks China to Better Differentiate between Scrap and Waste." Recycling Today. August 28, 2017. https://www.recyclingtoday.com/article/isri-comments-china-revisions-identification-standards-for-solid-wastes-general-rules/.

Richards, Simon. "The Antisocial Urbanism of Le Corbusier." *Common Knowledge* 13, no. 1 (2007): 50–66.

Richards, Simon. *Le Corbusier and the Concept of Self*. New Haven, Conn.: Yale University Press, 2003.

Sachs, Jeffrey D. *The Age of Sustainable Development*. Foreword by Ban Ki-moon. New York: Columbia University Press, 2015.

Sadler, Simon. *The Situationist City*. Cambridge, Mass.: MIT Press, 1998.

Sagan, Dorion. 2017. "Beautiful Monsters: Terra in the Cyanocene." In *Arts of Living on a Damaged Planet: Monsters of the Anthropocene*, edited by A. Tsing et al., 169–74. Minneapolis: University of Minnesota Press, 2017.

Sartre, Jean-Paul. *What Is Literature?* Translated by Bernard Frechtman. New York: Washington Square Press, 1966. (Orig. pub. 1947.)

Schmidt, Dennis J. "Of Birth, Death, and Unfinished Conversations." In *Gadamer's Hermeneutics and the Art of Conversation*, edited by A. Wierciński, 107–14. Münster, Ger.: LIT Verlag, 2011.

Schneider-Mayerson, Matthew. *Peak Oil: Apocalyptic Environmentalism and Libertarian Political Culture*. Chicago: University of Chicago Press, 2015.

Schumacher, E. F. *Small Is Beautiful: Economics As If People Mattered*. New York: Harper and Row, 1973.

Scott, James C. *Against the Grain: A Deep History of the Earliest States*. New Haven, Conn.: Yale University Press, 2017.

Scranton, Roy. *We're Doomed, Now What? Essays on War and Climate Change*. New York: Soho, 2018.

Shaviro, Steven. *The Universe of Things: On Speculative Realism*. Minneapolis: University of Minnesota Press, 2014.

Sheldon, Rebekah. "Form / Matter / Chora: Object Oriented Ontology and New Materialism." In *The Nonhuman Turn,* edited by Richard Grusin, 193–222. Minneapolis: University of Minnesota Press, 2015.

Singer, Peter. *Animal Liberation: A New Ethics for Our Treatment of Animals*. New York: Random House, 1975.

Smith, Mick. *Against Ecological Sovereignty*. Minneapolis: University of Minnesota Press, 2011.

Stengers, Isabelle. "Penser à partir du ravage écologique." In *De l'univers clos au monde infini,* edited by Émile Hache, 147–90. Paris: Dehors, 2014.

Stoekl, Allan. *Agonies of the Intellectual: Commitment, Subjectivity, and the Performative in the Twentieth-Century French Tradition*. Lincoln: University of Nebraska Press, 1992.

Stoekl, Allan. *Bataille's Peak: Energy, Religion, and Postsustainability*. Minneapolis: University of Minnesota Press, 2007.

Stoekl, Allan. "Marxism, Materialism, and the Critique of Energy." In *Materialism and the Critique of Energy*, edited by Brent Ryan Bellamy and Jeff Diamanti, 1–28. Chicago: MCM', 2018.

Stoekl, Allan. "Truman's Apotheosis: Bataille, 'Planisme,' and Headlessness." *Yale French Studies* 78 (1990): 181–205.

Swyngedouw, Eric. "Impossible 'Sustainability' and the Post-Political Condition." In *The Sustainable Development Paradox,* edited by David Gibbs and Rob Krueger, 185–205. New York: Guilford Press, 2006.

Thacker, Eugene. *Infinite Resignation*. London: Repeater Books, 2018.

Timofeeva, Oxana. "From the Quarantine to the General Strike: On Bataille's Political Economy." *Stasis* 9, no. 1 (2020): 144–65.

Tsing, Anna Lowenhaupt. *The Mushroom at the End of the World: On the Possibility of Life in Capitalist Ruins*. Princeton, N.J.: Princeton University Press, 2015.

Varela, Francisco, and Humberto Maturano. *Autopoiesis and Cognition: The Realization of the Living*. Dordrecht, Neth.: D. Reidel, 1980. (Orig. pub. 1972.)

Veblen, Thorstein. *The Engineers and the Price System*. New York: Viking, 1933.

Vernadsky, Vladimir I. *The Biosphere*. Translated by David B. Langmuir. Foreword by Lynn Margulis et al. Introduction by Jacques Grinevald. New York: Copernicus, 1998. (Orig. pub. 1926.)

Wackernagel, Mathis, and William Rees. 1996. *Our Ecological Footprint: Reducing Human Impact on the Earth*. Gabriola Island, B.C.: New Society.

Wernick, Andrew. *Auguste Comte and the Religion of Humanity: The Post-Theistic Program of French Social Theory*. Cambridge: Cambridge University Press, 2004.

Wilson, Thomas. *The Swastika, the Earliest Known Symbol, and Its Migrations*. New York: Wentworth Press, 2016.

Wohlleben, Peter. *The Hidden Life of Trees: What They Feel, How They Communicate.* Translated by Jane Billinghurst. London: William Collins, 2017.

Woods, Derek. "Scale Critique for the Anthropocene." *Minnesota Review* 83 (2014):133–41.

World Commission on Environment and Development. *Our Common Future (The Brundtland Commission Report).* New York: Oxford University Press, 1987.

Wright, Robert. *Why Buddhism Is True: The Science and Philosophy of Meditation and Enlightenment.* New York: Simon and Schuster, 2017.

Yelle, Robert A. *Sovereignty and the Sacred: Secularism and the Political Economy of Religion.* Chicago: University of Chicago Press, 2019.

Yong, Ed. *I Contain Multitudes: The Microbes within Us and a Grander View of Life.* New York: Ecco, 2018.

Young, John. 1990. *Post Environmentalism.* London: Belhaven Press, 1990.

Žižek, Slavoj. *For They Know Not What They Do: Enjoyment as a Political Factor.* London: Verso, 2002.

Index

ALLAN STOEKL is professor emeritus of French and comparative literature at Penn State University. He is also author of *Bataille's Peak: Energy, Religion, and Postsustainability* (Minnesota, 2007).